D0168665

LAW AND SOCIETY

STUDIES IN SOCIOLOGY

Consulting Editor:

CHARLES H. PAGE
University of Massachusetts

LAW
and
SOCIETY

A Sociological View

EDWIN M. SCHUR

Tufts University

RANDOM HOUSE   NEW YORK

To the memory of
R. C. D. and F. V. H.

teachers of law, whose
broad social perspectives helped
stimulate interdisciplinary analysis
of law and society

Acknowledgments

My teachers at the Yale Law School first made me aware of the important interrelationships between law and society. Richard Donnelly and Fowler Harper in particular, the men to whom this book is dedicated, were instrumental in nurturing my interest in such matters; and, inadvertently, they helped kindle in me the motivation to become a sociologist. In the course of my further training, contact with men alert to the social importance of law —men such as Otto Kirchheimer, Alfred Schutz, and J. E. Hall Williams—helped keep my interest in this field alive. This work in part reflects my residence during 1963–1964, on leave from Tufts University, at the Center for the Study of Law and Society, University of California, Berkeley; and I am most grateful to the Russell Sage Foundation and to Tufts for making my residency possible. Those familiar with their work will recognize my indebtedness to the ideas of Philip Selznick, Sheldon Messinger, Jerome Skolnick, David Matza, Jerome Carlin, and others at the Center. The book also reflects the development of a course on the sociology of law, which I have been teaching for Tufts undergraduates during the past few years. A Tufts Faculty Summer Research Fellowship assisted me in the preparation of the manuscript, which Mabel F. Adams typed with her usual care and diligence. Finally, I would like to express my appreciation to Charles H. Page for his careful reading of the manuscript

vii

and his many helpful suggestions, and also to Sybil Elman, Theodore Caris and others on the staff of Random House for their assistance.

F. M. S.

Medford, Mass.

Contents

Introduction: Sociology and the Law   3
    SOCIOLOGY'S NEGLECT OF LAW   5
    DEVELOPING LINES OF INQUIRY   8
    SOME CENTRAL CONCERNS   10
    AIMS AND LIMITS OF THIS STUDY   15

One: Jurisprudence and Sociology   17

    The Speluncean Explorers   19
    Some Influences from Jurisprudence   23
    FORMALISTIC APPROACHES   24
    CULTURAL AND HISTORICAL ORIENTATIONS   30
    UTILITARIANISM   33
    SOCIOLOGICAL JURISPRUDENCE   37
    LEGAL REALISM   43
    NATURAL LAW AND SOCIOLOGY   51
    Justice and Obedience to Law   58
    CIVIL DISOBEDIENCE   60
    WAR-CRIMES TRIALS   62

Two: Law and Order   68

    The Meaning of Law   70
    FUNCTIONAL APPROACHES   79
    CRITICISMS OF THE FUNCTIONAL APPROACH   82
    Law, Power, and Stratification   85
    LAW, CLASS, AND POWER IN THE UNITED STATES   92

ROLE OF THE LEGAL PROFESSION   101

Three: Law and Social Change   107

Some General Theories   108
THE SOVIET EXPERIENCE   116
SOME RECENT TRENDS IN AMERICAN LAW   121
THE LIMITS OF LAW   127
LAW AS AN INSTRUMENT OF CHANGE   135

Order, Conflict, and Law   139

Four: Law in Action: Selected Areas for
Research   141

Courts, Judges, and Juries   142
Administration of Criminal Justice   153
DEVIANCE AND SOCIETAL REACTIONS   154
ENFORCEMENT DISCRETION   157

Styles of Legal Work   163
THE LARGE LAW FIRM   165
INDIVIDUAL PRACTICE   168
LEGAL ETHICS AND ROLE STRAIN   172

The Public and the Law   177

Five: Scientific Justice and Legality   183

Evidence from the Social Sciences   184
Specialized Tribunals   188
THE JUVENILE COURT   189
PSYCHIATRIC COMMITMENT   194
THE LEGALITY ISSUE   198

Conclusion   202

Notes   205

Selected Readings   227

Index   231

LAW AND SOCIETY

Introduction

✻✻✻

Sociology and the Law

In modern industrial societies, systems of law have become so far-reaching that we find legal rules and procedures permeating all realms of social behavior. To recognize this situation, it is first necessary to cast aside the popular misconception of law that limits it to the control of criminal behavior (a belief undoubtedly nurtured and reinforced by the treatment of legal matters in the media of mass communication). Once we pass this roadblock, there is little difficulty in appreciating at least the social pervasiveness, and perhaps also the social significance, of law. A man's ownership or use of property both real and personal, his relations with his wife and children, his relations with employers or employees and the conditions and security of his job, his rights and duties in his interaction with the numerous other individuals and organizations that shape his network of social relations—all these aspects of his everyday living are governed by or subject to existing or potential rulings of the legal system.

Some of these rulings have been or will be expressed in the form of specific statutory provisions, others in the form of judicial holdings or dicta (statements by the court not necessarily required

3

in reaching the decision at hand), still others in the deliberations and findings of administrative agencies whose rulings may often be supported by judicial sanction. Indeed, when one realizes that *any* aspect of social relations can be brought within the legal system (that is, made subject to legal ruling) simply by an individual initiating a suit in court to establish the rights and duties involved in the situation in question, one sees quite clearly that the boundaries of law are, in at least one sense, coterminous with those of the full range of social interaction. From this perspective, it is evident that relatively few areas of social life can be fully understood in all their complexity without some appreciation of their legal aspects; this observation suggests one reason why the nature and operation of legal systems must be of considerable interest to the sociologist.

At the same time, it should be apparent that the legal system is sociologically important in its own right as a major institutional complex within society. A society's legal system is embedded in and generates a distinctive and more or less coherent (though continuously changing) set of legal roles, norms, and organizations, together with characteristic patterns of interrelation between the legal order and the other institutional realms of the society.[1] There are, in other words, specialized personnel and organized ways of doing things that are distinctively *legal*; furthermore, the procedures and substantive rules of this legal realm cut across, and hence may apply equally throughout, various sectors of the social order. It is the analysis and understanding of this legal system *as such,* rather than the mere recognition of legal aspects in selected areas of social life, that is the primary concern of the sociology of law. Certainly it is true that the sociologist cannot analyze crime and punishment, or marriage and the family, or labor unions, or political movements without some reference to legal systems. But no adding up of such diverse analyses can be expected to provide us with an overall view of the meaning and workings of specifically legal phenomena. For this purpose we must confront such phenomena directly—as the sociologist attempts to do when he undertakes research on the courts, the legal profession, the views of law (including concepts of "justice" and "legality") held within a society, the effectiveness of law as a mechanism of social control, the place of law in broader patterns of social change.

SOCIOLOGY'S NEGLECT OF LAW

Given these seemingly fruitful lines of inquiry, one might expect the sociological analysis of law to constitute a well-entrenched area of research and an important professional specialty within the discipline of sociology. Yet, at least in modern American sociology, until very recently such has not been true. Indeed, only a few years ago, the introduction to a collection of articles in this field described that effort as announcing "the birth of a new subdiscipline within American sociology." [2] Modern sociology's selective inattention to law is particularly surprising since several of the classic social theorists had already given legal phenomena a very important place in their still influential analyses.[3]

Several factors may have combined to produce this gap in our efforts to develop a comprehensive and systematic knowledge of social life. In the first place, to the extent that a legal system is viewed as a set of rules it seems to fall entirely into the realm of the "normative," a realm in which sociologists find themselves very uncomfortable. Furthermore, at least some sociologists may uncritically have accepted the popular notion that law consists of a static body of pronouncements, a view mirrored in the question constantly asked the lawyer, "What is *the law* on . . . ?" In short, sociology may have avoided the law partly because of a failure to recognize sufficiently its social nature. The realization that law (even if viewed primarily as a set of rules) is always an outcome of social processes—that men make and change law, and indeed that it is constantly changing—is an important step in breaking down the researcher's hesitancy to enter this area. At the same time, however, as David Riesman has aptly commented, sociologists may feel that there is "a certain intellectual impenetrability about the law, reflecting and resulting from the achievements of generations of jurists" as well as a "factual impenetrability resulting from the sheer overwhelming and opaque bulk of data that must be mastered. . . ." [4] While such feelings are not totally unfounded, they do not justify closing off the legal realm to the sociologist, any more than the social researcher's incomplete technical knowledge of medicine, science, or religion precludes research in those areas. In other words, as well as the admittedly complex and enormous body of legal doctrine and procedural forms, there are more general areas of legal organization, behavior, and belief, which can be empirically investigated and which may appropriately be analyzed from sociological perspectives.

Certain general tendencies in American sociology also help to account for the relative neglect of law. As Karl Mannheim noted, American sociology in its quest for truly scientific status sought to carve out new areas for analysis, areas that had not already been thoroughly investigated in the more fully established disciplines.[5] The long-standing and well-developed body of work in jurisprudence, and the fact that European scholars in various social sciences often had received formal training in the law, may indirectly have motivated American researchers to avoid becoming involved in this field. The possible association of much European legal study with "speculative" schools of social philosophy also may have deterred empirically minded sociologists. Although sociological research in America has often focused on areas in which there are significant legal aspects—areas such as crime and delinquency, slum neighborhoods, and problems of the family—attention was directed to behavior, ecology, and social organization and disorganization rather than to the legal issues. Likewise, American sociology generally has tended to place much greater emphasis on informal than on formal mechanisms of social control. It is natural that sociologists should have wanted to counteract the mistaken belief that formal sanctions are always necessary if norms are to be enforced. And certainly it is important to recognize that a legal rule requires broad social support to be effective. As MacIver and Page state, "a law which attacks a widespread custom, even though a majority support it, both lacks a ground of support that is essential to its effective operation and creates a force of resistance that endangers its authority." [6] The trouble is that many sociologists, aware of such facts and also of evidence suggesting the negligible deterrent effect of criminal law on crime (for example, of the death penalty on homicide), seem to have concluded that formal sanctions are without any social force or consequence whatever. As the discussion to follow should suggest, such an inference is not warranted.

Fortunately for the study of the sociology of law, general trends in American life are such that it is becoming less and less possible to ignore the social role of law. Not only does increased bureaucratization and centralization seem to imply the need for more law but also, as Philip Selznick has pointed out, the drift to an open, fluid, mass society "must inevitably increase the burdens of our legal institutions. If society cannot depend on an informal, autonomous, self-regulating, person-centered order for the maintenance of social control, it will turn to more explicitly organized agencies and to more powerful instruments of surveillance and regulation." [7] Similarly, some of the uses to which law is currently being put (such as to aid in the struggle for civil rights for the Negro) have created second thoughts about the related view of law as a completely dependent variable, a variable shaped by the social context in which it occurs (as it undoubtedly in part is) but without any significant shaping force of its own.

The development of a meaningful sociology of law has probably also been hampered somewhat by difficulties of interaction between sociologists and lawyers. In a sense, it is true that lawyers and sociologists "don't talk the same language," and this lack of communication undoubtedly breeds uncertainty in both professions concerning any involvement in the other's domain, much less any cooperative interdisciplinary endeavors. Then too, sociologists and lawyers are engaged in quite different sorts of enterprises—the lawyer's role being primarily one of advocacy and concern with issues of policy, the sociologist's centering around the disinterested and systematic quest for knowledge. This latter task may often seem "unreal," even incomprehensible, to the conventional lawyer. Similarly, the lawyer's characteristic need to make decisions, here and now, may render him impatient with the sociologist's apparently unlimited willingness to suspend final judgment on an issue, to refuse to take sides, to assert nothing more definite than "rebuttable hypotheses." These problems, however, should not be exaggerated. Not all sociological study of the legal system requires an interdisciplinary research team; nor is the sociologist's incomplete legal knowledge always a serious impediment to his work. At the same time, as sociologists and lawyers increasingly work with one another on problems of mutual interest, they begin to see that cooperative effort can be painless and also to appreciate that each specialty may well have something to learn from the other.

DEVELOPING LINES OF INQUIRY

If, then, sociological study of the legal system is possible and desirable, what lines of development should it take? Because this area of research is really still in the formulative stages, at present it comprises a variety of somewhat diverse strands of research and theory, partly reflecting the major interests of those particular individuals who have undertaken work in legal sociology. Such diversification should not be attributed to either professional disorganization or personal opportunism. On the contrary, it represents a useful searching out of key areas and may help to guarantee a broadly based and intellectually open-minded and modern sociology of law. While some sociologists are analyzing legal systems because of a long-held theoretical interest in their operation, and a few others have a background of dual professional training in sociology and law, the more typical researcher has entered this field as the result of a previous commitment to a related sociological specialty.

The possibilities for this kind of recruitment are so numerous that a complete listing is not possible. But a few of the more significant patterns may be noted. Much of the useful research on the legal profession now under way derives from the more general sociological interest in the study of occupations and professions. The investigation of the sociological aspects of criminal law and the administration of criminal justice is beholden, not surprisingly, to sociology's earlier interest and work in the areas of criminology, deviant behavior, and social control. Specialists in comparative social structure, historical sociology, and social change are using these perspectives to illuminate other vital aspects of legal systems. Organizational specialists tend to focus on decision-making processes, on the structure of legal organizations, and on the development in private, large-scale organizations of procedures that mirror (and that may even represent incipient forms of) strictly legal institutions. Social theorists attempt to develop analytical models of the legal system in order to determine the hallmark of the distinctively legal and to delineate clearly the lines of demarcation between the legal system and other subsystems of the social order.

We shall have occasion below to examine more closely some theories and findings developed from these somewhat different orientations. In presenting this material it would be misleading to attempt to impose an artificial organization that would neatly order the various lines of analysis and research. Sufficient unity is provided by the fact that all of the investigators share the overarching aim of expanding and systematizing our understanding of the legal order, and indeed their work is rapidly producing a body of knowledge that should help us to achieve that goal. At the moment, considering that empirical work in this field is of recent origin, we should require no more than that. There is certainly no reason for us to feel defensive about not being able to point to *the* theory of law in society. Likewise, the present writer holds that it would be a mistake to try to assimilate the entire enterprise of the sociology of law to any particular analytical model of the legal order. It would be most unfortunate indeed if in place of the admittedly significant but rather stultifying jurisprudential debate about "What is law?" sociology could do little more than substitute an endless haggling about the meaning of "the distinctively legal." Similarly, it should be apparent, and will indeed become clear as we survey actual research projects, that in the sociological study of law, as in sociology generally, we can put to good use a variety of empirical research methods, as well as theoretical perspectives; the appropriateness of particular techniques and perspectives will depend in each instance on the specific task at hand.

SOME CENTRAL CONCERNS

As we examine the work that has already been done in this field, and consider additional lines of inquiry that may just now be opening up, we shall find certain central themes and issues confronting us again and again. Some of the more important of these pervasive concerns are as follows:

1. *Law and Its Social Context.* In a sense, of course, the phrase "law and its social context" really encompasses the entire field of the sociology of law. There is little doubt among sociologists that a legal system reflects the broader social context within which it exists. There is a considerable need, however, for further specification of the conditions under and ways in which this influence

occurs. Furthermore, as already mentioned, there is the persisting question of whether, or to what extent, this process of influence is a reciprocal one. Can legal change (changes in the substance of law, changes in key legal procedures, or broad changes in the structure of a legal system) produce or at least reinforce more general patterns of social change? Again, it seems apparent that pronounced legal changes will rarely be without *any* effect. Nonetheless, there is room for a great deal more data and analysis bearing on the nature and extent of such effects. Notwithstanding the considerable methodological dilemmas facing the sociologist in such work (reflected, for example, in the near impossibility of "holding social conditions constant" in order to determine any independent effects of legal change), research aimed at illuminating these processes of change, particularly analysis proceeding from historical and comparative orientations, seems essential if we are to develop a comprehensive understanding of the nature of legal systems.

2. *Uniformities and Diversity in Legal Systems.* Although most recent empirical work in the sociology of law focuses on particular elements of specific present-day legal orders, and in particular the current American legal system, sociologists interested in law remain aware of the need to place these studies in broader perspective. There is always the lingering question of how far one can generalize from the particular and somewhat circumscribed setting examined. Clearly, analysis that cuts across specific legal systems is a prerequisite to any generalization about the nature of legal systems and to the development of meaningful theories in this area. The anthropologist, as well as the sociologist, has a real contribution to make in this regard.

3. *The Two-Edged Nature of Law.* Although the law might better be characterized as multiedged than two-edged, one dual-faceted aspect of legal rules and legal systems is particularly evident. Whether one views a legal system in terms of procedure or

in terms of substance, it is apparent that law, on the one hand, constitutes an important means of fostering individual freedoms, insuring human rights, and furthering broad social goals of equality and general well-being. On the other hand, law is a powerful tool for the control of the individual, a means by which some segments of a society can maintain social and economic superiority over others, a device with great potential for tyranni-cal rule. At least to some extent, then, the meaning of law (in terms of its relationship to the tenor and workings of any given society) may depend upon the uses to which law is put. Further-more, the freedom-enhancing and freedom-reducing aspects of law are not mutually exclusive. Except in extreme cases, we may expect to find them combining, in various ways, within particular legal systems. Actually this combining is inevitable, in view of the fact that an increase in the rights of some individuals will almost always entail some restriction on the rights of others. We find this same dual characteristic present in concrete legal dis-putes, where judicial or other rulings invariably imply both a winner and a loser.

4. *The Relation between Procedure and Substance.* Certain analyses have found the essence of legality to reside in a system of dispute-resolving institutions that adhere to a specified "adju-dicative" model. (See the section "Natural Law and Sociology" in Chapter One.) If one adopts this formulation, and the associated claim that elaboration of these distinctively legal entities should preoccupy sociologists in their studies of law, then research on legal systems will tend to concentrate almost exclusively on pro-cedures. An emphasis on procedure, and inattention to substance, may also result from the sociologist's legitimate desire to general-ize—to examine those elements that cut across, and operate similarly in, the various areas of substantive law within a given system. At the same time, if we are seeking a thorough under-standing of the legal order, it may be a mistake not to pay at least some attention to matters of substantive law. This would

seem particularly desirable in considering such matters as the effects of law, and the relation between legal development and social change. There are undoubtedly some meaningful generalizations that can be made about substantive law, as well as about legal organization and procedure. Indeed, it might be noted that Maine's famous statement of the trend from "status to contract," [8] to be discussed below, essentially concerns matters of substantive law. In any event, the relationship between procedure and substance will probably be a question confronting us frequently as we continue to develop empirical research into various aspects of legal systems. A special feature of this relationship is posed in a statement of our fifth central concern.

5. *Substantive and Formal Rationality.* In his writings on the sociology of law, Max Weber emphasized the tendency for modern Western legal systems to rely heavily on "formal rationality" (the systematizing of general rules and patterns of procedural regularity).[9] Although this development could be viewed as a protection against idiosyncratic or politically expedient decision-making, Weber also saw that the principle of formalism could conflict with the desirable aspects of "substantive rationality" (concern for the justness of outcomes in individual cases). Reinhard Bendix, discussing this problem as it applies to the system of "adversary procedure" (in which the conduct of the lawsuit depends largely on the steps taken by the adversary parties themselves), suggests some of the related difficulties encountered in our own legal system:

> . . . the formal rationality of the law guarantees only the formal rights of the interested parties. If, for example, an individual fails to remember an important fact or cannot afford the expense required to document it, he may be forced to forego the enjoyment of rights that are legally his. Thus fortuitous circumstances may produce substantive injustice under a formally rational system of law.[10]

This dilemma presents itself at numerous points in our examination of the workings of the law. Among other things, the dilemma is relevant first to the attempt to develop a legal system that provides "equality before the law" while doing justice to the peculiarities of individual cases; second, to the need for a system of laws that maintains at one and the same time consistency and flexibility in the face of changing social conditions; and third, to the desire of legal functionaries to make the greatest possible use of scientific knowledge as an aid to judicial determination while sustaining the formally legal character of their rulings.

6. *Limitations on a Science of Law.* Various legal philosophers have long hoped for the development of some kind of truly scientific legal system. Just what they meant by such a system varied depending on the approach of the particular theorist. Some legal analysts have hoped that a completely logical and exhaustive system of readily applied rules would produce automatically just and fully consistent decisions in legal disputes. Other jurists have seen salvation in a system of law that would be soundly constructed with the assistance of specialists in the various social sciences. In particular realms of law, sociologists themselves have sought to provide data that they believed might "improve" policies and procedures. Although science can make definite contributions to the effectiveness of a legal system in attaining specified goals, it cannot indicate what these goals shall be. This limitation simply restates the old issue of facts and values in sociology. The position taken by the present writer is that the scientist can never *prove* values. No matter how thorough an explication he can provide of the social consequences of alternative courses of action, an area of value choice always remains. Given such likely consequences, which course do we wish to take? This ineradicability of the policy realm will always place some limitations on efforts to develop, *scientifically,* a just and effective legal order.

7. *The Sociologist and Legal Policy.* The sociologist need not ignore questions of policy. By bringing to light underlying causes and functions of behavior and social arrangements, by specifying

social costs and consequences of competing policies, and by developing a general understanding of how different kinds of legal systems work, the sociologist may be in a good position to provide policymakers with highly relevant information and perspectives. Although systematic knowledge of legal systems is the sociologist's primary goal in this field, there is at least a legitimate secondary interest in seeing that relevant data are put to some socially beneficial use. One sociologist, accordingly, has criticized his colleagues for having done "virtually no work that is related to the substantive or procedural needs of the system of law." [11] Even if not primarily motivated by the desire to reform, many of the ongoing empirical studies in this area will undoubtedly produce findings that have significant policy implications.[12]

AIMS AND LIMITS OF THIS STUDY

As a final introductory comment, it may be useful to indicate briefly the aims and limits of the present study. To begin with, it should be stressed that this study is most definitely *not* intended to be an introduction to law in the guidebook or "book about law for the layman" sense. Thus, it does not contain detailed descriptions of the structure and operation of the American court system, an outline of how a lawsuit proceeds, or a summary of major principles of substantive Anglo-American law. There are available numerous well-written and highly informative books of this sort.[13] Nor is this an in-depth analysis of major philosophies of law, although we shall have occasion to examine the implications for sociology of some of these philosophies.

It is not even possible, in this brief compass, to touch on all the points concerning law that might be of interest to the sociologist—obviously these are myriad. What is attempted here is simply a discussion of those aspects of legal systems that seem most relevant to the development of a sociological understanding of legal phenomena, a summary analysis of some of the directions empirical research in the sociology of law has already taken, and an indication of the general issues that seem to the writer to be central to work in this field. It would be the height of presumption to claim to have covered the field of law and society in a volume of this size. If, then, a good deal of selection has been necessary, the author can only hope that it is intelligent selection and that the materials included will encourage further intensive and extensive research on many of the matters discussed herein.

Chapter One

✶✶✶

Jurisprudence and Sociology

Jurisprudence, or legal philosophy, has long occupied many
of the world's greatest thinkers. The theoretical heritage produced by this ancient quest to illuminate the meaning of law
includes much wisdom, and yet at the same time it reflects a
considerable amount of wishful thinking, misguided analysis, and
intellectual pretentiousness. It may be partly because of the latter
that modern students of the social aspects of law have often paid
insufficient attention to the former. Of course it is always likely
that one man's wisdom may be taken by another to be misguided
analysis. It is, however, the general questions posed in jurisprudence, rather than the answers provided by the particular competing schools of legal theory, that are of the greatest importance.
Such central issues as "What is law?" "What is justice?" and "Is
bad law, law?" continue to plague us today.

Most sociologists find it difficult to accept the *manner* in which
jurisprudence has sought to answer such challenging questions.
Many might even query whether the questions really are answerable by any means. Typically—even within those schools of legal
theory that place relatively heavy emphasis on social and cultural
aspects of law—the technique of analysis has been completely

17

nonempirical. In some of the analytical schemes, the attempt to determine the meaning of law has taken the form, either explicitly or implicitly, of specifying what the law should be. For those who study society empirically and insist that the "is" and the "ought" must be kept separate, this mode of operation will usually not be acceptable—at least not when presented as embodying more than the value preferences of the particular theorists. Although some legal philosophers have insisted that we must find out what the law "really is" rather than simply speculating about it, even these theorists have rarely had much feeling for what a truly empirical investigation of legal phenomena would entail; or if they did, they showed little inclination to pursue such investigation themselves. At its best, then, and no matter how sociological *in orientation,* jurisprudence has not approximated a real sociology of law.

This comment is not to say that the various theories have not had any influence upon or provided useful leads for the sociological study of legal systems. No matter how committed we are to an empirical orientation, it is impossible to avoid the socioethical dilemmas that continuously arise in the operation of legal systems. Individuals and groups within a society, including legal functionaries themselves, find it necessary to make ethical choices regarding legal matters, to assess in whatever terms they choose to adopt the meaning to them of "law" and "justice," to decide what stand they will take when a proposed legal policy is advanced or decision suggested. These choices—which, in turn, influence the actual shaping of the legal system and hence help to determine that which we are concerned with studying empirically—are not easy to make. There are always conflicting interpretations and alternative conclusions that can be reached. From a variety of philosophical perspectives and expressed or inarticulate premises, jurisprudence provides a rich storehouse of possible responses.

In order to provoke his students into confronting some of the perplexities of defining law and understanding legal processes,

Lon L. Fuller, professor at the Harvard Law School, has presented two intriguing hypothetical law cases. It may be useful to relate one of these here in brief summary form, covering the basic facts and the alternative grounds for decision and suggesting some of the features or problems of legal systems highlighted by Fuller's presentation. (The other case, which is equally stimulating and which raises some rather different but also very important issues, may be found as an appendix to Professor Fuller's recent book *The Morality of Law*.)[1]

The Speluncean Explorers[2]

Fuller tells us that five members of an amateur cave-exploring society were trapped inside a deep and isolated cave following a landslide. After some time, through the efforts of relatives and the cave-exploring society, rescuers located the cave only to encounter repeated obstacles to removing the trapped men. At great monetary expense and the cost of ten rescuers' lives (in a subsequent landslide), the rescue operation finally succeeded thirty-two days after the men entered the cave. On the twentieth day, communication between the rescuers and the trapped explorers had been established, when it was discovered that the latter had with them in the cave a radio transmitter-receiver. At that time, the trapped men asked for medical advice as to whether they could live without food (there was none in the cave) for the time engineers had determined would be required to rescue them. A physicians' committee at the rescue site stated that they could not. When the trapped men later inquired if they could survive by consuming the flesh of one of their number, the reply was ("reluctantly") in the affirmative. But the explorers could get no guidance at all (from the physicians or from any clergyman or judge) when they went on to ask about the advisability of casting lots to determine who should be killed and eaten.

When the men were finally released, the rescuers learned that on the twenty-third day one of them, Whetmore, had been killed and eaten by the other four. Although originally it had been Whetmore's idea (at first resisted by his companions) that such an act might be necessary for survival, and also that a casting of lots would be the fairest means of selection, just before the dice were cast, Whetmore changed his mind. His companions disallowed this sudden switch, however, and cast the dice for him, after obtaining his agreement that this procedure was fair; he lost and was put to death and eaten by the others. Following recuperation, the survivors were charged with Whetmore's murder, held guilty of that crime by the judge (after the jury had rendered a special verdict, leaving final decision to the court), and sentenced to be executed. Both judge and jury later recommended to the Chief Executive commutation of the sentence to six months' imprisonment.

Following this recital of facts, Fuller offers, in the form of "opinions" written by five fictitious justices (of the "Supreme Court of Newgarth, 4300"), some alternative lines of reasoning which such a situation might summon forth. The Chief Justice, noting that the relevant statute ("Whoever shall willfully take the life of another shall be punished by death") provides no exception appropriate to the case at hand, upholds the conviction and urges his colleagues to join in the recommendations for executive clemency. Indeed, he sees this outcome as highly desirable since "then justice will be accomplished without impairing either the letter or spirit of our statutes and without offering any encouragement for the disregard of law."

To a colleague on the bench, Justice Foster, this solution seems a sordid expedient. Arguing that "a case may be removed morally from the force of a legal order, as well as geographically," he maintains that the enacted statutes simply did not apply to this unusual situation. The men were in a "state of nature" calling for new legal principles; they were, in effect, required to create their own government—one appropriate to their condition. Noting that ten lives were lost in the rescue effort, he asks why the sacrifice of one member of the trapped group, a sacrifice that effectively saved the remaining four, should be considered so reprehensible. Finally, taking an alternative tack, Foster claims that even if the regular statute were held applicable to this case, reasonable interpretation of it (in line with earlier decisions, upholding the right of self-defense) requires a determination of innocence.

A third judge, Tatting, says that having struggled long over the perplexities of the case, he concludes that the established laws and legal principles must apply. "By what authority," he asks, "do we resolve ourselves into a Court of Nature?" He then denies the self-defense analogy, cites a case where hunger was not allowed as a defense against larceny (of a loaf of bread), and suggests further that one cannot assume that a guilty verdict in the case at hand might not serve some useful deterrent effect. Expressing regret that the prosecutor has found it necessary to seek a murder indictment, Tatting states he has found no formula whatsoever "capable of resolving the equivocations that beset me on all sides"; for this reason he announces, in a move unprecedented in the court's history, that he is withdrawing from the case.

Justice Keen, also writing a separate opinion, insists that it is not the court's job to decide whether executive clemency should be extended. He personally would favor a complete pardon for the defendants, but in his role as judge he cannot rule on such matters. Likewise, it is not up to the court to determine the rightness or wrongness of the defendants' act. All that is necessary is to apply the statute. Castigating his colleague Foster, whom, he claims, doesn't really like *any* statutes, Keen insists on the doctrine of legislative supremacy. For the judges to substitute their will for that of the legislature would be improper and would, in the long run, contribute to an undermining of the legal system. For these reasons, he states, the conviction must be affirmed.

Finally, we have the opinion of Justice Handy, who expresses amazement at the "tortured ratiocinations" of his colleagues. The problem, he asserts, is one of "practical wisdom" and "human realities," not reducible to abstract theories. Endless legal dissection of the issues only serves to drain "the life and juice" out of a very real and human situation. According to Handy, legal forms and concepts must be seen primarily as instruments, if flexible rule in the interests of the citizenry is to be maintained. And some practical facts must be noted: that the case has aroused enormous international publicity and that a large-scale opinion survey found 90 percent of the public in favor of a pardon or token punishment. Furthermore, if the verdict is upheld by the Supreme Court, executive clemency is most unlikely; the Governor (as was reliably reported by Handy's wife's niece, "an intimate friend of his secretary") is definitely resolved not to commute the sentence (as might be expected of him, "a man now well advanced in years, of very stiff notions"). Insisting on the importance of applying common sense in legal matters, and stating that the defendants "have already suffered more torment and humiliation than most of us would endure in a thousand years," Handy finds them innocent and declares that the sentence should be set aside. With the court evenly divided, and in the face of Justice Tatting's subsequent refusal to reconsider his withdrawal, the conviction and sentence of the lower court are upheld.

It has not been possible, in this short summary, to do full justice to Professor Fuller's fascinating and intricate interweaving of diverse themes and arguments. Nonetheless—and notwithstanding that on the face of it, the case may not seem "sociological" in any conventional sense of the term—we can see here certain recurrent questions confronting legal systems, questions that must be taken into account by anyone attempting to understand how such systems operate. Above all, the point is brought home forcefully that legal issues are not simple and clear-cut. Likewise, we cannot help but conclude that judges are human beings, whose varying orientations and propensities indeed represent an important factor contributing to the complexity of legal matters. A significant question on which these particular judges differ, in fact, is, To what extent, and in what ways, ought the judge's human feelings influence his decisions? (From a sociological standpoint, this question may be reframed to read, To what extent, and in what ways, *do* the judge's feelings influence his decisions?) Another key issue concerns the existence of some sort of "natural law" and the relation between any such law and positive law (enacted statutes and existing bodies of judicial precedent). Then too, if there is a natural law, when and where does it have jurisdiction? What are the appropriate roles of the legislature and the judiciary in the legal process? How should judges interpret statutes? To what extent should they take account of facts outside the litigation itself? The Case of the Speluncean Explorers indicates how all these issues (and others) can be posed by a single set of facts confronting one court at a given time and place. For a broader view of some of the general orientations reflected in the differing judicial opinions in that case, it may be useful to consider briefly some of the important schools of jurisprudence, in order to assess their influence on and relevance for a sociological approach to the law.

Some Influences from Jurisprudence

Few sociologists doing research on present-day legal systems specifically cite the work of leading legal philosophers of the past, and probably it is correct to say that the influence of the latter on the former has mostly been indirect and diffuse. Some of the more important lines of continuity between jurisprudence and sociological analysis of the legal order are depicted in Figure 1. This chart does not purport to show all possible jurisprudential influences on the sociology of law. And, again it should be stressed that the influences it does show have, in the main, been subtle ones. At the very least, however, we can say that many of the areas studied by sociologists of law do seem to coincide with the central concerns of the various schools of jurisprudence.

In the remarks that follow, no attempt is made to provide a comprehensive or depth analysis of jurisprudential theories. Since our concern is primarily with sociology and the law, it may be legitimate to lift out of the work of an individual thinker or even an entire school those central ideas that seem most germane to such a concern. With a focus on sociologically relevant themes, no attempt is made to trace out the strictly philosophical antecedents of particular positions. Similarly, it is not possible here to deal with the theorists' specific formulations relating to areas of substantive law. Many important theorists are omitted entirely. Virtually all the great philosophers have provided some sort of analysis of the meaning and place of law in human life. The present work cannot include much discussion of the work of such thinkers as Aristotle, Plato, Kant, Hegel, Locke, Hobbes, Rousseau, and Montesquieu. Readers desiring an analysis of their writings are referred to the numerous studies in philosophy and political science that cover this ground.[3] Another important body of legal theory that is not treated at length in this chapter— Marxist analysis—will be alluded to in later sections of the study.

FORMALISTIC APPROACHES

Some legal philosophers (in particular, the natural-law theorists, who will be singled out for special discussion following examination of the other antecedents of the sociology of law) have emphasized the relation of law to some overarching system of moral principles. Others, frequently labeled "positivists," have

FIGURE 1 *Some Antecedents of the Sociology of Law*

NATURAL LAW (*Aristotle, Aquinas, Grotius*)	FORMALISM (*Austin, Kelsen*)	CULTURAL *and* HISTORICAL SCHOOLS (*Savigny, Maine*)	UTILITARIANISM (*Bentham, Iaering*)	SOCIOLOGICAL JURISPRUDENCE (*Ehrlich, Pound*)	LEGAL REALISM (*Holmes, Llewellyn, Frank*)
Law and morals	Study of legal reasoning	Cultural contexts of law (including relationship between law and major value systems)	Social consequences of law	Law as a mechanism of social control	
"Legality" and "justice" as aims of the legal system (or even the hallmark of "the legal")	Emphasis on function of legal consistency	Law and social change	Inappropriate uses of legislation	Political and "interest" aspects of law (including law and stratification)	
	Formal role of legal functionaries ("sovereign")		Classification of human and social purposes	Relation between legal reality and law "in the books"	
				Law and public policy	
				"Human side" of the law	
				Studies of judicial decision-making and courtroom behavior	

Study of "Law in Action"

Less Pronounced Influence   More Pronounced Influence

considered the legal and the moral to constitute two quite separate realms. Contemporary experts on jurisprudence appear to
be in some confusion or disagreement as to precisely what points
are central to "legal positivism." [4] But at any rate, one important
offshoot or branch of this positivistic orientation is an approach
that can be termed alternatively a formalistic, conceptualistic, or
analytical theory of law. Most noted of the formalistic schemes is
that developed by the British legal philosopher John Austin
(1790–1859), which is usually termed "analytical jurisprudence." [5]

Austin is perhaps best known for his definition of law as the
command of a sovereign. While this definition has been an influential doctrine, it has been noted that Austin, compared with
other analysts who have used the terminology of sovereignty
(such as Hobbes and Bodin), was much less interested in dealing
with the substance of power and social relations. Austin's jurisprudence was labeled analytical because of one of his more central concerns—the development of a formal, logical closed system
of legal rules. As Julius Stone put it, Austin's main purpose was
"to suggest a framework for viewing law as a logically self-consistent system; it was not to provide a theory of how power was
or ought to be, distributed in society." [6] Austin was not concerned with the goodness or badness of legal rules, considering
such matters extralegal questions. Likewise, although he recognized that conceptions of a moral law or a law of nature might
influence people strongly, he insisted that such conceptions were
not *legally* important. According to one contemporary political
theorist, the essence of formalism, of which Austin's work seems
a prime example, lies in "treating law as an isolated block of
concepts that have no relevant characteristics or functions apart
from their possible validity or invalidity within a hypothetical
system." [7] The desire for such a self-consistent and fully exhaustive body of legal norms is understandable. As numerous writers
have noted, the search for certainty is an inarticulate premise

underlying man's development of systems of law. Then too, if there were such a readily applied system of rules, it would be possible for judges to act without any reference to their personal values.

Unfortunately, as critics of Austin are quick to point out, the reality of a legal system can never be fully contained within such a closed logical structure. Invariably any such hypothetical structure of norms would inhibit the flexibility needed for legal adaptation to changing social conditions and for dealing with totally new situations. And it would fail to account for the human as well as the social factors that invariably intrude themselves into the workings of an actual legal order. Nor is the emphasis on commands of a sovereign entirely helpful. Apart from any difficulty in tracing back the "commands" of judges and other subordinates of the "sovereign" to a supposed underlying command from the top, it could be argued, at least by normative critics, that Austin's scheme seems to provide all "official" action with an undesirable immunity from criticism.

Another influential example of the formalistic approach is the so-called "pure theory of law" developed by Hans Kelsen (1881–   ).[8] Kelsen views the legal system as a hierarchy of norms, with legal acts and rules at any level traceable to norms at still higher levels, culminating in the "basic norm" (*Grundnorm*), which is the major premise of the entire system. The validity of law is determined solely through this process of authorization by higher norms and ultimately by the basic norm. Kelsen's use of the term "pure" (indeed sometimes he refers to a "pure science" of law) is significant, because it indicates his desire to proclaim law as an independent, self-enclosed realm or discipline. To this end, he insists, along with Austin, on an absolute separation between the law and moral considerations. His theory has as its aim "to show the law as it is, without legitimizing it as just, or disqualifying it as unjust; it seeks the real, the positive law, not the right law. . . . It refuses to evaluate the positive law." [9] Similarly, although not emphasizing the concept of sovereignty, Kelsen asserts the "unity of State and law." He writes:

> The attempt to justify the State by law is vain, since every State is necessarily a legal state. Law, says positivism, is nothing but an order of human compulsion. As to the justice or morality of that order, positivism itself has nothing to say. The State is neither more nor less than the law. . . .[10]

While Kelsen's scheme, under which judicial and administrative acts represent the "concretization" or "individualization" of more general norms, might make some sense *given* an acceptable basic norm, critics wonder just what the basic norm consists of, and how its validity is to be determined. As one commentator states, "Kelsen refuses to answer, dismissing the question as irrelevant because it raises considerations which he regards as metajuristic. In the final analysis he assumes the validity of the basic norm *a priori*." [11] Although the basic norm seems to be viewed as residing in a given state's constitution, or in the principles on which such a constitution is based, beyond that, Kelsen is rather vague. Furthermore, the extreme positivism reflected in his equation of state action and law raises some disturbing questions. Kelsen writes:

> Any content whatsoever can be legal; there is no human behavior which could not function as the content of a legal norm. A norm becomes a legal norm only because it has been constituted in a particular fashion, born of a definite procedure and a definite rule. Law is valid only as positive law, that is, statute (constituted) law.[12]

Notwithstanding Kelsen's insistence that the basic norm is neither valid nor invalid (since, being at the top of the ladder of norms, it cannot be checked against any higher norm), his system obviously permits the designation "legal" to apply to measures of great iniquity as well as to those that seem either innocuous or of obvious social value. Kelsen doesn't say that evaluation of such norms is impossible, just that such effort lies quite outside of "legal science."

The impact of these formalistic and positivistic outlooks on modern legal thinkers and students of the social aspects of law has been a mixed one. At the risk of oversimplifying, one is tempted to say that the dominant approaches to law today, at least in the United States, embrace many of the positivistic tenets of these theories but tend to reject the attempt at formalism. Most sociologically oriented legal theorists and most sociologists interested in law insist on the separation of law and morals, the gulf between the "is" and the "ought." Similarly, it is usual to identify the legal, and to distinguish it from mere custom, primarily in terms of the state's power to enforce certain norms and establish certain procedures, even if the term "sovereign" is rarely mentioned. On the other hand, as already noted, modern legal analysts (and certainly sociologists) consider the formalist's search for a self-enclosed body of legal concepts an exercise in wishful thinking. It fails to recognize both the inevitable openness of a legal system and the system's need for flexibility to cope with changing social conditions and legal situations.

At the same time, formalism has had a definite impact on legal thinking and behavior, and even on the social scientist's selection of areas for inquiry. The very real "legal acts" of judges and others directly concerned with developing and interpreting bodies of substantive law are in part shaped by the desire to maintain formal consistency within the legal system. Legal education, particularly in the United States, was for many years (and to a more limited extent, still is) concerned with the searching out of the central legal principle believed to be embodied in each judicial decision, with the key importance of judicial precedent, and with the formal analysis of lines of doctrinal development. Social scientists trying to determine how the judicial process works—no matter how much they may wish to emphasize the social backgrounds of justices, general patterns of social change to which the courts must adjust, and so on—have to take into account the ways in which judges may be constrained by doctrinal considerations and by formal analysis of legal concepts and issues. It is noteworthy that many of the social scientific efforts to predict judicial decision-making are built around the judges' *doctrinal* predilections and past decisions. Although the strain toward formal consistency may sometimes conflict with substantive justice and with the general pressures for legal change it is, in short, a potent factor always to be kept in mind in studying the legal domain.

CULTURAL AND HISTORICAL ORIENTATIONS

In sharp contrast to formalism are those theories that emphasize that a legal order cannot be understood apart from the cultural and historical context within which it occurs. An outstanding theorist of this persuasion was Friedrich Karl von Savigny (1779–1861), who is generally credited with being the founder of "historical jurisprudence." According to Savigny, law is an expression of the common consciousness or spirit of a people (*Volksgeist*). He insisted that all law "is first developed by custom and popular faith, next by jurisprudence—everywhere, therefore, by internal, silently-operating powers, not by the arbitrary will of a law-giver." [13] In line with this view, Savigny stressed the danger that arbitrary legislation might be out of line with the underlying spirit of the people, and he opposed major proposals for the systematic codification of the German law of his time. Reacting against both universalistic and formally abstract theories of law, he insisted on the importance of examining the peculiar relationship between law and the structure and value system of any given society. Savigny was, in other words, alert to what any sociologist would now assert—that a legal system is but part of a larger social order, the various elements of which are interdependent. A major contribution of Savigny's work was to emphasize the dynamics of legal development, even if his approach to law seemed somewhat heavily focused on historical antecedents (as contrasted with the possible *future* lines of legal development examined in some other dynamic interpretations of law, to be noted shortly).

Critics of Savigny's approach have questioned his concept of the *Volksgeist*. Is there actually such a common or public consciousness, and if so, how important a factor is it in shaping law? Noting a minor difference in the principles of contract law as applied in Massachusetts and New York in the early 1900's, the American jurist John Chipman Gray asked:

> Is the common consciousness of the people of Massachusetts different on this point from that of the people of New York? Do the people of Massachusetts feel the necessity of one thing as law, and the people of New York feel the necessity of the precise opposite? In truth, not one in a hundred of the people of either State has the dimmest notion on the matter [whether a contract by letter is complete when acceptance is mailed or when acceptance is received]. If one of them has a notion, it is as likely as not to be contrary to the law of his State.[14]

Other issues raised concerning this theory include the following: Does law simply reflect a common consciousness, or does it at the same time help to shape such consciousness? How can we know just what the common consciousness is? Is there a tendency, in this approach, to evaluate positively that which has emerged historically? Is there a danger that the notion of *Volksgeist* will take on mystical notions of the historic mission of a nation or even racial group—as seen in the use of similar terminology during the Nazi regime? Notwithstanding these caveats, however, Savigny's attempt to place law in historical perspective must be viewed as an important step in the development of broadly social conceptions of the legal system. The sociologist who attempts to study the interrelationship between law and the value system of a society, or to examine public attitudes toward particular laws or aspects of legal procedure, or to analyze patterns of sociolegal change, is pursuing major lines of inquiry suggested by Savigny's work.

Another major figure in the development of historical approaches was Sir Henry Maine (1822–1888), author of the classic work *Ancient Law*.[15] Significantly, Maine stated that unverified theories had enjoyed an unfortunate preference over "sober research into the primitive history of society and law"; this situation was undesirable not only because it diverted attention from the true facts, but also because, once accepted, the theories themselves exercised a definite influence on the subsequent course of development in jurisprudence.[16] Attempting a general historical analysis of the stages of social and legal development, Maine found the dominant trend to be an increase in the basing of rights on free agreement between individuals. Hence his famous assertion that "the movement of the progressive societies has hitherto been a movement *from Status to Contract*." [17] Particularly with respect to the family, but in other realms of law as well, relationships determined solely on the basis of the social positions of the individuals involved gradually gave way to systems of rights and duties determined through contractual arrangements grounded in the voluntary consent of the parties. Clearly Maine was on the mark in citing a major sociological trend. His distinction is similar to those drawn by various sociologists in attempting to portray the differences between simple, relatively static, homogeneous groups and societies and more complex, dynamic, and heterogeneous ones. It is noteworthy that sociologists often cite the legal contract, which is formal, specific, and limited, and in which the parties seek to maximize personal advantage, as a prime example of the "secondary" (impersonal, fragmentary, instrumental) relationships dominating social interaction in modern society.

Various social and legal analysts have pointed to a recent

and reverse trend—from contract back to status—as seen in government regulation of relationships once left to "free competition," for example, in the realms of wages and hours regulation, workmen's compensation laws, and the like. Indeed, it has been suggested that Maine did not examine the ideal of contractual freedom with quite the objectivity he applied to the concept of status. As a result he went rather far in asserting the supreme value of the contract principle. Carl Friedrich states that "Maine looked upon freedom of contract as a kind of crowning achievement of legal development." It should also be noted, however, that "The more recent trend showing a marked renewal of regulation and limitation of freedom of contract was not yet apparent, of course, at the time Sir Henry Maine wrote." [18]

The relevance to the sociology of law of these historical and cultural perspectives should be obvious. As we shall see, such leading sociological theorists as Durkheim and Weber considered the cultural and historical aspects absolutely essential to an understanding of legal phenomena.

UTILITARIANISM

Yet another strain of legal theory that has had (and continues to have) considerable impact is utilitarianism. From the standpoint of studying law sociologically, Jeremy Bentham (1748–1832) is probably the most important representative of this school. An extremely active legal reformer as well as a philosopher of human nature, Bentham combined a strong and avowed interest in what the legal system *should* do, with his efforts to portray its actual workings. Bentham applied in the legal realm the general principles of the utilitarian approach—most notably the proposition that men act in such a fashion as to maximize pleasure and minimize pain, and the ethical rule that an assessment of the happiness produced by a human act should be the

major criterion for approving or disapproving of it. His significant work *An Introduction to the Principles of Morals and
Legislation* opens with the following statement:

> Nature has placed mankind under the governance of two sov-
> ereign masters, *pain* and *pleasure*. It is for them alone to point
> out what we ought to do, as well as to determine what we shall
> do. On the one hand the standard of right and wrong, on the
> other the chain of causes and effects, are fastened to their
> throne.[19]

While Bentham's interest in reform ranged across the entire
legal system, his most substantial legal contributions related to
crime and punishment. These contributions included proposals
in the area we would now call "penology and corrections," work
on the classification of criminal offenses, and a general theory
of punishment. Criminal offenses, he believed, should be coher-
ently classified in terms of the social "mischief" involved and
should be accorded specified punishments, the severity of which
should be no more than the precise amount needed to inhibit
the particular offenses. Punishment, Bentham asserted, is an evil,
and "if it ought at all to be admitted, it ought only to be admitted in as far as it promises to exclude some greater evil."
Furthermore, punishment definitely ought not to be inflicted in
cases where it is "groundless," "inefficacious," "unprofitable," or
"needless." [20]

Certainly, not all of Bentham's formulations are fully acceptable today. Many social scientists would question the application to human behavior of any simplified pleasure-pain
psychology, although the assumption that an individual does
rationally assess consequences before acting continues to be a
basic theme underlying much of our present criminal law. While
sociologists might agree that legislators ought to seek to promote
the "greatest happiness of the greatest number" (Bentham's expansion of the individual-happiness principle), they would be
hard put to say just how this goal can be achieved and would

definitely be reluctant to accept it as a description of the principle on which legislators indeed work. Bentham made a valiant attempt to spell out the kinds of factors that would have to be considered in assessing the pleasure or pain produced by an act, but by the standards of empirical science his system is clearly inadequate. The overwhelming problem, of course, is that what one person views as pleasure another sees as pain; that different groups and segments of society may hold incompatible social goals, not all of which can be achieved at the same time. But despite these difficulties, it is highly significant that Bentham saw the analysis of legislation as a scientific enterprise, that he advocated a systematic assessment of the social consequences of legislation.[21] This emphasis on the likely consequences of alternative policies later appealed greatly to the "sociological jurists" and the "legal realists" (see below). It also presaged a line of inquiry that is increasingly being taken up in sociological studies of law, as, for example, in attitude surveys relating to existing or proposed legislation.

Bentham's strictures concerning inappropriate uses of legislation are also highly relevant to a social analysis of the legal order. In the light of more recent controversies, it is interesting to find Bentham asking:

> With what chance of success . . . would a legislator go about to extirpate drunkenness and fornication by dint of legal punishment? Not all the tortures which ingenuity could invent would compass it: and, before he had made any progress worth regarding, such a mass of evil would be produced by the punishment, as would exceed, a thousandfold, the utmost possible mischief of the offence.[22]

This same line of reasoning also has been developed by representatives of various other schools of legal philosophy, as well as by major sociological theorists (for example, Sumner's discussion of law and mores). Similarly, contemporary students of the legal order are displaying considerable interest in the relationship between legislation and private morality.

Another important juridical thinker placing emphasis on the consequences of law was Rudolph von Ihering (1818–1892), whose philosophy is sometimes termed "social utilitarianism." In his major work, translated under the title *Law as a Means to an End*,[23] Ihering viewed law essentially as the means whereby the organized purposes of society are achieved. Unlike Bentham, he concentrated more on social than on individual purposes. He viewed the law as a device for controlling individual purposes and bringing them into line with social goals. Ihering developed a classification of purposes that was later adopted by the American jurist Roscoe Pound. Ihering's emphasis on purpose can, furthermore, be seen as an antecedent to the policy-oriented approach of the American legal realists. To Ihering, law was a significant instrument for promoting social change. He emphasized its positive effects, writing for example that "it is not the sense of right that has produced law, but it is law that has produced the sense of right."[24] (As mentioned in the Introduction, this question of the effects of law, especially in relation to social change, is a crucial one for sociological analysis.)

Ihering repudiated absolutist standards of good law, arguing instead that a legal order should be assessed in terms of the conditions and aims existing in a particular society and at a particular time. Indeed this relativism even contained the hint "that justice was itself only a relation between human purposes for the time being and the means, legal or other, existing for their fulfilment."[25] Although there are those who would challenge an unabashedly utilitarian conception of law, the appeal to utility exemplified in the work of Bentham and Ihering is extremely attractive to the nonabsolutists, who continue to dominate American conceptions of the legal order.

SOCIOLOGICAL JURISPRUDENCE

The Austrian jurist Eugen Ehrlich (1862–1922) is sometimes called the founder of "sociological jurisprudence," and indeed his major work is titled *Fundamental Principles of the Sociology of Law*.[26] Ehrlich is probably best known for his distinction between the "positive law" and the "living law." Here again, we find a concern for the central issue of the relation between law and more general social norms. According to Ehrlich, the positive law could only be effective if it was in line with the living law, or "social law," grounded in the "inner order of the associations." As one noted interpreter of Ehrlich has suggested, this concept of the inner ordering of social groupings was quite similar to what anthropologists now mean by "culture pattern"; as a result, it would not be entirely inappropriate to consider Ehrlich's work a kind of "anthropological jurisprudence." [27]

Ehrlich stated that "the centre of gravity of legal development lies not in legislation, nor in juristic science, nor in judicial decision, but in society itself." [28] In its relation with more general social forces, law tended to be, in Ehrlich's view, a relatively dependent factor. It could not provide control where the broader social basis for control was absent, and no amount of official proclamation and enforcement could, by itself, make a rule "law" in the truly social sense. Likewise, Ehrlich asserted that order in human society is grounded in the social acceptance of certain rules for living, not on sheer compulsion by the state. Such order "is based upon the fact that, in general, legal duties are being performed, not upon the fact that failure to perform them gives rise to a cause of action." [29] Such law-following, in turn, is attributable to the underlying social rules and regularities which the legal measures tend to reflect.

Ehrlich's work had the merit of directing the attention of

legal analysts to the larger social world. It was here rather than in legal documents, doctrines, or even courtrooms that the forces governing legal phenomena would be found. Unfortunately, it is not always easy to know just which living law should be adopted as a guide to formal legal action. Within a modern, heterogeneous society, there are diverse living laws relating to particular sociolegal issues, as well as to more general social goals that might be implemented through the legal system. As an example of testing the positive law against the living law, F. S. C. Northrop cites the work of Underhill Moore, who went to considerable lengths to examine the actual practices of people in various law-related realms, including violations of parking regulations in New Haven, Connecticut, and the actual behavior of individuals in connection with certain commercial transactions.[30]

A more recent example of this process, presumably, would be the comparison of the norms embodied in current American statutes relating to sexual behavior with the actual (living-law) norms of sexual behavior revealed in systematic empirical inquiries. While such comparison is obviously a useful technique for *explaining* the ineffectiveness of certain official norms, and might even, under a utilitarian ethic, provide a basis for policy, the *application* within the legal system of such findings clearly takes us beyond *scientific* questions. Thus Ehrlich's doctrine of the living law should be recognized as an important aid in understanding the legal order; it should not be mistaken for a principle on which to base a legal science. Even Northrop, who seems at times to invest the concept of living law with a kind of moral validity, is forced to recognize its limits. As he rightly notes, the living-law norms of one people are not necessarily those of another.[31] This comment is as true when it is applied to subgroups and categories within any one society as when it refers to the problems of developing a really effective international legal order, the object of Northrop's statement.

Sociological jurisprudence became a major force in American legal thought through the extensive writings of Roscoe Pound (1870–1964).[32] Pound asserted that law had to be viewed as a social institution designed to satisfy "social wants," and he considered it a task of jurisprudence to develop a scheme whereby the maximum satisfaction of socially worthwhile purposes might be accomplished. This theme is evident in his view of legal history as

> the record of a continually wider recognizing and satisfying of human wants or claims or desires through social control; a more embracing and more effective securing of social interests; a continually more complete and effective elimination of waste and precluding of friction in human enjoyment of the goods of existence—in short, a continually more efficacious social engineering.[33]

At the heart of Pound's entire program for developing a sociological jurisprudence lay the call for a study of law as it actually is—the "law in action," which Pound distinguished from the law in the books. As a leading disciple of Pound has noted, this distinction is applicable across the entire realm of legal substance and procedure. It encompasses the question of whether the enacted law is in line with prevailing behavior patterns (Ehrlich's living law), but extends to other possible discrepancies as well, for example, those between what courts say and what they actually do, and between the express aim of a statute and its actual effects.[34]

Needless to say, this emphasis on legal *reality* is absolutely central for the sociologist who intends to study legal phenomena. (Indeed, on this particular point, sociological jurisprudence and the sociology of law are virtually indistinguishable.) There is little likelihood of this concern for discrepancies between the stated and the actual becoming outdated. That professed law and actual law may diverge sharply is evident at many points in the present-day American legal system. The discrepancies between America's professed belief in equal justice before the law and the legal treatment of the Negro in some jurisdictions, between the stated requirement that divorce be only for "fault" and the actualities of marital dissolution, and between the ostensible and covert aims of the trial lawyer in the examination of prospective jurors, are but a few examples.

Also eminently sociological were Pound's recognition that law is but one of a number of mechanisms of social control and his appreciation of the web of conflicting interests calling forth, lying beneath, and continually challenging the legal order. And in his discussion of "jural postulates" (a concept drawn largely from the work of the German legal philosopher Kohler), Pound sought to formulate the crucial values of modern civilization which the law, in its attempts to reconcile conflicting interests, should, or must seek to, maintain. Although the details of applying this scheme may not have been entirely clear, nonetheless it constituted an important recognition of the necessary relation between law and systems of widely held human values.

Gilbert Geis has pointed out[35] that the sociological emphases in Pound's writings are attributable partly to the direct influence upon him of several leading American sociologists—Edward A. Ross, Albion Small, and Lester Ward. Although as noted in the Introduction, interest in law did not become a major focal point in American sociological research, these three sociologists did maintain such an interest. In his book, *Social Control* (1901), Ross, even while considering public opinion a more potent controlling agent, referred to law as "the most specialized and highly finished engine of control employed by society." [36] Pound was a commissioner of the Supreme Court of Nebraska at the same time that Ross was on the faculty of that state's university; they became friends and Pound was later to report that Ross's sociological thinking had influenced him greatly.[37] From the writings of

JURISPRUDENCE AND SOCIOLOGY   41

Lester Ward, Pound may have received reinforcement of his belief in the efficacy of using scientific study to reform the legal
order. A radical advocate of government intervention to control
the affairs of men, Ward saw sociology as providing the guidelines and even the implementation of such action. He foresaw a
day when legislation would become

> a series of exhaustive experiments on the part of true scientific
> sociologists and sociological inventors working on the problems
> of social physics from the practical point of view. It will under-
> take to solve not only questions of general interest to the state.
> . . . but questions of social improvement, the amelioration of
> the condition of all the people, the removal of whatever priva-
> tions may still remain, and the adoption of means to the positive
> increase of the social welfare, in short the organization of human
> happiness.[38]

The same emphasis on social reform or "engineering" was present
in Albion Small's work—along with a focus on categories of human interest, a matter that also was to occupy Pound. According
to Small:

> . . . the most reliable criterion of human values science can
> propose would be the consensus of councils of scientists repre-
> senting the largest possible variety of human interest, and co-
> operating to reduce their special judgments to a scale which
> would render their due to each of the interests of the total
> calculation.[39]

The above comments are not intended to suggest that the
sociological and legal worlds of the time were, in general, working closely together. As Geis has noted, on each side there was a
considerable resistance to the other's perspectives. Furthermore,
while both the sociologists and some lawyers felt that sociology
might help resolve *legal* problems, few sociologists believed that
their main work (that of understanding society in general) would
benefit greatly from a knowledge of, or contact with, the law.

Pound's work did help, however, to promote more cooperative and understanding outlooks.[40] A tremendously prolific writer, Pound ranged across the entire field of legal topics. He displayed a strong interest in judicial organization and procedure, as seen in a pioneering paper on "The Causes of Popular Dissatisfaction with the Administration of Criminal Justice" (1906).[41] On issues of legal substance, an article often cited by current researchers is his "The Limits of Effective Legal Action" (1917),[42] in which, tackling a problem that had also concerned Bentham, Ehrlich and others, he considered the conditions under which law loses its effectiveness as an agency of social control. In more specific areas of substantive law, Pound's many contributions had an enormous impact on American law, both influencing theory and generating specific legal reforms.

It is noteworthy that Pound placed great faith in social research. He called directly for systematic study of legal phenomena, deploring the lack of "endowments for juridical research" or "laboratories dedicated to legal science." [43] We may also attribute largely to sociological jurisprudence the practice of using "evidence" from the social sciences in actual court cases, a matter that is discussed extensively below. This practice is often said to have begun with the so-called Brandeis brief, initiated by Justice Louis D. Brandeis, who is usually considered to have been a sociological jurist. The Brandeis brief used social data in support of judicial rulings on the constitutionality of welfare legislation. As we shall see, this practice was certainly a major innovation with highly significant implications for the relationship between the social sciences and the legal order. But it should also be recognized that on this point as on others, there is a somewhat confusing mixture of normative and scientific aims to be found in sociological jurisprudence. For, as Edmond Cahn has persuasively noted, "Shrewd, resourceful lawyers can put a Brandeis brief together in support of almost any conceivable exercise of legislative judgment." [44]

In short, sociological jurisprudence left an indelible mark on American legal thought and also provided suggestive guidelines for social research on the law. While it was not, in its own right, a purely scientific "sociology of law"—for it clearly embodied in large measure specific normative prescriptions for the legal order —it came very close to being one, both in theoretical orientation and in some of its proposed lines of investigation. Unfortunately, many of Pound's most important proposals, such as creation of special interdisciplinary institutes to engage in large-scale research on the legal system, did not really catch fire at the time. We are just now beginning to see Pound's remarkable schemes coming to fruition.

LEGAL REALISM

Another lasting influence on modern thinking about law was provided by the so-called legal realists. Two of the most notable of the American realists were Karl Llewellyn (1893–1962) and Jerome Frank (1889–1957). Justice Oliver Wendell Holmes (1841–1935) may also be included under this designation, although the "sociological jurists" such as Pound insisted that Holmes was really an early representative of their school.[45]

The realists' approach was grounded in a radical conception of the judicial process. They asserted, with varying degrees of emphasis, that judges *make law rather than find it*. The judge always has to choose. He has to decide which principle will prevail and which party will win. According to the realists, this decision (as to the outcome of the case or the policy that shall be advanced) often *precedes* the recourse to, and elaboration of, formal legal principle. Judicial precedent and legal doctrine can be found or developed to support almost any outcome. The real decision is made first—on the basis of the judge's conceptions of justness, determined partly by his predilections, personal background, and so forth—and *then* it is "rationalized" in the written opinion.

Similarly, at the trial court level, juries decide cases as they do because of their feelings about right and wrong and about whatever in the trial makes a special impact on them, rather than in terms of the strictly legal points advanced by the attorneys and conveyed to them by the judge. Thus, to the sociological jurists' insistence on heeding the law in action, legal realism added a still further stress on the *human* nature of such action.

Since the law is always human, it cannot be absolute. Hence the grounds for Holmes's famous comment that the law "is not a brooding omnipresence in the sky. . . ." [46] Accepting the positivistic tenet that we can never prove values and hence cannot scientifically establish what is just law, the realists nonetheless were greatly concerned with justice. Indeed they argued not only that the legal functionary does in fact decide cases according to his sense of justice, but also that he must face up to the responsibility of deciding as best he can what legal rules and policies *should be* in force. Through their recognition that policy issues always are at stake, and always are resolved, in legal determinations, the legal realists, whose critics sometimes condemn them for blatant relativism, were, in a way, facing most directly the ethical implications of legal rules.

Justice Holmes's often quoted and widely reprinted essay "The Path of the Law" [47] set forth some of the basic propositions of the realist outlook. Stating that "a legal duty so called is nothing but a prediction that if a man does or omits certain things he will be made to suffer in this or that way by judgment of a court," [48] Holmes asserted that if we really want to know the law we must look at it "as a bad man" does, that is, as one who cares nothing for general moral pronouncements and abstract legal doctrines. What is important to the "bad man" is "what the Massachusetts or English courts are likely to do in fact. I am much of his mind. The prophecies of what the courts will do in fact, and nothing more pretentious, are what I mean by the law." [49] Applying this reasoning to some specific areas of the law,

Holmes argued, for example, that there is nothing mystical about the basic principles of the law of contracts: "The duty to keep a contract at common law means a prediction that you must pay damages if you do not keep it—and nothing else." [50]

If abstract moralism was anathema to Holmes, so was the effort to work out a purely logical system of legal rules. He saw this effort as a natural consequence of the lawyer's training in logic and of the general human search for certainty, but felt that any sense of absolute certainty about the law was bound to be illusory.

> Behind the logical forms lies a judgment as to the relative worth and importance of competing legislative grounds, often an inarticulate and unconscious judgment, it is true, and yet the very root and nerve of the whole proceeding. You can give any conclusion a logical form.[51]

Lawyers and judges, Holmes believed, should face up to these underlying policy issues and replace their absorption in abstract reasoning with an effort to get to the bottom of the subject of the legislation or proposed legal rule. Along with the usual search for relevant legal principle they should, quite openly, "consider the ends which the several rules seek to accomplish, the reasons why those ends are desired, what is given up to gain them, and whether they are worth the price." [52]

Karl Llewellyn, who placed strong emphasis on the relation between legal rulings and the general and changing social context within which they occur, developed a moderate version of the legal-realist theory. Llewellyn's interest in sociological perspectives led him to team with an anthropologist, E. A. Hoebel, to produce a pioneering interdisciplinary analysis of "primitive" law, *The Cheyenne Way* (1941).[53] The emphasis in this work on "the law-jobs" (major functions of legal institutions, having both a "pure survival" or "bare bones" aspect for the society and a "questing" or "betterment" value as well)[54] contributed significantly to the development of a modern, functional approach to the legal system. With respect to the judicial process, Llewellyn called for attention to the *actual* behavior of courts; he stressed the need to determine "how far the paper rule is real, how far *merely* paper." [55] Recognizing that the judge is both human and (usually) a lawyer, Llewellyn noted the continuous interplay between value judgment and rule by precedent. It is the business of the courts, he wrote:

> . . . to use the precedents constantly to make the law a *little* better, to correct old mistakes, to recorrect mistaken or ill-advised attempts at correction—but always within limits severely set not only by the precedents, but equally by the traditions of right conduct in judicial office. [56]

A more radical version of legal realism, and one of perhaps special interest to the sociological student of law, was developed by Jerome Frank. In *Law and the Modern Mind* (1930) and more especially in *Courts on Trial* (1949), Frank asserted that jurisprudence had been unhealthily preoccupied with the nature of appellate decision. He urged that increased attention be paid the work of the trial courts, for only if one examined the roles of judge and jury at this lower court level could one gain a comprehensive understanding of the judicial process. On the basis of what really goes on in the court trial, Frank concluded that one must add what he termed "fact skepticism" to the "rule skepticism" already propounded by Llewellyn and others.

As Frank indicated, the essential work of the trial court is the determination of facts, a reconstruction of the past situation that has given rise to a dispute. There is no simple way of being certain just what those facts really were; and the adversary nature of the trial proceedings, in which the lawsuit becomes a kind of combat, may often serve to obscure rather than reveal the true facts. The notion that through such confrontation of adversaries the "truth will out" glosses over the numerous elements of subjectivity and chance, the many sources of possible error on the part of witnesses, the fact that judges and juries are themselves "silent witnesses of the witnesses [who] suffer from the same human weaknesses as other witnesses." [57] Since the trial can only be an extremely imperfect process of reconstruction, "fact finders," Frank insisted, really make the facts every bit as much as they find them.

Even the conscientious judge is likely to reach his basic decision in one essentially subjective grasp of the entire situation (a "gestalt") and then to rationalize it through legal doctrine. Where a jury is to "find" the facts, the obstacles to objective reconstruction are still greater. The jurors are in no way specially qualified to assess dispassionately and intelligently the conflicting claims. And the combat of the trial makes it almost impossible for them to remain detached. As Frank pointed out:

> . . . the lawyer aims at winning in the fight, not at aiding the court to discover the facts. He does not want the trial court to reach a sound educated guess, if it is likely to be contrary to his client's interests. Our present trial method is thus the equivalent of throwing pepper in the eyes of a surgeon when he is performing an operation.[58]

With this dual skepticism of abstract legal rules and of actual courtroom ways, and drawing on his own long experience as a practicing lawyer and later a judge, Frank proposed various practical reforms. He urged that legal education should include exposure to real court trials and should emphasize the human and policy aspects of the law. He also advocated special training for trial judges, including intensive self-analysis. And he advocated limiting the role of the jury, and wherever possible transferring the function of fact-finding to impartial experts or at least to honest, well-trained judges. Frank's most significant contributions, however, were probably more general ones of outlook and emphasis. He leveled a devastating challenge against the adversary nature of the court trial, alerted his readers to the difficulties (almost the impossibility) of determining the true facts, and pioneered in recognizing the role of subjective elements in the decision-making process.

Eventually, and under the prodding of critics, Frank and other legal realists came to admit that there was a good deal more to the process of judicial decision-making than subjective whim colored by personal-background characteristics. Interestingly, Frank's own experience once he had been elevated to the bench appeared to mellow his view of the matter. Nonetheless, at least a moderate version of the realists' general thesis—that judges do not simply "find" the law—has received widespread acceptance. While some social analysts would insist that the judge's role in the legal system exerts a constraining influence upon him, the assertion that judges in fact "make" much law is one that most sociologists can easily accept. Similarly, the realist thesis that policy issues are central to legal disputes, and that every outcome constitutes a form of policy, is generally consistent with sociological views. For example, sociologists at least since Max Weber would insist that "nonaction" is itself a form of social action; this point comes across nicely in the realist analysis, with the realization that following past precedent is as much a policy act as rejecting it—in neither case can the need to make policy be avoided.

The notion of "law as prediction" developed by the legal realists also has relevance for the sociologist, although its meaning is somewhat blurred. On the one hand, there is the realist insistence that law is *nothing but* a prediction of how particular courts will actually behave. Here the emphasis is on undermining the idea of any absolute sense of certainty in legal matters, such as formalists might see imposed through a logical system of principles and through a strain toward consistency and the following of precedent. On the other hand, there is the social scientist's desire to predict (for a class of cases or in diverse situations, as compared with the "bad man's" interest in his specific case) how courts behave. A prerequisite to such analysis is that there is an ascertainable degree of regularity and consistency in judicial behavior. Actually, these aspects of "law as prediction" do not necessarily contradict each other. Except in their most extreme statements, the legal realists themselves recognized that a combination of continuity and reaction to the individual case characterizes decision-making. Furthermore, the consistency required for sociological prediction need not be, though it can be, either in whole or in part, consistency based on application of legal principles. Indeed, the regularity in a judge's or a court's behavior may be attributable largely to personal-background characteristics or to general policy predilections of the judges themselves, thus rendering the two aspects of prediction quite compatible with each other. In any case, the efforts by social scientists to develop predictive analyses of judicial decisions are very likely indebted, in one way or another, to the doctrines of the legal realists.

Frank, in particular, provided very helpful leads for the sociologically minded student of law when he called for increased focus on the trial courts and on the difficulties involved in ascertaining the legally relevant facts of a case. Analyses of law from the point of view of the social sciences have, at least in the United States, paid inordinate attention to appellate courts, and especially to the content of particular decisions, as in much of the work of political scientists on the U.S. Supreme Court. Now we are beginning to see, even in studies of appellate courts, an interest not only in particular lines of public-policy development but also in the factors involved in the general *process* of reaching decisions. Similarly, and particularly among sociologists, increased attention is being paid to the work of the lower courts. In research on the court trial, the perspective characterized by skepticism of the facts cannot be ignored. Frank's insistence that careless or biased testimony, missing evidence or unavailable witnesses, honest mistake and outright perjury, are all possibilities to be reckoned with in any trial—compounded by the fact that both juror and judge are cast in the role of a kind of secondary observer, assessing the attorneys' competing efforts to reconstruct the past—rings true for the sociologist. No understanding of the workings of law at the trial-court level is conceivable unless we recognize that the courtroom itself is an arena of ongoing social action.[59]

Together with sociological jurisprudence, legal realism had a pronounced impact on American legal education—leading at least the nationally oriented law schools to offer courses on the interrelations of law and the social sciences and to develop a less formalistic and more policy-oriented conception of the judicial process and the nature of law. From Holmes on, the realist approach to law reflected an important general development in American thought, which the philosopher Morton White has termed "the revolt against formalism." [60] It also signaled the influence of Freudian psychoanalysis on legal thinking, as seen in Frank's *Law and the Modern Mind,* where the author stated:

> Why do men seek unrealizable certainty in law? Because . . . they have not yet relinquished the childish need for an authoritative father and unconsciously have tried to find in the law a substitute for those attributes of firmness, sureness, certainty and infallibility ascribed in childhood to the father.[61]

Through the active participation in Franklin Roosevelt's New Deal government of such men as Frank, Thurman Arnold,[62] and William O. Douglas, the orientation of legal realism made a very definite contribution to the shaping of American public policy in a crucial period of stress and change. This contribution suggests one of the most interesting features of the realist outlook —that it combined a strong belief in relativism with a powerful desire to reform, and hence, make more "just," the existing legal and social orders.[63] It is this combination that has led one commentator[64] to see in legal realism a kind of synthesis of positivism and the philosophy of natural law.

NATURAL LAW AND SOCIOLOGY

As we have seen in Figure 1, natural-law theory, along with formalism, in a way its most radical opposite, has not, to date, greatly influenced sociological research on the legal order. Nonetheless, it is in connection with this school of legal theory that some of the most challenging questions of the interrelation between sociology and jurisprudence arise. Among some sociologists there is a renewed interest in natural-law perspectives, stemming in part from a stimulating and influential essay by Philip Selznick, in which he asserts that the low reputation of natural law among sociologists is sad, "because sociology should have a ready affinity for the philosophy of natural law." [65] Before considering Selznick's argument in more detail, a few general points about the natural-law approach are in order.

The idea of natural law is possibly as old as philosophy. Clearly we cannot here explore the concept in depth or consider in detail the many varieties of thought it covers. But as Kessler has cogently stated, all philosophies of natural law share a basic common belief "in the existence of certain fundamental legal principles and institutions deeply grounded in the general plan of life and inherent in all ordered social existence. These principles laying down absolute standards of justice are open to man's cognition." [66] Among the most noted classic definitions of natural law are those of Aristotle ("Of political justice part is natural, that which everywhere has the same force and does not exist by peoples' thinking this or that"; also, "reason unaffected by desire"); Cicero ("There is in fact a true law, namely right reason, which is in accordance with nature, applies to all men and is unchangeable and eternal"); Thomas Aquinas ("an ordinance of reason for the common good, made . . . by him who has care of the community"); and Grotius ("a dictate of right reason which points out that an act according as it is or is not in conformity with the social and rational nature of man has in it a quality of moral baseness or moral necessity . . . such an act is either forbidden or enjoined by the author of nature, God").[67]

The theory of natural law is always grounded in the assertion that through reason we can know the nature of man and that this knowledge should be the basis for the social and legal ordering of human existence. Sometimes the positive (enacted) law has been said inevitably to reflect natural law. More often the natural law is viewed as a higher order against which to assess the positive law. When positive law is found to be out of line with such higher principles, it is said to be "unjust law" or "not law at all." Although we tend today to associate the natural-law approach with Roman Catholicism (since the Roman Catholic Church not only asserts such principles but seeks to apply them through rules governing various spheres of common human behavior), the central idea of natural law is not necessarily tied to any particular theology, or even to theology in general. Conceptions of the nature of man, which might serve as ethical yardsticks for the legal order, are many indeed. Recently the psychologist Erich Fromm has attempted such a formulation of the basic qualities of man, a formulation that could well be conceived of as one variety of secularistic and humanistic natural-law theory.[68] Another modern version of nontheological natural law is offered by Robert Hutchins, who asserts that "there are actual, existing, universal human ends" to which legal systems should be geared— "self-preservation, self-perfection, self-propagation, and social fellowship." [69] Similarly, the legal philosopher H. L. A. Hart finds a certain "minimum content of natural law" in the basic needs of all societies for control of aggression, principles of reciprocity and mutual forebearance, and allocation of limited resources— roughly what sociologists have recognized as the "functional prerequisites of societies." [70] And as we shall see shortly, still other theorists suggest a kind of "procedural natural law," in which requirements of the "rule of law" are taken as the universal criteria against which to measure legal acts and institutions.

Some of the criticisms of natural law have probably been based on confusions and mistaken impressions, as when a critic attacks a particular application of natural-law principles by the Roman Catholic Church, yet believes this attack to constitute a sufficient refutation of the entire natural-law approach. At the same time, other criticisms are quite central. Basically, the critic challenges the natural-law adherent to demonstrate how we can determine the nature of man, where we can obtain verification of the supposedly absolute moral principles, and how we can have assurance as to the proper application of such principles in the legal order. That men in fact do seek certain ends in their own behavior and do assess enacted laws and legal institutions against their conceptions of justice does not satisfy the critic as to the reality of natural law. As one philosopher notes, "That there are purposes *in* life does not at all show or even suggest that there is a purpose *to* life or a purpose *of* life or that man was made *for* a certain purpose." [71] Likewise, the critics of natural law do not deny that laws may be considered just or unjust, rather they merely insist that such assessments are in no sense scientifically validated or susceptible of validation.[72] Such criticisms tend to weigh heavily with sociologists, who usually take a highly relativistic view of values and ethical principles. Nor do the efforts to secularize natural law ordinarily convince them that what they believe to be the inability to "prove" values is being surmounted. Even a writer who is at great pains to distinguish natural-law theory from conventional theology admits that the former requires "accepting a moral universe—a universe whose laws have as much claim on men as those of the physical universe itself." [73] Many sociologists cannot accept such assertion of universal moral principles.

Critics sometimes insist further that natural-law theory has been a bastion of conservatism, that it has invariably been used as a rationale for resisting social reform. Here again to a certain extent, though this may not be entirely unjustified, criticism has tended to center around the most systematic and widely proclaimed of present systems of natural law, as reflected in Roman Catholic policy on certain social issues. Advocates of natural law insist, on the other hand, that the basic idea is "neutral"; that just as it can justify the status quo so too it can and has been used to justify resistance to totalitarianism and to insist on equality of rights for all humans. But even a sympathetic student of natural law states that conservative uses of the natural-law concept have been more frequent than progressive ones:

> Rarely are the advocates or practitioners of natural law to be found on the frontiers of ethical thought. Historically, natural law has been far more in evidence as a limiting and restraining factor in human activity than as a liberating principle making for growth and development.[74]

In urging a rapprochement between sociology and natural law, Selznick claims that sociologists have gone too far in their attempt to separate fact and value. Much of their work, whether they recognize it or not, deals with "normative systems," realms of behavior in which values are so central that sociological analysis inevitably involves the assessment of actual social conditions in terms of their approximation of a "master ideal." [75] He suggests, for example, that even where the sociologist seeks to avoid terminology that smacks of values, as when he uses the term "primary relation" rather than "friendship" or "love," a normative standard or "framework for diagnosis" is implied; we consider to what extent the ideal of primary relation is reached in the experience of actual persons. Since this engagement with normative ideals is inevitable, Selznick asserts, there should be no reason for the sociologist to consider it "unscientific" to assert similar ideals in the legal realm. There the relevant master ideals are "justice" and "legality," perhaps particularly the latter, the essential element of which Selznick describes as follows:

> . . . the governance of official power by rational principles of civic order. Official action, even at the highest levels of authority, is enmeshed in and restrained by a web of accepted general rules. Where this idea exists no power is immune from criticism nor completely free to follow its own bent. . . . Legality imposes an objective environment of constraint, of tests to be met, of standards to be observed, and, not less important, of ideals to be fulfilled.[76]

Essentially, the distinctive contribution of legality is "a progressive reduction of the arbitrary element in positive law and its administration." [77]

In discussing legality, Selznick cites with approval the work of Lon Fuller and appears mainly to have in mind as a normative standard the procedural sort of natural law advanced in the latter's book *The Morality of Law*. Fuller states that he is trying to articulate "the natural laws of a particular kind of human undertaking, which I have described as 'the enterprise of subjecting human conduct to the governance of rules.'" In seeking the law's "internal morality," according to Fuller, "we are concerned not with the substantive aims of legal rules, but with the ways in which a system of rules for governing human conduct must be constructed and administered if it is to be efficacious and at the same time remain what it purports to be." [78] In brief, the requirements of this internal morality of law are as follows:

1. There must be general rules.
2. These rules must be made known.
3. They must not be retroactive.
4. They must be reasonably clear.
5. Laws should not be contradictory.
6. Laws should not require the impossible (or the extremely unreasonable).

7. Insofar as possible, laws should be constant through time.
8. Legal rules and administration of the law should not conflict.

Fuller views these requirements simply as ideals toward which
legal systems should strive. On the other hand, he asserts that a
total failure on any one of these points "does not simply result in
a bad system of law; it results in something that is not properly
called a legal system at all. . . ." [79] According to Fuller, a legal
system geared to *adjudication under adversary court procedure* is
most likely to attain these goals. He finds many of our system's
failures to meet these requirements (such as the lack of general
and clear rules and the existence of laws requiring almost the
impossible, as through "strict criminal liability," that is responsibility without "criminal intent") arising where traditional adjudicative methods are modified, as in some of the procedures of
federal regulatory agencies.

Whether Selznick would limit his "natural law" to such procedural requirements or would include some minimal substantive
guidelines for law is not entirely clear. But in any case, he feels
there are some absolute legal ideals, which can be grounded in
our understanding of human nature. In this connection, he states
that sociology's extreme acceptance of cultural relativism (the
notion that one way of life is as "good" as another) has been
misguided. He admits that the diversity of cultures is impressive
and that many early efforts to identify essential traits of human
nature have rightly been discredited. Nonetheless, this diversity
does not mean that such a quest has no merit. Asserting that
apart from generally acknowledged basic drives and potentialities,
there are other features "of man's psychic unity . . . more directly relevant to what is universal in social organization and
pervasive in human values," he mentions "such motivating forces
as the search for respect, including self-respect, for affection, and
for surcease of anxiety; such potentialities as the union of sex
and love, the enlargement of social insight and understanding,

reason and esthetic creativity." [80] "If there is to be a legal order," he insists, "it must serve the proper ends of man." [81]

Selznick's presentation serves to warn the sociologist that analysis of the legal order may be incomplete if no account is taken of men's notions of justness or of the broad ideals they may seek to attain through their legal institutions. Similarly, it underscores the fact that neither the ruler of a society nor the official who adjudicates particular disputes in that society is absolutely free from constraint in the administration of the law. At the same time, empirically oriented researchers will be likely to find some of the implications of this natural-law formulation troublesome.[82] It is not entirely clear just how we can use the ideal of legality to assess actual legal conditions and at the same time stay within the limits of scientific investigation. As already noted, Fuller goes so far as to say that a serious failure of "legality" means that there really is no legal order. Similarly, Selznick seems willing to determine the "maturity" of a legal order in terms of its approximation of the ideal of legality. If we could define legality precisely and operationally, then presumably we might measure the amount present under any given set of conditions, and through such measurement draw some conclusions about the state of the legal system. Whether we can make such measurements and conclusions is questionable. There is no universal consensus about what constitutes legality, any more than about what constitutes justice. One man's justice is usually another man's injustice, and few sociologists are prepared to claim that science can assess such conflicting claims. Defining legality in terms of relatively neutral *procedures,* as Fuller does, may help a bit; but as we shall see in Chapter Five, there is not really any consensus among specialists even as to the procedures through which justice and legality are best served.

Such concepts as "degrees of legality," and "maturity of a legal order" appear to be middle-of-the-road substitutes for the blatantly nonempirical notion that "bad law isn't law." Yet it seems no more scientific an operation to call a legal system we don't like "immature" than to say it isn't a legal system. Conceivably, further research into the social development of law may reveal a basis for some kind of evolutionary evaluation; but at the moment no such basis exists. Similarly, many empirically minded scientists will question how a nonevaluative search for the "psychic unity of mankind"—which presumably might provide a basis for further elaboration of natural-law principles—can be conducted. Commenting on Selznick's work, Robert Gordis states the basic problem:

> Human nature exhibits the qualities of friendship, love, cooperation, the appreciation of beauty, the hunger for righteousness. But it also reveals aggressiveness, greed, lust, irrationality. Which constellation of attributes is to be regarded as the norm of human nature and which as aberrations or perversions of the essential nature of man? Which traits accordingly can be made the basis of natural law?[83]

Justice and Obedience to Law

The very idea of law implies rules that are more often obeyed than violated, for if this were not the case we would have to speak of lawless behavior rather than a legal order. (In the same sense, we could not speak of society unless there were a tendency to conform to general social norms.) Man's obedience to law has long interested jurists and political and social philosophers, and there are many explanations of this intriguing phenomenon. At one extreme, some would insist that man obeys simply because he is forced to. At the other extreme, it could be argued that man sees in law the reflection of a natural order that morally compels obedience. In between are various theories citing such factors as an internalization of norms, habit, a sense of the need for reciprocity and fair play, a "compact" among the citizens through which public order is attained, the rational acceptance of particular rules as desirable, obedience to particular rules with a view to maintaining the integrity of the overall system of laws, and so on.

Relatively few observers would assert that men obey laws *simply* because of coercion by the state; that is an entirely negative conception of law, applying only imperfectly to the criminal law, where it may be most relevant, and having even less usefulness when we consider other kinds of legal rules and institutions. As Hart points out, modern legal systems include not only coercive orders but "power-conferring" rules as well.[84] And underpinning the entire legal order is a claim to legitimate authority. Selznick would even go so far as to state that, "An authoritative act asserts a claim to obedience, and the reach of that claim determines whether and to what extent a legal system exists." In similar vein, he notes that just as coercion is a significant *resource* for legal systems, so are education, symbolism, and an appeal to reason: "Coercion does not make law, though it may indeed establish an order out of which law may emerge. In the authoritative use of coercion, whether by public or private agencies, the distinctively legal element is not the coercion itself but the invocation of authority." [85] A related point, emphasized by some natural-law theorists in particular, is that just as the individual in a legal order is not merely submitting to naked power, so the ruler or other legal functionary cannot exercise unlimited power—the existence of law implies some limits, "natural" or otherwise, on arbitrary rule. To a certain extent a ruler may recognize "higher" principles, which he cannot with impunity violate;[86] or at least we may say that he must (whether he would prefer to or not) make concessions in the direction of the sort of legal order that can "command" the willing obedience of those "subject" to it.[87]

CIVIL DISOBEDIENCE

If substantial obedience and a grounding in legitimate authority are key features of the legal system, so too, however, is disobedience. Disobedience may be intentional or nonintentional, individual or collective, haphazard or systematic, violent or nonviolent. It may be directed against particular legal rules or against an entire legal order, and may on occasion, of course, be part of a broader social rebellion. For present purposes, the practices that are usually described as "civil disobedience" hold some special interest.[88] In the United States at the present time, various sorts of nonviolent demonstrations and public acts challenging legal rules are being used by advocates of peace and disarmament, civil rights, and other ameliorative social goals. Such challenges may be directed against general abuses in the legal system (for example, police brutality against Negroes), or against specific legislation believed to be unjust (such as the selective service or racial segregation laws), or against an aspect of administering a particular law (such as the use of tax funds to finance warfare), or against the absence of a specific law (such as fair-housing legislation). Civil disobedience may attempt direct interference with some official act considered unjust, or it may instead simply seek to have an indirect impact upon legal processes. But invariably it goes beyond private law-violation; for it involves an attempt to dramatize publicly what is considered to be a major injustice within the legal order.

Although it is usually said that the term "civil disobedience" should apply only to a principled act of objection and challenge, the possible sources of principle are varied; they range from classic natural-law theories to strongly held personal and group codes of morality, drawing at times on the teachings of Thoreau and Gandhi and at others on supposedly neutral requirements of a rule of law. The "right to resist" in a society which flagrantly and generally flouts the most elemental principles of legality is frequently asserted by philosophers of democracy.[89] And even within a generally democratic order, the persistent inability to correct flagrant injustice through ordinary legal processes, and the need to shame a majority into recognizing its obligations to justice, may sometimes be said to justify civil disobedience. At the same time, it is generally recognized that the legal order, by definition, cannot provide for its own violation. Those who civilly disobey must be prepared to accept penalties for such action. Indeed, sometimes such acceptance of punishment is viewed as a central aspect of achieving the goal of dramatizing a legal wrong.

Clearly, it is beyond the purview of sociology as a scientific enterprise to attempt any statements as to whether or when civil disobedience may be "justified." Nonetheless, from the standpoint of a sociologist's attempt to understand the legal order, it certainly seems a noteworthy phenomenon. It is, for one thing, a significant indicator of the viability of notions of justice as an influence on individual and group behavior with reference to the legal system. And, whether we see this influence as suggesting the "reality" of natural law or not, it is a fact that for some men the belief in such a higher order may motivate such behavior. Thus, Martin Luther King, in his "Letter from Birmingham City Jail," declared:

> One has not only a legal but moral responsibility to obey just laws. Conversely, one has a moral responsibility to disobey unjust laws. I would agree with Saint Augustine that "An unjust law is no law at all."
> . . . An unjust law is a code that is out of harmony with the moral law. To put it in the terms of Saint Thomas Aquinas, an unjust law is a human law that is not rooted in eternal and natural law. Any law that uplifts human personality is just. Any law that degrades human personality is unjust. All segregation statutes are unjust because segregation distorts the soul and damages the personality. . . .[90]

As we shall see, sociologists have tended to emphasize very strongly the positive functions of law in holding a society together. In civil disobedience we find at least one type of exception to such a generalization; others will be touched on below. If we do accept the idea that such activities are more or less normal to the legal order, then presumably analysis of actual civil-disobedience movements—their causes, development, organization, leadership, techniques, and impact—could be an important area for research within the sociology of law. In any case, it seems necessary to recognize the existence of disobedience as well as obedience. We may even come to decide that this apparently "dysfunctional" phenomenon in fact serves certain positive functions in strengthening the legal order. Certainly one major aim, and potential effect, of civil disobedience is the promotion of social change, which often may be required if the law is to maintain flexibility and be relevant to contemporary social conditions. It has even been argued that disobedience is sometimes really a kind of necessary and recognized "legal" procedure, for under our system of judicial review the line between violation of a law and testing a law's constitutionality may often be a hazy one.[91] As one philosopher notes, the existence of individuals and groups who are civilly disobedient makes us

> painfully aware that we too are implicitly making choices, and must bear responsibility for the ones we make. . . . They remind us that the man who obeys the law has as much of an obligation to look into the morality of his acts and the rationality of his society as does the man who breaks the law.[92]

WAR-CRIMES TRIALS[93]

These questions of obedience and responsibility, and indeed of the very meaning of "law" and "legality," were most perplexingly posed by the activities of the Nazi regime prior to and during World War II, and also by the subsequent legal action taken against the Axis leaders in the name of international law. It was, in fact, the inhumanity of Nazi policies and acts that led many social and legal relativists to rethink their positions and to show a renewed interest in natural-law perspectives in the postwar period. Could we, in the face of such systematic atrocities, largely perpetrated in "legal" form, maintain the assertion that no matter how bad law is, it is still law? Many felt this position was no longer possible, that an appeal to higher principles of *some* sort was necessary, and that such appeal in effect invalidated the pseudolegal acts of the Nazis.

In 1945 the principal Allies in World War II executed an agreement, later accepted by nineteen other nations, creating an International Military Tribunal for the purpose of trying Axis war criminals. The most notable trial resulting from this charter convened in the same year in Nuremberg, Germany. Prosecutors representing the United States, the United Kingdom, France, and the Soviet Union jointly filed an indictment against twenty-four Nazi leaders; the indictment charging war crimes (slave labor, mistreatment or execution of prisoners, and the like), crimes against peace (planning and waging of "aggressive war"), and crimes against humanity (what would now be termed "genocide").[94] Twenty-two of the Nazis were brought to trial, nineteen of whom were convicted—eleven being sentenced to death and the others to imprisonment for terms ranging from ten years to life. Three of six Nazi organizational units proceeded against were adjudged to be criminal organizations, thus paving the way for further prosecutions of individual members of such units.

There was and still is wide agreement among students of these proceedings that bringing the Nazi leaders to justice for their unparalleled crimes was absolutely essential, both to avert a blood bath of unofficial reprisal and because basic principles of decency required formal public accountability and punishment for such infamous acts. At the same time, various questions have been raised concerning such war-crimes trials. Were the trials really anything more than the dispatching of the vanquished by the victors? A strong effort was made to portray the tribunal's work as something quite different, as a disinterested adjudication of the charges; but not all the critics were convinced. One jurist suggested that if "Nuremberg was an example of high politics masquerading as law, then the trial instead of promoting may retard the coming of the day of world law." [95] Such critics argued that the political nature of the judgments should have been faced up to and that—at least with respect to the more unconventional offenses in the indictment—some form of more summary, non-judicial, openly political determination of guilt would have been appropriate. On the other hand, framers of the tribunal's charter, in particular the representatives of the United States, considered it especially important that a strictly "legal" means of acting against the war criminals be adopted. Such procedure would distinguish the judgments from acts of mere political expediency, would demonstrate the Allies' commitment to the rule of law and reason rather than to the authority of sheer power, and hopefully would establish some sort of precedent for bringing future transgressors to justice through similar international tribunals and according to similar principles of law.

These very principles of law, however, as well as the possible precedents established by the proceedings, formed a major basis for criticizing the trials. As well as challenging the tribunal's jurisdiction, critics attacked the doctrine of collective guilt, noting also the difficulty of establishing at what level of action and complicity the guilt should begin; and they claimed that some of the most important charges were formulated *ex post facto,* hence placing the proceedings in violation of accepted principles of legality or rule of law. Crimes against peace ("aggressive war") and even more clearly crimes against humanity were said not to have "existed"—that is, not to have been established in recognized principles of law—prior to the enactment of the tribunal's charter. Hence these charges could not be applied to acts committed before that time. Prosecutors at Nuremberg were quite aware of this problem and accordingly were at great pains to try to state a basis for such charges in previously existing international agreements and in "customary international law." (The concept of natural law was not relied on at Nuremberg, though it did enter heavily into the proceedings in a separate trial of Japanese war criminals.) This attempt was not fully convincing. One commentator refers to the effort "to build on the fiction of a positive international law envisaged as analogous in its formal structure to the legalistic image of municipal law in matured systems." [96] Yet the underlying premise seems to have been that even if such "crimes" had not already been "enacted," decent men everywhere recognized their existence. Furthermore, the monstrosity of the acts involved, and the widespread agreement that severe punishment was called for, overshadowed the technical objection that some charges were retroactively applied.

But the possible implications of such retroactive legal action troubled many observers. The prosecution of individual offenders against the charter depended crucially on retroactive determinations. The only basis for proceeding against the individual was that he should have known his acts were "unlawful" and therefore, even if ordered to commit them, he had a legal obligation to refuse. Yet how could an individual always know which particular acts would subsequently be held illegal? With respect to many of the most blatantly indecent acts of the Nazis there was ample reason to override such an argument. But where was the line to be drawn? And if we were to allow retroactive formulations of this sort, how could the individual ever find guidance in the law?

That the concern about possible precedent was not totally unwarranted is seen in the fact that today we find opponents of United States military actions in Vietnam asserting the "Nuremberg principle" (that is, that since one can be held legally responsible for obeying orders to commit war crimes and crimes against humanity, one must refuse to obey such orders) as grounds for refusing to accept military service. While many might consider this argument, along with the Nuremberg trials themselves, quite reasonable and in accord with valid principles of justice, clearly its legal standing is uncertain at best. One of the consequences of Nuremberg appears to be a considerable confusion as to who is to determine, and on what grounds, which military orders and actions are lawful and which unlawful. Furthermore, it now seems to be established international law that waging "aggressive" warfare is a crime against peace. But who is to say which war and which party is aggressive? And *how* aggressive does a war have to be before it violates the prohibition?

Similar issues, compounded by special jurisdictional questions raised by the official kidnapping of the defendant and his forcible removal from Argentina to Israel, arose in the more recent trial of Adolf Eichmann.[97] At the present time, it is difficult to say what the overall historical meaning of such trials will be. In one sense, they represent an attempt to justify punishment of political-military opponents under color of legal proceedings. In another sense, they reflect a sincere desire to come to grips with historically unique behavior extremely offensive to principles of human decency and to develop just legal forms for this purpose. As a leading student of political trials concluded: "In spite of the Nuremberg trial's infirmities, the feeble beginning of transnational control of the crime against the human condition raises the Nuremberg judgment a notch above the level of political justice by fiat of a successor regime." [98]

From the standpoint of sociology, the debate about such trials underscores once again the uncertainties involved in defining "law" and "legal system" and indicates the special moral dilemmas facing the extreme legal relativist. In the Nazi experience and its aftermath, we see the individual citizen's opposition to and rejection of the ostensibly legal order raised from a mere possibility to a compelling moral and perhaps even legal obligation. Comforting as the idea might be, however, neither actual opposition nor the phenomenon of the war-crimes trials provides a basis for believing that legal systems are inherently or automatically self-correcting. On the contrary, a view of the uses of law in the Nazi era seems to compel the belief that legal phenomena are inevitably social, that is, human, in nature and have the capacity to facilitate both good and evil. At the same time, the persistence of broad legal ideals does seem to exert a certain amount of influence on men in their assessments of actual legal rulings and institutions. "Rule of law" and "rule of men" are not mutually exclusive. Nor is there a one-sided influence of either on the other. The relation is reciprocal.

Chapter Two

✷✷

Law and Order

Jurisprudence, as we have seen, touches on many questions of interest to the sociology of law. Nonetheless, and perhaps partly in reaction to the speculation and generality characteristic of some legal philosophy, the researcher in sociology today seems drawn to somewhat detailed and limited studies of down-to-earth aspects of the "law in action." To a certain extent, this has been a very desirable development. For one thing, it would be most unfortunate if the seemingly endless jurisprudential debate about the *philosophical* meaning of law were simply replaced by an equally endless haggling over the correct *sociological* definition of law. Furthermore, it may well be that only through fairly specific and intensive studies of the law in action can we gain a meaningful knowledge of the sociologically important features of legal phenomena. It would probably not be wise, however, to allow this valuable concentration on detail completely to over-whelm interest in the broader picture. One commentator has recently asserted: "True, research on the legal profession and the problematical aspects of law within a particular legal system is defensible, but somehow the field has lost sight of the original paramount question: What is the relation between law and social order?" [1]

It was this broad perspective that intrigued the classic social theorists, and actually not all contemporary students of law from the point of view of sociology have abandoned interest in such matters. Despite a tendency toward considerable specialization even within the realm of the sociology of law, most systematic analysts of the legal order do feel compelled, for example, to formulate or accept a particular definition of "law" or "legal." Indeed such efforts by both classic and modern social analysts of law leave us with a rather confusing variety of alternative definitions. This writer thinks that it would be a mistake to single out one of these definitions and label it "the" definition of law. Instead, several definitions will be noted in the discussion that follows, so that we may see the points that different theorists have emphasized and consider possible advantages of alternative formulations.

If our exclusive interest is in empirical research on a particular, present-day legal system in action, then no very complicated quest for a definition is necessary. For example, we know pretty well what we mean by law in modern American society—rules established by legislatures, or by courts, or backed up through sanctions imposed by courts. To some extent this definition of law is quite adequate, at least for certain limited purposes. Yet if we wish to develop a precise theoretical analysis, it may not suffice. The problems of meaning lie at the borderland of those rules and institutions we all tend to recognize as distinctively legal. There is, to put it another way, a lack of clarity as to just where law or the legal begins and where it ends. Is law more than merely a strongly enforced custom? Most observers seem to feel that it is. But if we point to state or official enforcement as the differentiating factor, a new dilemma emerges: how are we to distinguish the "legal" from the "political"? Special difficulties arise when we attempt to analyze systems in which we feel that something "like" law is present yet are not sure that that something "really is" law. As we shall see, the two most notable examples of these difficulties are primitive society and the modern international order.

The Meaning of Law

Is law an inevitable component of social life, a cultural universal and imperative? We would probably all be willing to agree that complex modern societies have and need legal systems. But might there not be simpler or differently organized schemes of social life in which legal mechanisms would not be necessary? Anarchists have advocated abolition of all law. Orthodox Marxist theory, which viewed cultural values and social institutions as fundamental reflections of the underlying economic arrangements in a society, also inclined to the view that law is not a social necessity. In modern capitalist society, Marxism maintained, law was a tool used by the bourgeoisie to further their exploitation of the workers. A return to more normal, cooperative modes of living would, it was asserted, cause law, along with the state, to "wither away." [2] More of this later; suffice it to say now simply that existing modern governments professing to be grounded in Marxist principles have in fact been forced to acknowledge that a legal system is something more than a capitalist device. Law has yet to wither away in the socialist societies.

At the same time, sociology recognizes that the need for formal mechanisms of social control, as exemplified in legal institutions, may be closely related to the nature and effectiveness of informal social controls, the sanctioning of norms through informal group processes. Sociologists, for example, have long cited the difference in dominant forms of social control as one hallmark of the distinction between *gemeinschaft* (close-knit, homogeneous, communal) and *gesellschaft* (impersonal, hetero-geneous, associational) collectivities. Gossip and informal group pressures are major techniques of social control in the small rural town; in the modern city we find instead a dominance of such formal mechanisms as the clock, the traffic signal, and the policeman, who is a symbol of the legal order.[3] It may be that formal control mechanisms such as we find in legal institutions come into play primarily in situations where informal mecha-nisms have proven inadequate.

Some evidence for this situation was uncovered by the so-ciologist Richard Schwartz in a study comparing two Israeli agri-cultural settlements—one community organized around a system of economic collectivism (a *kvutza*), the other a semiprivate property settlement (a *moshav*).[4] Whereas the *moshav* was found to have a special Judicial Committee for settling disputes, no comparable specialized agency was present in the *kvutza*. Al-though the "legislature," or General Assembly, of the cooperative (*kvutza*) made decisions which affected specific individuals, there was no organized enforcement. Looking into the general nature of social control in the two communities, Schwartz found the collective community to be extremely close-knit with continuous interaction between all members and with a system of social norms that was "detailed, generally unambiguous, applicable to wide, clearly defined segments of the population, and well known to the members." Members of the *moshav*, by contrast, did not engage in such continuous and intimate interaction; nor was there in that settlement a similar consensus about explicit and uniformly applied social norms. While it was not possible to trace out the complete histories of control mechanisms in the two settlements, Schwartz reached the reasonable conclusion that the *kvutza* was able to get along without legal controls because of the strong system of informal norms and sanctions. Even when this system seemed threatened, the tendency was to strengthen the generally effective, informal mechanisms rather than to develop formal ones. The absence of an effective framework of informal control in the *moshav,* on the other hand, seemed to have been at least partially responsible for the development of specialized legal institutions in that settlement.

Of course the main point of Schwartz's analysis, that legal controls may arise when other social controls are inadequate, can be turned around as well. Sometimes informal control in effect replaces unworkable legal control. (When we consider below instances in which enacted law exceeds the limits of effective legal control, we shall find behavior actually governed by new sets of informal norms and sanctions.) Furthermore, it should be noted that Schwartz was dealing with communities only. It is questionable whether his findings provide a basis for believing that entire societies, even relatively simple ones, can rely entirely on informal control mechanisms, although perhaps for a few exceptionally close-knit types of social system the possibility may have to be held open.

We know that mechanisms of social control are required in all societies. The problem remains of determining whether or when a particular type of control mechanism we choose to call "legal" is necessary. Similarly, if we follow Llewellyn and Hoebel in viewing law as a means of dealing with "trouble cases," [5] we are forced to recognize that "trouble" arises in all social systems. Thus increasingly, it is being stressed that conflict and deviance, rather than constituting unusual or idiosyncratic occurrences, constitute integral aspects of social life.[6] Yet we know that trouble can be and is controlled through informal and nonlegal processes as well as through formal, legal ones. Nor does Hart's "minimum content of natural law," referred to above, help us very much. It is quite true that all societies have certain basic problems to solve, such as scarce resources and control of aggression, and that there are "functional prerequisites" for the maintenance of a social system. Still, the question persists: To what extent must these problems be solved or functions served through "legal" mechanisms?

We come back, then, to the question of distinguishing law from other social norms, a matter that has plagued and continues to plague numerous anthropologists and sociologists. For the anthropologist,[7] the analysis of "primitive law" is complicated by a general methodological dilemma present also in the study of other primitive social institutions. On the one hand, the anthropologist cannot insist on evidence of the specific sorts of legal institutions we find in modern society before admitting that law exists. On the other hand, he must be wary lest he read law into arrangements not really warranting that description, simply because he expects to find it. Notwithstanding these problems, many efforts have been made to seek out and examine primitive legal rules or institutions. Although there is considerable variety among the resulting definitions, a general consensus seems to have emerged, to the effect that virtually all societies have had something we can reasonably term "law." A few cultures have been examined that seem to come very close to the "no-law" category,[8] but generally some collective enforcement of norms or specialized machinery for the general settling of disputes has come to light.

One of the best-known works on primitive law is Bronislaw Malinowski's *Crime and Custom in Savage Society* (1926). Drawing on his studies of the Trobriand Islanders of Melanesia, Malinowski saw the essence of law to be embodied in the principle of reciprocity. He wrote: "The rules of law stand out from the rest in that they are felt and regarded as the obligations of one person and the rightful claims of another. They are sanctioned not by a mere psychological motive, but by a definite social machinery of binding force, based . . . upon mutual dependence, and realized in the equivalent arrangement of reciprocal services. . . ."[9] Law and legal phenomena, according to Malinowski, were not to be found in special, independent institutions or in a special system of decrees. Rather, "Law is the specific result of the configuration of obligations, which makes it impossible for the native to shirk his responsibility without suffering for it in the future." [10]

There is little doubt that in calling attention to the role of reciprocity, Malinowski was highlighting one of the most basic processes in social relations.[11] His analysis is useful too in suggesting that law operates not merely in violent dispute situations, but in the realm of common, everyday activities as well. Yet in his effort to play down the factor of sheer coercion, and to picture instead a complex and broadly social system of control, Malinowski failed adequately to distinguish law from custom. If reciprocity is present in many legal relations or reinforces legal control at certain points, that does not mean that everything legal comes under the reciprocity principle. In emphasizing the subtle interlocking social arrangements that facilitated harmonious relationships, Malinowski may have paid insufficient attention to the serious disruptions of social life that his research on the Trobriand Islanders had indeed made quite evident. One commentator even suggests that Malinowski had a distinct distaste for conflict and coercion and for that reason de-emphasized them in his analysis. It does appear that some years after writing *Crime and Custom,* Malinowski came to acknowledge that some norms require enforcement by central authority, thus moving toward a definition of law under which the legal and the merely customary might be distinguished.[12]

Perhaps partly because Malinowski tended to confuse custom and law, many other theorists have been at great pains to distinguish the two, usually doing so in terms of the source of sanctions and enforcement—individuals and groups in the case of custom, the central authority of the society at large in the case of law. Hence law becomes the administration of state power. This emphasis is seen in Radcliffe-Brown's definition of law as "the maintenance or establishment of social order, within a territorial framework, by the exercise of coercive authority through the use, or the possibility of use, of physical force." [13] In a similar vein is Hoebel's more recent, and quite influential, formulation: "A social norm is legal if its neglect or infraction is regularly met, in threat or in fact, by the application of physical force by an individual or group possessing the socially recognized privilege of so acting." [14] As already noted, a difficulty with this approach is that under it law and government seem indistinguishable. Not only does this seeming indistinguishability make their separation for analytical purposes almost impossible, but also it renders the notion of a government *subject to* law meaningless.

Max Weber's definition of law also emphasized enforcement through central authority. Starting with the notion of an *order,* endowed with legitimacy ("the prestige of exemplariness or obligatoriness"), he stated further:

> An order will be called *law* if it is externally guaranteed by the probability that coercion (physical or psychological), to bring about conformity or avenge violation, will be applied by a *staff* of people holding themselves specially ready for that purpose.[15]

Weber emphasized that the sociologist is not to judge legal systems or rules, but only to understand them. According to an eminent interpreter (and translator) of his work, Max Rheinstein, Weber held that the sociologist must "concern himself with any kind of organizationally coercive order, regardless of whether or not he is pleased by its contents or by the ends for which it is used by those who have the power to manipulate it." [16] Although Weber's approach clearly is quite positivistic (his definition is not unlike that of Austin), it is significant that he refers simply to a specialized staff, rather than to "the state" or "the sovereign." Weber conceived of the enforcement staff in a very flexible way, stating, for example, that in cases of blood vengeance and feud the clan is the enforcement body.

This broad concept permits us to discern law in different types of social systems, including collectivities other than those we call "societies" (for example, large-scale organizations, as will be seen below), and also covers such possible border areas as ecclesiastical law and international law. Nor did Weber use the term "command," but rather "order." Placed together with his theory of legitimate authority, this use of terms may indicate that he did not view law solely as an application of centralized power. Selznick sees Weber's contribution in this broader light and, as pointed out in the last chapter, rejects coercion as the hallmark of the distinctively legal. According to Selznick, the key word in the discussion of law is authority. Going somewhat beyond Weber, he asserts that

> legality presumes the emergence of authoritative norms, norms that are themselves "guaranteed" not, as Weber put it, by the probability of sanction by a specialized staff, but rather by evidence of other consensually validated rules that confirm the legality of the immediately relevant norm.[17]

Similarly, H. L. A. Hart tries to develop a balanced "concept of law," recognizing the element of centralized authority and yet also stressing the special qualities of obligation intrinsic to legal phenomena. Obedience to law, he insists, is not the same as obedience to a gunman's order. Furthermore, law consists of particular kinds of rules. According to Hart, the essence of a legal system lies in the "union of primary and secondary rules." Primary rules are informal rules of obligation through which the basic conditions of social existence are satisfied. It might be possible to live by primary rules alone in an extremely stable and close-knit community; but under more typical conditions, the nature and scope of such rules become uncertain, the rules fail to cope with changing conditions, and their administration by informal social pressure becomes inefficient. In response to these characteristic problems, secondary rules appear: *rules of recognition,* to clarify what the authoritative primary rules are and, where necessary, to order them in a hierarchy of importance; *rules of change,* which authorize the introduction of new primary rules; and *rules of adjudication,* "empowering individuals to make authoritative determinations of the question whether, on a particular occasion, a primary rule has been broken." [18]

Although Hart discusses law primarily in terms of rules, it should be clear, especially from his reference to rules of change and of adjudication, that the sort of development he considers essential to law presupposes *specialized social institutions,* which we may term *legal.* This same point is elaborated in an interesting way by the anthropologist Paul Bohannan, who also, in his notion of "reinstitutionalization of norms," comes very close to Hart's idea of the union of primary and secondary rules. Bohannan states:

> A legal institution is one by means of which the people of a society settle disputes that arise between one another and counteract any gross and flagrant abuses of the rules . . . of at least some of the other institutions of society. Every on-going society has legal institutions in this sense, as well as a variety of nonlegal institutions. [19]

Law consists of rules, or customs, that are "reinstitutionalized" —"some of the customs of some of the institutions of society are restated in such a way that they can be 'applied' by an institution designed (or, at very least, utilized) specifically for that purpose." [20] Only rights that are upheld through norms that have undergone this "double institutionalization" can be termed "legal." As Bohannan states, legal institutions differ from other social institutions in at least two ways. First of all, they provide some regularized way of dealing with trouble situations arising in connection with the workings of the nonlegal institutions. Second, legal institutions combine two sorts of rules: "modifications or restatements of the rules of the nonlegal institution[s]" (substantive law) and rules governing the activities of the legal institutions themselves (procedural law). Here, Bohannan is focusing on a crucial characteristic of legal phenomena, the fact that legal rules and institutions *cut across* the various realms of social behavior. Not only are there laws dealing with the family, owner-ship of property, wills and trusts, taxation, negligence, and will-fully anti-social behavior, but potentially there are some legal principles and certainly there are some legal processes that apply in several or even all of these areas.

As Bohannan notes, in ordinary municipal (that is, state) systems of law, the central political authority provides a more or less unified power base for the secondary or legal institutional-ization of norms. But in other situations where we may still think of law as existing, there is no such single and central focus of power. Likewise, sometimes there is no single, relatively unified "legal culture," which Bohannan defines as "that which is sub-scribed to" by a people. To clarify these diverse sets of conditions under which law may exist, Bohannan developed the four-fold diagram shown in Figure 2. One particular merit of this typology is that it makes clear the dual nature of the problems facing attempts to develop international legal rules and institutions—

FIGURE 2   *The Legal Realm*

	UNICENTRIC POWER	BICENTRIC (*or Multicentric*) POWER
One culture	Municipal systems of law	Law in stateless societies
Two (*or more*) **cultures**	Colonial law	International law

SOURCE: Paul Bohannan, "The Differing Realms of Law," in Laura Nader, ed., *The Ethnography of Law*, special pub-lication, *American Anthropologist*, 67, 6, Pt. 2 (December 1965), 38. Reproduced by permission of the author and the publisher.

complexity on the dimensions of both power and culture. According to Bohannan, in international law "there is a *treble* institutionalization: once at the level of custom, once at the level of the legal institutions of states, and again at the level of the bicentric, bicultural 'international' accord." [21]

FUNCTIONAL APPROACHES

It is also possible to approach the question of the meaning of law from the standpoint of the basic functions served by legal institutions. Here, we are not quite so much concerned with spelling out the identifying *characteristics* of legal phenomena as with indicating how legal institutions fit into the workings of the overall social structure. (Of course, we may conclude that in a sense such functions in themselves constitute the primary characteristics of legal systems.)

Elaborating on the theme of "the law-jobs," which he and Llewellyn had set forth in *The Cheyenne Way,* Hoebel concludes that law serves certain basic functions "essential to the maintenance of all but the very most simple societies." These are as follows: (1) defining relationships among the society's members, indicating which types of behavior are permitted and which proscribed; (2) allocating authority and specifying who may legitimately exercise coercion over whom, together with the selection of appropriate and effective sanctions; (3) the disposition of trouble cases; and (4) maintaining adaptability by redefining relationships when life conditions change.[22]

It is significant that a broad interdisciplinary consensus about basic legal functions seems to be developing. However their terminology may differ, anthropologists, legal philosophers, and sociologists are in general agreement that a legal order must, at the very least, provide for the authorization and recognition of legitimate authority, provide means of resolving disputes, and provide mechanisms for facilitating interpersonal relationships, including adaptation to change. Some indication of such a consensus may be seen in Figure 3, setting forth a few of the basic concepts about

FIGURE 3   *Basic Functions of the Legal System*

GENERAL FUNCTION	HART	HOEBEL	PARSONS
Provision for ascertaining rules and defining relationships	Rules of recognition	Allocation of authority, who may coerce	Legitimation, jurisdiction
Provision for applying rules	Rules of adjudication	Disposition of "trouble cases"	Sanction, interpretation, jurisdiction
Provision for legal change	Rules of change	Redefine relationships and maintain adaptability	Interpretation

SOURCE: adapted from H. L. A. Hart, *The Concept of Law* (London: Oxford Univ. Press, 1961), Ch. V; E. Adamson Hoebel, *The Law of Primitive Man* (Cambridge: Harvard Univ. Press, 1954), Ch. XI; and Talcott Parsons, "The Law and Social Control," in William M. Evan, ed., *Law and Sociology: Exploratory Essays* (New York: Free Press, 1962).

law found in the work of H. L. A. Hart, E. A. Hoebel, and Talcott Parsons. Hart's specification of the types of "secondary rules" in a legal system (perhaps phrased in that way precisely because Hart is a legal philosopher and hence intimately concerned with the nature of legal rules) is in effect a formulation of essential legal functions. While Parsons approaches the legal order in terms of a general functional theory of social systems, he too identifies roughly the same central problems.

Viewing law as "a generalized mechanism of social control that operates diffusely in virtually all sectors of the society," Parsons asserts that the major function of a legal system is *integrative:* "It serves to mitigate potential elements of conflict and to oil the machinery of social intercourse. It is, indeed, only by adherence to a system of rules that systems of social interaction can function without breaking down into overt or chronic covert conflict." [23] If a system of rules and specialized institutions is effectively to provide such integration, it must, according to Parsons, deal with four problems: (1) legitimation (providing a basis for adherence to the rules); (2) interpretation (establishing rights and obligations by determining the applicability of particular rules); (3) sanctions (specifying what sanctions will follow from conformity to and deviation from the rules and by whom they will be applied); and (4) jurisdiction (establishing the lines of authority by which legal norms will be enforced and also designating those "classes of acts, persons, roles, and collectivities" to which given sets of norms apply).

While Parsons recognizes that the "legal system" and the "political system" are closely interrelated (particularly as regards the problems of sanctions and jurisdiction, since in both these matters the ultimate recourse for enforcing law is to the central political authority), he insists that analytically they are separable. This separation is made possible by concentrating on the key work of the courts in providing, through the function of "interpretation," perhaps the *most* basic of the legal functions, a more or less consistent body of rules, and by noting that in well-developed legal systems the courts may enjoy a significant measure of independence from political authority.[24] Analytically, then, the work of the courts becomes the central feature of the legal order, whereas the formation of policy, as through the legislature, lies at the core of the political domain.

This distinction has been further elaborated by Harry C. Bredemeier, who attempts, using general concepts developed by Parsons, to trace out in some detail the "inputs" and "outputs" involved in the functional interchanges between the legal system and the other major subsystems of a society. In the analytical scheme developed by Bredemeier, the political ("goal pursuance") system, primarily, the legislature, "provides" the legal ("integrative") system, the courts, with policy goals "in exchange for" interpretation and with enforcement in exchange for legitimation.

Likewise the "adaptive system" (economic system, science, and technology) contributes an input of specialized knowledge designed to facilitate the ascertaining of truth. It receives in exchange from the legal order authoritative decisions, which influence the adaptive sphere mainly through their impact on the organization of roles in the division of labor ("an imposition of rights and obligations *in the interests of efficient organization*"). In its interchanges with the socialization ("pattern maintenance") system, the legal order receives the motivation to turn to law instilled in the citizenry as part of the society's value system and in return provides an output of "justice," the meeting of individuals' "internalized expectations." [25]

CRITICISMS OF THE FUNCTIONAL APPROACH

Bredemeier acknowledges that such interrelationships do not work perfectly smoothly, and in fact he specifically discusses some possible difficulties. Thus he mentions, for example, that there may develop in the legal realm "goal-conceptions inconsistent with the polity's," that there may be a lack of communication of accurate knowledge to the courts, and that legislatures may be unduly responsive to "short-run fluctuations in private interests." [26] These problem areas may provide a point of departure for some general criticisms of the functional approach to law.[27]

How are we to determine, for example, the polity's goal conceptions? Is there a monolithic set of values in a society, which can be "fed into" and applied through the legal system? Certainly, a reasonable amount of broad value consensus is necessary if a society is to continue as a going concern. Nonetheless, the far from complete nature of this consensus, and the fact that specific social and legal outcomes must to some extent reflect a continuing struggle between conflicting interests, may suggest the inadequacy of an exclusive emphasis on law's integrative function. (As we saw earlier, the new natural-law theories also seem to flounder in the absence of a public consensus as to what specific policies or procedures will maximize justice and legality.) Similarly, it could be argued that the short-run, private interests that Bredemeier mentions as constituting an intruding difficulty are in fact an integral part of the workings of a legal system. Furthermore, if real conflicts of interest and value clashes are central to the processes of law, improved "communication" in the legal system may not be very effective in furthering its integrative consequences.

Nor is it clear that the proposed analytic distinction between the legal and political systems can be upheld without qualification. (Again, the neo–natural-law proponents hold this point in common with the functional theorists, when they postulate a process of adjudication as the ideal form of the distinctively legal.) It is true that courts and legislatures do not operate in precisely the same way. But it is certainly difficult to find judicial decisions, at least with respect to any area of substantive law, that do not have any political aspects or ramifications. And to place the entire law-originating and law-making process, that is, legislation, outside the realm of the legal (because it lies in some other realm labeled "political") forces us to go against the dictates of common sense. Besides, as Arnold Rose has noted,[28] many problems that might be of great interest to the sociologist of law concern the legislative process and related matters.

As already suggested, there may be a danger that the functional approach exaggerates the integrative contribution of the legal order. Undoubtedly it is true that in a very general sense a legal system does tend to contribute to the orderly workings of society. Nevertheless, particularly when we examine specific legal systems, a recognition of potential and existing dysfunctions becomes necessary. As law professor Harold Berman has pointed out, a legal system has "many qualities or tendencies which contribute to social disorder, to disintegration, and to discontinuity." [29] It is at least theoretically conceivable that a social order might reach a stage in which its legal institutions became so inadequate that the society could no longer survive. But short of that, and in many actual social situations, one can see many potentially dysfunctional features of the legal system.

The strain between formal and substantive rationality or justice has already been alluded to. While legal formalism seems to play a valuable role in social ordering, it can get out of hand. In such instances we may find that excessive formality produces denials of substantive justice. Indeed, it is not beyond the realm of possibility that legal formalism may at times make specific everyday transactions more complicated than they would otherwise need to be. Similarly, we have to recognize that many legal disputes and areas of dispute are, in effect, produced by the law. Although it is probable that legal substance and procedure usually emerge *in response to* situations of conflict or potential conflict, it is also true that individuals "develop" new conflict through their attempts to obtain new legal rulings and to seek previously nonexistent legal solutions to their specific problems.

Another major area of dysfunction is seen in the social consequences of relying on substantive law in areas where informal social control might suffice, as in the various efforts to use law for the enforcement of morality. Finally, potential or actual dysfunctions may be found in connection with the relation between the legal order and the distribution of power in a society (the topic to which we turn next). All of these indications of potentially negative aspects of the legal system suggest how important it is always to specify the unit of society from the standpoint of which one is asserting functions or dysfunctions.[30] Laws would not exist unless they served *some* functions, manifest or latent, for society at large or for important elements within the society. But what is positively functional for one unit may be dysfunctional for another. In the area of legal outcomes and policies, in which we may assume there are always "winning" and "losing" parties or interests, such specification is absolutely essential. We can see this need most clearly, perhaps, when we consider the power and stratification aspects of the legal order.

Law, Power, and Stratification

This is not the place for a comprehensive analysis of the meaning of power,[31] but a few of its general characteristics should be noted. If we define power very broadly as "the ability to determine the behavior of others in accord with one's own wishes," then we must recognize it to be "clearly an ubiquitous social phenomenon."[32] No real understanding of legal phenomena can be achieved if the power dimension is ignored. We have seen that analysis of law in terms of its functions tends to take stability as a point of departure. As Schermerhorn points out, an approach to social relations in terms of power "reverses the emphasis by assuming that change is the starting point and that order or equilibrium is a by-product of the ceaseless quest for power by individuals, groups, institutions, and nations."[33] This view is a particularly useful corrective to overly static and positive conceptions of the legal order.

The legal system reflects or incorporates relationships of power in at least two major ways. First, it should be understood that the makers, interpreters, administrators, and enforcers of law themselves hold positions of considerable actual and potential power in a society. We have already seen that such individuals are not completely free to use this power according to personal whim. The legal functionary is constrained by the societal definition of his role, by the ideals of justice held in the community, and by the practical limitations on the effectiveness of absolute power-wielding. As we saw earlier, in considering grounds of obedience and disobedience to law, the effectiveness of legal power is determined largely by its authoritative character. Although the sources of legitimation may be various, only legitimated power has the compelling quality of authority. It is in this sense that a rule of law may be claimed to exert a checking influence on the rule of men.

MacIver has stated: "Not only in primitive society but also in the ancient civilizations and in the mediaeval world it was accepted doctrine that the ruler was subject to the laws, not above them, and that the body of laws was something scarcely touched by the fiat of authority. The law is the law of the community, not the law of the ruler." [34] While this assessment of the limits of state power may be phrased in a somewhat overly optimistic way, it is widely acknowledged by social theorists that power (in social relations generally, as well as in legal contexts) always requires a kind of validation through obedience or acquiescence. Simmel emphasized the reciprocal aspect of superordination-subordination and even applied this concept specifically to the realm of legal relations.[35] At the very least, and no matter how committed we are to hardheaded realism, we are forced to recognize the invariable presence of *some* limits on the uses of legal power. As a leading American student of political power expressed it, "The morale of the community depends in large measure on the sense of justice in the political society, and the widespread feeling of injustice is the deadliest foe of political power." [36] At the same time, it is interesting to consider how fashions in social and legal theory may influence our assessments of the role of power in law. Bertrand de Jouvenal has suggested that the growing commitment to relativistic and positivistic conceptions of law has permitted an easier equation of power and law and has actually made it much more difficult effectively to criticize unprincipled power. Law, he claims, "has lost its soul and become jungle." [37]

The other major power aspect of the legal system lies in its creation or elaboration of the rights and duties accruing to the various constituent elements of the society. Whereas certain kinds of rights may be claimed by individuals or groups lacking in the power to exercise them, some sort of power usually supports a claim to rights.[38] Furthermore, it seems clear that formal, societal recognition that a legal right exists necessarily implies power—the power of individuals or groups to enforce such right through the legal institutions. A seller's legal right to satisfaction under the terms of a sales agreement, either through adequate compliance or through the receipt of payment for damages in the absence of such compliance, means quite simply that the seller is accorded a particular kind of effective and legitimate power over the buyer.

Since legal rules are crucially concerned with such power-related aspects of social life as the distribution of scarce resources and the control of the use of aggressive means, it can hardly be denied that in a general sense the legal order establishes (or at least recognizes and legitimates) the broad patterns of power relationships in a society. As Gerth and Mills state, the legal institutions are responsible for regulating "the power that may be wielded by and in the other institutions." [39] The work of the legal system in defining and applying the concept "property rights" is but one major example of law's inevitable relation to the distribution of power. The consequences of such determinations are felt at different levels of social life, affecting as they do both the everyday interaction patterns of particular individuals and the more general standing of major groups and social categories within a society. In the words of MacIver:

> Every conferment of rights, civil or political, on an originally subject class narrows the distance between rulers and ruled and involves a change not only in the distribution but also in the character of power. The investment of a subject class with rights is a conferment of a degree of power on them, the power to pursue new opportunities, to seek new objectives, to give expression to their opinions.[40]

MacIver's statement suggests the ever present if subtle interplay among law, power, and social class. Through the legal system rights are conferred, and equally, duties imposed, on the occupants of specified social positions or on all members of social categories. Rights and duties are reciprocal; one party's right implies a duty imposed on another, and vice versa. Similarly, an expansion of liberty for one group invariably means a limitation on the liberty (or license) of another. Although it is difficult to appreciate these matters fully without reference to patterns of social and legal change, this matter will be deferred to a later section. Suffice it to say here that, through its impact on the distribution of power, especially in the economic and political realms, law invariably reflects and influences the ordering of social strata within a society.

This is not to claim that the legal functionaries themselves (judges, legislators, administrators, lawyers) necessarily wield legal power primarily for their own benefit. Such may at times be the case; but the more cogent point would seem to be that the legal system as a whole, even where jurists are at great pains to proclaim its neutrality, can hardly be viewed as completely aloof from the patterns of power and the structuring of class positions. It is quite true that in their substantive impact, the rulings in a legal order may seem to balance out; some may favor workers for example, whereas others favor employers and managers. Yet in another sense, the legal order at any time and place must overall be considered to support the prevailing stratification order; the relative positions of the various strata are, after all, upheld by law, either positively or negatively, through the failure of the legal order to invalidate such an ordering. Lest these statements suggest that the law is somehow simply a "tool" of any particular form of stratification, it should hastily be added that the concept of a "prevailing" stratification order is really somewhat misleading, just as is the notion that one can stop and assess a legal system at any time and place. Since both social change and legal change are continuous, the substantive relations between law and stratification are always shifting. That these two key elements of social order are always in a *general* relationship of *functional interdependence,* however, seems unquestionable.

Earlier in this study, reference was made to the dual nature of law—its potential for both expansion and curtailment of man's freedom. There can be little doubt that down through the ages ruling groups in diverse types of societies have used legal forms and processes to realize various ends, some of which we would classify as good and some evil. While ideals of justice and the concept of an overriding "rule of law" undoubtedly have at times helped to limit arbitrary and unjust rule, it is also unfortunately true that great and systematic iniquity has been done by men who claimed to be acting under law and whose actions were facilitated by those institutions (legislatures, courts, and so on) that we would generally characterize as legal. It seems somewhat beside the point to insist that such actions were not *really* legal. While we might well prefer that law should be capable only of expanding man's freedom (and indeed it often has served nobly in this cause), it is a fact of history that the legal order can with almost equal ease be made to provide the underpinning of a highly inequitable social order.

The most glaring modern example of this use of law was perhaps the use of ostensibly legal methods under the Nazi regime in Germany. It has been suggested that one of the essential characteristics of totalitarian dictatorship is a transition from a state based on the rule of law, in which the presumption is in favor of the rights of the citizen, to a police state, in which the presumption favors the coercive right of the state.[41] Although this may be an accurate statement, it is nonetheless also true that totalitarian regimes frequently proclaim a legal basis for their actions, however perverse by democratic standards, and also utilize conventionally legal institutions. Thus it must be admitted that in Germany under National Socialism the court system, along with legislative and executive departments, was pressed into the service of the regime's goals, however unorthodox and improper specific rulings and procedures adopted at that time may seem to us.[42] In such a situation, virtually the entire apparatus of law is mobilized to serve the state; it is "the use of legal procedure for political ends," in Otto Kirchheimer's apt phrase.[43] This statement is true not only in the narrow sense, of using court trials to dispose of the regime's specific political foes, but in the broader sense too, of developing a comprehensive program of "legal" repression. Part of such repression may well be blatant "class legislation," in which a category of persons is arbitrarily defined as antisocial and subjected to discriminatory punitive action. The so-called Nuremberg Laws singling out the Jews as categorical ("racial") enemies of the Third Reich,[44] constitute an excellent example of this phenomenon.

A similar use of law is found currently in the Republic of South Africa, where the relatively small white population maintains a suppressive regime under which the much larger African population is kept in a social "minority" position by virtue of the legally enforced *apartheid* policy.[45] Here again, and notwithstanding assertions by democratic jurists the world over that such policy violates the essential requirements of justice,[46] legal forms are maintained and legal justifications advanced. The same courts that rule in everyday, nonpolitical disputes indiscriminately apply a "Suppression of Communism Act" to squelch all enemies of the regime. A system that insists on calling itself "legal" adopts repressive techniques of preventive detention, waives the various rights of suspects, and makes little pretense of providing equal justice. The entire legal system is marshalled to support the actual minority's determination to maintain that stratification order that best accords with its own interests—an order in which Africans, Cape Coloureds (a racially mixed population), and a minority of Indians, are all kept in legally, as well as socially, subordinate positions.

The example of the Soviet Union is also instructive on the question of the relation of law to power and stratification. We are generally familiar with the fact that, especially during the period of Stalin's rule, the Soviet leaders used the nation's legal institutions to administer a system of control through terror and ruthlessly to oppose all political foes.[47] Furthermore, throughout the various stages of postrevolutionary Russian history and in line with Soviet ideology, the sternest measures invariably have been reserved for individuals labeled "counterrevolutionary." It is noteworthy that social-class background has often influenced the likelihood of an individual's being so labeled, with nonproletarian origins tending to render him suspect.

Apart from the periods of ruthless suppression and the labeling of certain social categories as "class enemies," the Soviet system of law has had a pronounced impact on the general shaping of the society's stratification order. There was at one point among Marxists a hope for the eventual withering away of both state and law. Such law as might be necessary in the interim was to be in the service of eliminating class differentials, rather than establishing any. Yet it seems clear from the Soviet experience that neither law nor stratification can be eliminated, and perhaps it is inherent in that truth also that the two must always be interrelated. If the Soviet system has eliminated certain kinds of social and economic inequities, it has created others. Above all, a definite system of stratification (albeit a quite different one from that existing in prerevolutionary Russia) has emerged,[48] supported at every level by the authority of law. To a great extent, the relation between law and stratification in the Soviet Union illustrates the specially close intertwining of these two elements to be found under any system of government based on the principle of centralized planning. We have seen that the need for legal control over allocation of resources in a society implies an invariable connection between the legal and the stratification orders. When it has been consciously determined to plan rationally the workings of all or much of the socioeconomic order, including, crucially, the distribution of wealth among individuals, then clearly the relation between law and stratification becomes all the more pronounced and more intricate.

It should be emphasized, however, particularly since this discussion has focused also on the power element, that central planning does not imply the necessary abridgment of the rule of law or any other of the trappings of a totalitarian regime.[49] The experience of recent governments in the Scandanavian countries and Great Britain, where considerable central planning has occurred without accompanying disturbance of legality, should make this point clear. Indeed, as Karl Mannheim properly emphasized,[50] the recent course of development of industrial societies seems to make clear the necessity of governmental planning in one form or another. If this statement is true, then we should expect (on that ground, as well as on others) to find a close intermeshing of law and stratification not only in dictatorially controlled societies but also in democratic ones such as our own.

LAW, CLASS, AND POWER IN THE UNITED STATES

As we shall see when we examine some patterns of social and legal change, the relationship between law and stratification is borne out by various American trends in the substantive law, where we find the socioeconomic positions of various groupings in American society advancing or declining along with their "legal" status. And with the growth of governmental control of industry and intervention in the economy, law (including legislation, court-interpretation, and enforcement) has indeed become an instrument for a conscious reordering of the entire stratification system.

Apart from these trends in specific areas of substantive law that bear on economic power and social status—such as minimum-wages and maximum-hours legislation and recognition of collective bargaining—the intimate relationship between law and stratification is clearly evident in the overall differential legal standing of the several social strata in American society. The most striking case in point, of course, is the treatment "under law" accorded the Negro American.[51] Although lynching of Negroes has presumably never occurred with the official sanction of law, since by definition lynching involved "taking the law into one's own hands," it is nevertheless clear that such informal and summary executions of Negro suspects or other "troublemakers" often did occur in the South with the more or less explicit approval or even cooperation of local law-enforcement officers. On a reduced scale, and with perhaps somewhat less overt official condonation, similar brutality continues in certain Southern states to the present day.[52] Likewise, and particularly in those states where racial segregation has hitherto been the norm, patterns of law enforcement and judicial discrimination against Negro suspects and defendants in criminal cases have long been evident.

It is widely accepted among sociologists that in many (if not most) jurisdictions a set ordering of the seriousness of offenses has existed, based on the racial membership of offender and victim. In this scheme, Negro offenses against whites are most serious, offenses committed by whites against whites next most serious, Negro offenses involving Negro victims somewhat less serious, and least serious (and hence dealt with least stringently) offenses by white persons against Negro victims.[53] In line with such differential evaluations and corresponding differences in enforcement and judicial practice, a more general situation often has developed in which Negroes may be said to have a greater "categoric risk" of experiencing contact with law-enforcement processes at all levels.[54] They are more likely than whites to be arrested, if arrested to be prosecuted, if prosecuted to be convicted, if convicted to receive heavy sentences, if imprisoned to have difficulty being paroled. Although such an "actuarial" picture of the Negro's position under the law partly reflects the fact that Negroes much more than whites are subject to all the social and psychological conditions and pressures believed to cause criminal behavior, the risk factor definitely reflects as well a large measure of differential, discriminatory treatment under the law.

Other measures, such as the general disenfranchisement of Negroes in many jurisdictions (now being partly rectified, under the directive of federal law), the exclusion of Negroes from jury duty (another area in which change is gradually taking place), and the existence in a large number of states of "antimiscegenation laws" (prohibiting interracial marriage)[55] have contributed to giving the term "second-class citizen" legal as well as social meaning. A revealing indicator of the significant impact of "legal" discrimination is found in the negative attitudes toward law that, not surprisingly, have developed among American Negroes. Relatively few Negroes appear to view the formal legal institutions in our society as an avenue through which to redress wrongs[56] or as a means of facilitating interaction with their fellow men. The law is apt to be thought of as an agency of the white man's oppression, the white policeman constituting the prime symbol of the legal for much of the Negro population. James Baldwin has described the situation as follows:

> None of the Police Commissioner's men, even with the best will in the world, have any way of understanding the lives led by the people they swagger about in twos and threes controlling. Their very presence is an insult, and it would be, even if they spent their entire day feeding gumdrops to children. They represent the force of the white world, and that world's real intentions are, simply, for that world's criminal profit and ease, to keep the black man corraled up here [Harlem], in his place. The badge, the gun in the holster, and the swinging club make vivid what will happen should his rebellion become overt.[57]

An important side effect of second-class justice for the Negro has been a low level of motivation among educated Negroes to enter the legal profession,[58] although as the patterning of justice undergoes change, professional recruitment may be expected to follow.

Of course, there is nothing *inherent* in the overall American system of legal rules and institutions that requires these conditions; indeed our legal ideology expressly condemns them, as in the maxim "equality under the law." The legal system's neutrality with respect to specific patterns of outcome is shown by the fact that currently we find legal form and substance contributing significantly to the expansion of rights for Negroes, to the correction of the injustices just mentioned. At the same time, it is noteworthy that while recent efforts in the civil-rights movement have been making appreciable advances on the legal front as well as on others, one by-product of such efforts has been a deeper realization of, and more direct confrontation with, the continuing patterns of systematic injustice by agencies of the law in certain American jurisdictions.[59] In any event, the point to be kept in mind is not that a legal system necessarily upholds any *particular* patterns of class subjection in a society, but rather that whichever patterns prevail or emerge, they will importantly incorporate some degree of support from legal institutions. As we shall see, there is debate as to whether the law simply reflects the changing class structure or, on the contrary, may also constitute an important instrument for the shaping and changing of that structure.

Although the discriminatory treatment of Negroes in the area of criminal justice is perhaps unparalleled in this country, in some other respects the subordinate position of Negroes in the American system of law is primarily a reflection of the more general sociolegal subordination of the poor. This subordination can perhaps best be conceptualized as a glaring discrepancy within our society between the distribution of legal needs and the distribution of legal resources or access to such resources. Recently, sociologists Jerome Carlin and Jan Howard have presented a comprehensive survey of research on this question. Asserting that "a distinctive characteristic of the poor, and an essential condition of their predicament, is their lack of participation in the legal and governmental process," Carlin and Howard insist further that "the contention that the problems of the poor are inherently nonlegal is based on an extremely narrow view of the law and of the lawyer's role." [60]

It is often held that the poor have little need for lawyers, and research has in fact shown that about two-thirds of lower-class families have never employed a lawyer for any purpose whatsoever. Likewise, studies reveal that the poor are less likely than the middle class to make wills, enter into contracts, make lease or deed agreements, and sue or be sued. But as Carlin and Howard cogently point out, such findings "do not necessarily indicate that the poor have fewer legal problems" and "do not necessarily represent different *needs* for legal services. They represent differences in legal *faits accomplis*." Such data tell us something about the recognition and exercise of certain legal rights, though clearly not all areas of possible legal action are covered in such surveys; but they tell us little about the overall distribution of problems for which legal solutions or actions might be appropriate.[61] As Carlin and Howard ably document, the poor are often hampered by their failure to realize that there may be legal solutions to their problems, by their reluctance to take legal action even if they realize the possibility of some legal solution, by their lack of access to private attorneys and their ignorance of free legal services, and, sometimes, by the difficulty of obtaining legal help even when they have reached the point of getting in touch with a lawyer.

The failure of the poor to seek legal aid reinforces the false impression that the poor have few legal difficulties, notwithstanding the existence of numerous, quite real legal problems cutting across various areas of their everyday lives. Among the areas (in addition to that of criminal justice) in which legal needs are especially striking are those of family law,[62] landlord-tenant relations,[63] consumer problems,[64] and welfare-law administration.[65] Mention of welfare administration as a problem area strikes a somewhat ironic note, since the proliferation of government welfare programs has of course been aimed at ameliorating many of the most pressing problems of the poor. Unfortunately, along with the gains established through such programs, many new problems for the poor have arisen. Not only do lack of communication, ignorance, and hostility often characterize the relations between the poor and welfare administrators, but the poor are greatly hampered in their dealings with such administrators by an overall philosophy under which "welfare is viewed by the agencies as a *privilege* rather than a *right*. This theory consequently permits a significantly wide scope of administrative discretion and a relative absence of procedural safeguards." [66] Welfare recipients, many people seem to feel, should be happy with whatever they get. They should expect to undergo the utmost scrutiny by authorities to determine their initial and continuing eligibility (including the notorious, surprise "midnight raids" of apartments of women on relief, to see if a man, who is presumed to be a source of income and would hence render her ineligible, might be present). There has been, in some instances, almost a presumption of fraud in welfare applications, a point suggested by the rigid, and sometimes discriminatory, residence requirements established in some jurisdictions.

Increasingly, lawyers and social workers have become alert to the injustices built into welfare programs, injustices that provoked law professor Charles Reich, in a path-breaking article, to urge complete repudiation of the prevailing handout philosophy and the repressive practices such philosophy entailed. Proclaiming that the modern era of the welfare state had heralded in "The New Property"—in the form of such benefits as unemployment compensation, public assistance, and old age insurance—Reich insisted that substantive and procedural justice for welfare recipients would be forthcoming only if the concept of legal "right" were applied to these special forms of "property." "Only by making such benefits into rights can the welfare state achieve its goal of providing a secure minimum basis for individual well-being and dignity in a society where each man cannot be wholly the master of his own destiny." [67]

One of the few existing sociological research projects focusing directly on law and stratification is reported on by David Caplovitz, in his book *The Poor Pay More*. As the title suggests, the research concerned consumer behavior, an area in which exploitation of the poor has been both harsh and systematic. Based on a sample survey of 464 low-income families in New York City, Caplovitz's study reveals that shady and illegal sales practices are virtually the norm rather than the exception in transactions with such consumers. Low-income buyers are routinely subjected to "bait advertising and the switch sale," in which they are lured by an offer of low prices and then tricked by high-pressure salesmen into purchasing much more expensive items; outright misrepresentation of prices, particularly in credit transactions; and misrepresentation of quality of goods, sometimes with the surreptitious substitution of merchandise at some stage of the transaction. They are sold shoddy goods at exorbitant prices; but any complaints they make meet a deaf ear, and sometimes they are even unable to locate the (anonymous) salesman they dealt with, receiving all correspondence subsequent to the sale from a remote finance company.

Because in this group most major purchases are made on an installment basis, a major area of difficulty concerns failure to meet payments and the repossession of merchandise. As Caplovitz states:

> Many consumers have almost no idea of the complex set of legal conditions embodied in the contracts they sign. The penalties that can be brought to bear on them, such as the loss of possessions already paid for, the payment of interest on money owed, the payment of lawyer and court fees, are matters that some families become rudely aware of only when—for whatever reasons—they miss their payments.[68]

A special problem facing low-income buyers is that, whatever the merits of their cases, failure to appear in court when proceeded against results in automatic and adverse judgment. In the Caplovitz study it was found that "a number of consumers in this group only learned of the court action taken against them after the fact, when, for example, they were informed by their employer that they were being garnisheed. Under the law, the consumer is given seven days to answer the summons issued him and if he does not reply in that time, a judgment by default is entered." [69] According to Caplovitz, the majority of court cases involving low-income consumers probably end this way. Sometimes the consumer's ignorance, forgetfulness, or reluctance to take time off from work may be involved; at other times the consumer may never even have received the summons (failure of process servers to deliver summonses is so frequent that a special term, "sewer service," is applied to the practice).

Perhaps even more distressing than the existence of widespread exploitation, is the lower-income consumer's inability to cope with improper or illegal practices when he experiences them. Caplovitz's findings on reactions to cheating are striking. Families who reported having been cheated were asked what they had done about their problem. Half had done nothing at all, not even complained to the merchant, 40 percent had tried to deal directly with the merchant; and only 9 percent had sought professional help. Similarly, *all* respondents in the survey were asked, "Where would you now go for help if you were being cheated by a merchant or salesman?" Some 64 percent said they did not know. Of this finding Caplovitz notes that these two out of three respondents

> could not name any of the community agencies equipped to deal with these problems, such as the Legal Aid Society, the State Banking and Finance Department, the Small Claims Court, or the Better Business Bureau. The Better Business Bureau was the agency most often cited by the minority who had some idea where they could go for professional help. Quite significant . . . is the fact that only 3 percent of the families said they would turn to a private lawyer for help.[70]

Not surprisingly, Caplovitz found that the newest migrants to the city, the Puerto Ricans, were much less knowledgeable about sources of professional aid than the longer-resident Negroes and whites.

Such studies are helpful in alerting policymakers to the fact that not all the legal problems of the poor lie in the area of criminal justice. Although the confrontation between the indigent and our apparatus of criminal law has many extremely disturbing features, the active public debate surrounding criminal procedures and the considerable publicity given key U.S. Supreme Court decisions relating to such matters (for example, the celebrated *Gideon v. Wainwright,* in which the court held that every indigent defendant in a criminal trial is entitled to be provided with defense counsel by the State)[71] have tended to overshadow other legal needs of the poor. That a broadly based awareness of these needs is now developing can be seen in the efforts to build plans for "the extension of legal services to the poor" into the various government or government-supported "poverty programs." [72] Here once again we see an attempt to develop in the legal system, measures to counteract exploitative uses and impacts of legal process. Although the details of the specific schemes vary, basically the aim of these programs is to provide the poor with free, easily accessible legal advice and assistance.

Usually building on some variant of the idea of a "neighborhood law office," the hope is to bring preventive legal action to bear on the poor person's problems by providing an agency or office he can easily reach, manned by persons with whom he can deal openly and without suspicion or the feeling he is being patronized. Such persons should also be able to explain his rights to him and help him to implement them in appropriate ways. There is much discussion at the moment of various specific issues concerning these programs—including the composition of the staff of such an office or agency, the extent to which the problems to be dealt with are necessarily legal problems, the appropriate financing of such programs, whether the programs involve solicitation of legal business (disapproved by the organized bar's canons of legal ethics) or (in some schemes) improper practice of law by nonlawyers, and the relation of such programs to existing, local law firms and bar associations. But it is significant that some such programs are already in effect and that on the basis of limited experience with them it appears they may constitute an important vehicle for mediating undesired "stratification effects" in the American legal system. As well as focusing on the legal problems of the urban poor, the special legal needs of the rural and migrant poor are also now receiving increased governmental attention.[73]

ROLE OF THE LEGAL PROFESSION

As noted above, the power of the legal functionaries themselves may represent one aspect of the relationship between the legal system and the stratification order. It is unquestionable that judges wield power; their decisions invariably affect the structure of power, whatever their personal intentions may be and whatever constraints they feel owing to the nature of their judicial role. On the other hand, the power factor as it relates to the legal profession as a whole is somewhat more elusive. There have been, over the years, numerous assessments of the role of the American lawyer—some admiring, others caustic and contemptuous. To Alexis de Tocqueville, the lawyer embodied a certain aristocratic outlook and spirit, which would have a salutory influence on American democracy: "Lawyers belong to the people by birth and interest, and to the aristocracy by habit and taste; they may be looked upon as the connecting link between the two great classes of society." It was only in the profession of law, Tocqueville maintained, that the aristocratic element could be "amalgamated without violence with the natural elements of democracy and be advantageously and permanently combined with them." [74] A strikingly different view was expressed by the iconoclast Thorstein Veblen. Placing the law among the "pecuniary employments" (having to do with ownership and acquisition, and to be contrasted with the "industrial employments" involving workmanship and production) he stated:

> The profession of the law does not imply large ownership; but since no taint of usefulness, for other than the competitive purpose, attaches to the lawyer's trade, it grades high in the conventional scheme. The lawyer is exclusively occupied with the details of predatory fraud, either in achieving or in checkmating chicane, and success in the profession is therefore accepted as marking a large endowment of that barbarian astuteness which has always commanded men's respect and fear.[75]

Whether by outlook aristocratic or predatory, there is little doubt that some lawyers in modern American society (those at the top echelons of the profession) do maintain positions of considerable power. C. Wright Mills asserted that "men of the higher legal and financial type from the great law factories and investment firms" act as "professional go-betweens" for the dominant corporate, political, and military interests and hence serve to "unify the power elite." [76] Another student of "strategic elites" has noted that the lawyer's familiarity with rules and regulations and with formal procedures may help to explain the importance of legal training as a stepping stone to top posts in business, diplomacy, and the civil service: "Within the business elite of 1950, one sixth were trained as lawyers; within the diplomatic elite for the century, two fifths; and within the political elite, one half." [77] In his study, *The Wall Street Lawyer,* Erwin Smigel makes clear the extensive and ramifying influence of those lawyers who hold major positions in the largest and most prestigious of New York law firms. Such lawyers hold the confidence of the major corporate interests they represent and hence both directly or indirectly guide business policy. Through the unlimited resources at their command they can push disputes to the highest appellate courts, thus gaining an opportunity to shape the course of judicial policy. Their prestige exerts influence on legislation as well, and their active personal participation in government service has a direct impact, both domestic and international.[78]

Without much doubt these particular lawyers feel an identity of interests with big business and thus tend to exert a conservative influence on the development of public policy. It has also been found that the selective recruitment policies of these important law firms tend to result in the exclusion of persons of lower-class or minority-group background, who might be ideologically disposed to challenge conservative outlooks and practices. At the same time, one has to recognize that these same corporation-linked law firms have often contributed men to the top echelons of government—some of whom, as in the Roosevelt New Deal era, proved to be extremely liberal in their work as federal administrators or appellate justices and in other positions of national importance. Similarly, partners in these top firms often have been in the forefront of the effort to provide adequate legal services for the poor and to enforce high ethical standards of conduct within the legal profession. Indeed, as Jerome Carlin has shown in an important recent study of ethical standards and behavior within the metropolitan bar, there is (following the formulation of Everett Hughes) a kind of "moral division of labor" within the profession; according to this division, the large-firm lawyers, having no need, financial or otherwise, to involve themselves in legal dirty work, can well afford to maintain high standards of conduct in their own practice and to seek to impose such standards on the entire legal system.[79]

It is difficult, then, either on the basis of social background or in terms of professional role, to assert unequivocally that even these especially influential lawyers further only the dominant economic interests in our society. Nor do we find much evidence for a kind of inherent conservatism bred of training in formalism and consistency, such as some observers claim afflicts the legal profession. Furthermore, if the Wall Street lawyer comes from a relatively "elite" social background, and has intimate and continuous contact with other elements of the ruling interests in society, this factor is considerably offset by the existence, already well documented in various studies,[80] of a pronounced system of stratification *within* the legal profession. It has consistently been found that lawyers' social background and legal training are closely related to such matters as organization of their legal practice (individual practice, small firm, large firm), income earned, type of legal work in which engaged, extent and type of court and agency contact, and nature and affluence of clientele. Since perhaps two-thirds of the practicing lawyers in major cities (64 percent in the Carlin survey of New York) are concentrated in small firms and individual practice, have relatively low incomes, and handle routine and nonrecurrent matters for an essentially low-status clientele, it seems quite inaccurate to place the profession as a whole within any presumed "ruling class" in American society.

Perhaps the ultimate test of the legal profession's position relative to the overall stratification order in American society is the extent to which it facilitates or hinders the development of a system of equal justice for all. Hence the crucial point is not simply whether lawyers tend to be liberal or conservative on a multitude of diverse social issues. Equally important is their degree of commitment to the ideals underlying the entire legal system and to the explicit professional ethic of denying no man his day in court or other legal assistance because of his social status, his ability to pay, or the nature of his legal difficulty. Such commitment is perhaps best described as uneven.

It is noteworthy that the federal government's current plans and programs for antipoverty legal assistance are encountering pronounced opposition from some local bar associations and particularly from organized groups of trial lawyers (who handle the bulk of personal injury and small claims suits and who, with individual exceptions, of course, tend to be situated rather low in the socioeconomic hierarchy of the profession).[81] The frequent charge that such schemes embody or will lead to "socialized law" suggests vested interests, which some elements of the bar fear (in a sense, quite accurately) may be threatened by the new programs. At the same time, however, it is equally significant that large numbers of lawyers forego more lucrative private practice to work full-time in legal-assistance agencies and projects, and a great many more devote part of their time and energy to such efforts. Then too, it is lawyers who have been largely responsible for the new governmental emphasis on the legal needs of the poor, and for insisting that their profession must work to develop effective mechanisms for meeting those needs. Similarly, whereas some local bar associations and fellow practitioners in the South have harassed, and even formally disciplined, lawyers, both white and Negro, representing clients in civil-rights cases,[82] it is also true that lawyers from both the South and the North have at considerable professional and personal risk taken up such unpopular cases and worked hard to promote legal and social reform in the field of race relations. Increasingly, too, legal education is recognizing the social stratification factors that influence the administration of justice and is stressing the lawyer's responsibility in this area.

On balance, we may say that while lawyers play an important role in shaping patterns of rights and duties in a society, and hence indirectly tend to contribute to its ordering along socioeconomic lines, there is no single clear-cut pattern with respect to the functions of the American legal profession in upholding or challenging existing socioeconomic differentials. That the bar is itself stratified seems to be as important to a sociological understanding of the profession as is the broader issue of whether the profession as a whole reflects and furthers any particular class interests. On the other hand, this internal stratification of the profession does, in a sense, at present contribute to an overall patterning of legal work in which lower-income clients are disadvantaged. Under the "moral division of labor" such clients are largely relegated to the poorly remunerated, lower-echelon lawyers, who tend to be less well trained, who have fewer legal skills and resources at their command, and who may often be likely to approach a legal problem as a one-shot business transaction in which the client's interests, as well as conformity to high ethical standards, are secondary considerations. Again, the developing programs of free legal assistance may ensure more competent and scrupulous representation for the poor.

Although membership in the legal profession (and especially the holding of some of the more distinguished positions within the profession, such as judgeships) certainly has high social prestige in the United States,[83] it seems unlikely that many individuals enter on a career in the law with a view to manipulating the broad course of public policy in any particular direction. We may safely assume a broad distribution of political orientations and attitudes among individuals entering the profession. Furthermore, any strong preference for particular political ideals may be somewhat modified by a generalized commitment to the rather neutral values of legality and of the profession's disinterested public responsibilities, a commitment instilled, at least in some law schools, during the formal socialization processes of a legal education.[84] While some individuals, especially members of ethnic minorities, enter the law out of an upwardly mobile striving for professional status,[85] a number of somewhat disparate and even conflicting factors may motivate other would-be lawyers. Perhaps the mixed nature of the profession's role in relation to the power and stratification orders is mirrored in these findings from a recent survey: "future lawyers consider the following values important: making a lot of money; a chance to help others and to be useful to society; freedom from supervision; and an opportunity to work with people." [86]

Chapter Three

�֍✳✳

Law and Social Change

In our consideration of historical jurisprudence and also at various other points, we have seen that theorists of law and society have often been preoccupied with efforts to spell out the broad historical course of development of legal institutions. Needless to say, the historical and comparative data bearing on the development of law are overwhelming in amount and complexity. No attempt at any chronological and specific summary of the course of law up to the present time will be undertaken here. Any such effort would inevitably involve gross oversimplification. Instead, a few of the major theoretical formulations about law and social change will be noted, some modern trends that seem to have particular theoretical significance will be discussed, and the general issues of law's limits and its social dependence or independence will be analyzed.

Some of the difficulties of determining the "beginning" and "evolution" of law were noted in our discussion of some of the work on primitive legal systems. Very likely the following recent assessment of the overall trend in development of the law is, notwithstanding its noncommital and bland nature, a succinct and accurate statement of our knowledge in this area: "The idea that law follows the same sequence of development in all societies has not been demonstrated, but it seems clear that law has become more complex whenever societies have grown more specialized." [1] If there is more or less general agreement that societal and legal complexity have gone hand in hand, beyond that there is little consensus. Particular theorists differ as to details and interpretation of the general relationship between social and legal change.

Some General Theories

As noted in the Introduction, one of Max Weber's most important contributions to an understanding of law was his emphasis on the peculiarly "rational" quality of legal institutions as they developed in modern Western societies. Weber stated that the development of law and procedure could be seen as passing through several stages (which we cannot consider in detail) ranging from "charismatic legal revelation through 'law prophets'" up to the most advanced stage, "systematic elaboration of law and professionalized administration of justice by persons who have received their legal training in a learned and formally logical manner." [2] It does not appear, however, that he had in mind any suggestion of a universal and orderly evolutionary sequence. For as Bendix has pointed out, these "stages" were really theoretical constructs:

> Actually, the rationality of the law increased in many different sequences, not only in this one. Not all of these "stages" have occurred—regardless of sequence—even where the process has gone furthest, as in the Occident. Also, elements from each of these "stages" can be found in ancient as well as in modern legal practice, as Weber showed by a profusion of illustrations. [3]

These stages more nearly represent generalized forces at work in various times and places in shaping legal phenomena, and they are in essence ideal types. The same can be said of Weber's statements concerning types of irrationality and rationality that may characterize legal systems.[4] According to Weber, legal *irrationality* (a failure to be guided by general rules) may be *formal,* as in decisions determined by means beyond the control of reason, such as oracles or ordeals; or it may be *substantive,* when, for example, the decision-maker is guided only by reaction to the individual case. (Weber saw this ideal type of decision-making approximated by the tyrant and also by the *kadi,* or Moslem market-place judge, who rendered decision without recourse to general norms.) Likewise, he elaborated both substantive and formal types of rationality in law. A legal system exhibits *substantive rationality* when it bases decisions on some general principles drawn from outside the legal system itself. The crucial characteristic of substantively rational law, in Weber's scheme, is that decisions are no longer arbitrary, but are now at least grounded in some considerations of substantive justice or even political expediency. In such a legal system, however, there is still no restraint imposed by procedural formality or by the need to maintain doctrinal consistency. This is where *formal rationality* in law enters the picture. It is this procedural and logical rationality that Weber termed formal and that he found to be uniquely emphasized in the legal systems of modern Western civilization. Of course, this development is closely associated with the bureaucratization of modern industrial society, as seen in the fact that the terms "rational" and "legal" or even "rational-legal" often are considered synonyms for "bureaucratic" in Weber's well-known typology of major types of authority (the other two being "traditional" and "charismatic").[5]

There is little doubt that Weber did in fact capture, in his concept of formal rationality, a crucial feature of modern legal systems. While doctrinal or logical consistency may be a quality more sought after than achieved, procedural formality on the other hand is certainly a key feature of present-day, Western legal institutions. The likely conflict between legal formality and substantive justice, recognized by Weber himself, has already been noted. But if formality may have its dysfunctional aspects, it may also operate to facilitate substantive justice; and indeed this is the premise underlying much of the procedural technicality of our system. Thus, in the American system of criminal justice, enforcement officers sometimes complain that the courts are free-ing "guilty" defendants because of some procedural finepoint, that is, because of the demands of formal rationality. Yet the ideology underlying the system refutes such argument, insisting that the occasional freeing of an actual offender is more than balanced out by procedures that guard against the danger of imprisoning innocent persons. We shall encounter other examples of the tendency toward formal rationality, and the search for it, in later sections of this study.

Another major sociological statement concerning law and social change was that of Emile Durkheim. Durkheim's basic thesis, presented in his *On the Division of Labor in Society*,[6] was that a society's law reflects the type of social solidarity existing within that society. According to Durkheim, there are two basic types of societal cohesion or solidarity: *mechanical solidarity* (which he saw prevailing in relatively simple and homogeneous societies, where cohesion was ensured by close interpersonal ties and identity of aims) and *organic solidarity* (that which charac-terizes more heterogeneous and differentiated modern societies, where "mechanical" cohesion gives way to a sort more consonant with the functional interdependence produced by the complex division of labor). Associated with these two forms of integration are two types of law, *repressive* and *restitutive*. In a mechanically integrated society, Durkheim asserted, law is essentially penal and repressive. An act is criminal, he stated, "when it offends strong and defined states of the collective conscience." The community at large reacts passionately, rather than through rational deter-mination, against offenders, because in such cohesive states of society each member feels himself directly threatened by every violation of a major norm. Crime, Durkheim believed, "brings together upright consciences and concentrates them." The collective reaction to the deviant, in other words, enhances solidarity among the reactors and helps to bind the group together. Deviance, then, which appears to threaten the community, at the same time indirectly serves to strengthen it.

With society's increased differentiation, the strong collective reaction to "offenses" becomes a less central feature of the legal system, as repressive law tends to give way to restitutive law, in which restitution to the injured person becomes a major way of settling disputes. What distinguishes the restitutive sanction, states Durkheim, is

> that it is not expiatory, but consists of a simple *return in state*. Sufferance proportionate to the misdeed is not inflicted on the one who has violated the law or who disregards it; he is simply sentenced to comply with it. If certain things were done, the judge reinstates them as they would have been. . . . Damage-interests have no penal character; they are only a means of reviewing the past in order to reinstate it, as far as possible, to its normal form.[7]

Actually, it is not at all clear that Durkheim's thesis of a development from repressive to restitutive law can be systematically demonstrated. A negative finding on this point was one of the outcomes in a recent comparative analysis of legal institutions found in a large sample of societies.[8] Richard Schwartz and James C. Miller studied Human Relations Area Files (a cross-cultural survey) data on fifty-one societies, which varied on a previously developed, societal complexity scale. The researchers examined several "characteristics of a fully developed legal system" including *counsel* (regular reliance on "non-kin advocates" in dispute-settling), *mediation* ("non-kin third-party intervention") and *police* (a specialized armed force used partially or wholly to enforce norms). These three characteristics were found to exist in a neatly ordered sequence of combinations ("near-perfect Guttman scale") in the various societies. Of the fifty-one societies, the following "scale types" emerged, closely associated with the progression from lesser to greater societal complexity: eleven societies showed none of the three characteristics; twenty had only mediation; eleven had only mediation and police; seven had mediation, police, and specialized counsel. There were two "deviant" cases in which police, but not mediation, were present. Societies lacking even mediation were found to be the simplest of those studied, with small community size and in most cases no use of money. Such symbolic exchange was present, on the other hand, in three quarters of the societies with mediation, almost all of which also had a concept of damages, which "appears to be virtually a precondition for mediation." Since twenty societies had mediation but no police, it is clear that these two developments do not inevitably occur together. Those societies that did have police were economically advanced with a substantial degree of specialization; most had full-time priests, teachers, and government officials.

As the authors noted, these findings seem to contradict Durkheim's thesis of progression from repressive to restitutive laws. The finding here was, on the contrary, "that police [the more "repressive" institution] are found only in association with a substantial degree of division of labor. . . . By contrast, restitutive sanctions—damages and mediation—which Durkheim found to be associated with an increasing division of labor, are found in many societies that lack even rudimentary specialization." [9] Use of counsel was found to occur only in the most complex of the societies studied, and it did not automatically accompany the use of mediation. The authors suggest that more than just economic strength and specialization seem needed for the use of counsel to occur; they surmise that level of literacy may be an important factor in this development. Schwartz and Miller maintain that their findings support the belief that *some* sort of evolutionary sequence does occur in the development of legal institutions. They also see their study as possibly bearing on the question of developing an effective international legal order. Their findings suggest "the need to build certain cultural foundations in the community before a central regime of control . . . can develop. . . . Compensation by damages and the use of mediators might well contribute to the development of such a cultural foundation, as well as reflecting its growth." [10]

If Durkheim's specific scheme does not hold up fully in empirical terms, it does not by any means follow that his formulations on law are not worth our attention. On the contrary, some of the points he emphasized have great relevance for a consideration of present-day legal systems. His discussion of the meaning of repressive law is particularly useful to an understanding of the social significance of crime and punishment. Indeed, we now realize that in modern society as well as in less complex forms of social organization, punishment of the criminal or deviant continues to incorporate a significant element of passionate reaction and moral outrage. Crime and the reaction to it may serve important personal functions for the reactors and punishers, as well as help to enhance cohesion in society at large.[11] Repressive law, then, exists and indeed thrives in all societies. At the same time, however, Durkheim's emphasis on restitutive law in modern industrial societies provides a corrective to the tendency to think of *all* law as punitive. Actually, in most commercial litigation in our society, the nonpunitive aspect is evident; ordinarily a party can collect damages only if he shows that, and to what extent, he has in fact been damaged. Since the bulk of Western law has to do not with criminal offenses but with civil disputes arising in various realms of everyday social and particularly business life, a recognition of the *dominance* of nonrepressive sanctions is important.

The writings of Weber and Durkheim, then, continue to illuminate our understanding of legal systems. So too does the work of Maine. As noted earlier, Maine's status-to-contract theme usefully highlighted the significant and broad social trend from homogeneous, close-knit forms of social organization to hetero-geneous ones in which interpersonal relations tended to be attenuated, impersonal, and instrumental. On the other hand, while many legal relationships have come to be based on free agreement of the parties rather than on fixed social status, critics noted a recent reverse trend, in which new types of "status" have been legally created for the *protection* of the "contracting" par-ties. Nonetheless, even this supposed countertrend may not really undermine Maine's thesis. In discussing status, Maine had in mind particularly the subservient position of wives and children within the family, as well as the institutions of slavery and serf-dom in general. Maine may have exaggerated the benefits of free contract. Yet it is quite possible that he never supposed that *all* specific social relationships could be governed by contractual agreement. As one defender of Maine insists: "The tendency to multiply specification of right and duty by overriding legislation, . . . does not restore anything remotely like the personal status to which Maine referred, nor anything like the social and to some extent legal stratification, transmitted from ancestor to descend-ant, of some archaic systems." Under our present system, the in-dividual has a tremendous range of free choice as to which particular relationships and transactions he wishes to enter, and it is primarily the specific details or conditions governing certain particular relationships or transactions that are fixed through regulatory legislation.[12]

Other theorists have contributed their own special versions of the evolution and development of law. The original Marxist formulation, envisioning the eradication of the need for law, today has virtually no acceptance, even among Marxist-oriented observers. Nevertheless, the general influence of Marxist perspec-tives should not be completely discounted. Dynamic and conflict-oriented analyses of the legal order often are indebted to Marxist theories. And a Marxist or Marxist-like emphasis on the broad structuring of economic relations has provided the foundation for various specific studies of legal trends, ranging from the area of property law to that of criminal law and penology.[13]

A rather different persisting sociological effort to express legal development, as well as other social development, in terms of distinct stages of society is represented in the work of Pitirim Sorokin. According to Sorokin, societies pass through stages in which the values he terms *ideational* (absolute truth, as revealed by God), *sensate* (reliance on sensory experience alone), or *idealistic* (an intermediate, mixed category) predominate. Law, as well as all other sociocultural phenomena, is shaped according to the dominating theme of the era or stage. Since modern Western society is in a sensate stage, sensate law predominates. Although this formulation has not had much impact on current work in the sociology of law, Sorokin nicely captures some of the quality of modern views of law. He states that law is viewed by a sensate society as

> man-made, frequently, indeed, as a mere instrument for the subjugation and exploitation of one group by another. Its aim is exclusively utilitarian: the safety of human life, security of property and possession, peace and order, the happiness and well-being of either society at large or of the dominating faction which enacts and enforces sensate law. Its norms are relative, changeable, and conditional. Nothing eternal or sacred is implied in such a system of law. It does not attempt to regulate supersensory values or man's relationships toward them.[14]

We see mentioned here, of course, some of the major jurisprudential themes (considered in Chapter One) that have exerted a powerful influence in modern times. Many sociologists would dispute Sorokin's insistence that the dominance of "sensate" values poses a severe threat of our society's downfall, moral or even physical.[15] Nonetheless, his work underscores the significant truth that ways of viewing law in general, as well as specific content of substantive law, undoubtedly are associated with and reflect broader societal value orientations.

Even if we do not have any one, fully satisfactory scheme setting forth the development of law, it is indeed true, as Sorokin noted, that modern law is generally acknowledged to be "relative, changeable, and conditional." The legal order changes, both in its substance and its forms, for the simple reason that it cannot remain unresponsive to changing social conditions.

THE SOVIET EXPERIENCE

Legal developments in the Soviet Union during the half-century since the Russian Revolution provide a good illustration of this necessary responsiveness. In his thorough discussion of Soviet legal development,[16] Harold Berman discusses trends during five major periods:

1. *The Period of War Communism (1917–1921).* During the period immediately following the Revolution, there were radical attempts to alter the existing economic, political, and legal institutions. Previously existing courts were abolished; and new People's Courts established, which were to be guided by a general norm of "revolutionary legal consciousness." There was little civil litigation during this period, and criminal law was administered largely through the special secret police (Cheka) and special revolutionary tribunals, which dealt with offenses against the Revolution on a more or less ad hoc basis. Except for a statement of principles of criminal law, emphasizing the need to repress class enemies, legislation was largely negative. For example, the new Family Code was mainly a repudiation and abolition of existing laws controlling marriage, divorce, and other family matters.

2. *The NEP (New Economic Policy) Period (1921–1928).* The key characteristic of the NEP period was a mixture of socialist and capitalist elements in the economy. As Berman comments, the partial restoration of a market economy implied "a restora-

tion of bourgeois law—there being no other kind." A large
number of legal codes were enacted during the NEP period.
These were, interestingly, based on a combination of prerevolutionary Russian law and that of other bourgeois countries modified in line with Soviet conditions and goals. The purposes of the
Revolution were evident in provisions under which civil transactions and criminal acts considered detrimental to the state were
singled out as being of the greatest concern. In criminal law, the
doctrine of analogy, under which a person could be punished for
acts "analogous to" acts specifically prohibited, was approved;
and again the general principle of "revolutionary legal consciousness" was to apply in doubtful cases in all realms of the law.

3. *The Period of the First and Second Five-Year Plans (1928–
1937).* In the years of the first two five-year plans, the Soviet
regime emphasized rapid industrialization, collectivization, and
militarization—all supposedly coordinated through centralized
planning. Early statements about the demise of law were re-
asserted, with the hope expressed that ultimately the Plan would
replace Law. Various philosophical and economic controversies,
having legal implications, arose at this time, but it is not possible
to detail them here. Perhaps the key theoretical point that
emerged was the need to subordinate law to political control.
There was a reversion to ad hoc rulings and procedures, and a
prevalent reliance on considerations of political, economic, and
administrative expediency. Neither abstract principles of law nor
the intent of the parties in a dispute (or personal guilt, in criminal cases) received much emphasis. Berman concludes that during
this period "the general deterioration of the legal system was
strikingly evident."

4. *Soviet Law under Stalin (1936–1952).* By the mid-1930's,
Soviet officialdom recognized that neither social institutions such
as law, family, and property, nor the need for criminal sanctions
were, after all, likely to "wither away"—at least not in the fore-

seeable future. Therefore an attempt would be made to re-establish them on a new, socialist basis. This decision led to many abrupt shifts and reversals in public policy. Family laws were tightened up; in particular, regulations on abortion were re-imposed, and judicial requirements for divorce were established. In the economic realm, there was a certain amount of decentral-ization, a new degree of flexibility concerning personal-property ownership, and increased emphasis on competition and incentives ("socialist emulation"). Law was recognized as having a legitimate and important role to play in socialist society, and many new legal codes and provisions were adopted. There was some tighten-ing up of legal definitions and procedures, use of the principle of analogy was limited, relatively traditional court procedures were reintroduced, and legal education was expanded. Ironically, this reassertion of the law in certain realms occurred alongside the well-known Stalinist reign of terror against actual and sus-pected political enemies; Berman refers to the "duality of law and terror" in this period. In any event, it was seen that a new and more positive conception of law was required: "Without a legal system and a legal order . . . the Stalinist regime could neither control the social relations of the people nor keep the economy going nor command the political forces in the country as a whole. It was rediscovered that law is not a luxury but a neces-sity. . . ." [17]

5. *Soviet Law after Stalin* (*1953–1962*). Berman cites seven major tendencies during the post-Stalin period: (1) a tendency toward elimination of political terror; (2) some liberalization of procedural and substantive norms, including final elimination of the principle of analogy in criminal cases; (3) increased system-atization and rationalization of the legal system, including court reorganization and adoption of Fundamental Principles in vari-ous realms of law; (4) a tendency toward decentralization and democratization of decision-making; (5) introduction of popular participation in administering justice (for example, in local Com-

rades' Courts, which might meet in factories and apartment houses to consider minor offenses); (6) a return, in 1961–1962, to harsh criminal and administrative penalties for certain offenses (typified by the so-called antiparasite laws, which were not always administered through rigorous legal procedures, and by the extension of capital punishment to a variety of crimes, especially offenses against state property); and (7) a new theory of law and the state, calling for strengthening of the "socialist legal order." [18] It is noteworthy that in the years since Berman's analysis was published, the emphasis on "socialist legality" has continued. Thus in two recent articles, Soviet legal experts called for a strengthening of the role of the legal profession, including improvement of the work of defense counsel, better legal education, and dissemination of legal information among the working people, and repudiated theories and procedures under which the Stalinist regime had used "pseudoscientific concepts" to "conceal violations of rights and legitimate interests of citizens and to justify unfounded repressions and other gross violations of socialist legality." [19]

While Berman's assessment tends to emphasize the favorable trends toward reform, other analysts present more negative interpretations. Critics note that the basic deficiency—subservience of the legal system to party control—has not really been eliminated. Furthermore, such extrajudicial or quasi-judicial arrangements as the Comrades' Courts and other specialized tribunals may invite the danger of informal action without procedural safeguards. It may, therefore, be misleading to consider such machinery an advance toward "popular participation." Above all and notwithstanding some undoubted degree of reform, it has been questioned whether Soviet citizens "will consider it in any significant sense 'their' legal system, since it remains one imposed from above, one dependent for its elements of stability and decency on the fateful caprice of an elite ultimately responsible to no one but itself." [20] (Of course it is an intriguing empirical question how the citizens in *any* modern society view their legal system; as we shall see, this is an important area for research in the American sociology of law.)

The Soviet experience is significant not only because of the failure of the original plans to abolish law. It is interesting that Soviet law reflects a mixture of influences—Marxist, Russian (that is, prerevolutionary), and Western (bourgeois).[21] Clearly, we see here evidence that no amount of ideological commitment and planning can override completely the need for the legal system to relate to the general social context, both past and present. Furthermore, the startling fluctuations, both in the organization of legal institutions and procedures and in substantive law, demonstrate that the aims and processes of a legal system can never really remain static, with the possible exception of a few extremely broad ideals and a few very general neutral kinds of procedure. (It is noteworthy that similar fluctuations have occurred in another major legal system grounded in Marxist theory, that of Communist China.)[22] As already mentioned, some analysts attach particular significance to the trend away from rule by analogy and in the direction of the rule of law (in the technical sense of nonretroactivity, specificity, uniformity of application of rules, and the like). Whether or not one finds here a "strain toward legality" in modern legal systems, or an indication that the Soviet system is approaching a stage of legal maturity, certainly this is an interesting development. Also to be noted is the development in the Soviet Union of what Berman calls "parental law," that is, reliance on the judicial system not merely for resolution of specific legal disputes but also to serve a more general function as an agent of socialization for the entire citizenry, educating the public to the major values of society and of the legal system.[23] It may be that a similar trend is evident today in the United States, particularly in some quasi-judicial and administrative settings. If so, perhaps this trend too is a general feature of legal development in modern industrial societies. And clearly the potential function of law as a socialization mechanism has important implications for the attempt consciously to use legal form and substance in the promotion of more general social change.

SOME RECENT TRENDS IN AMERICAN LAW

Various developments within the American legal system similarly illustrate the responsiveness of law to changing social forces and conditions. In large measure such developments reflect three "master trends" highlighted by Selznick: (1) the decline of kinship and fixed status as key points of orientation in social control and the emergence of a mobile and socially fragmented "mass society" (as already noted, Selznick sees in this trend an inevitable increase in the work formal agencies of regulation and control will be called upon to do); (2) emergence of the large-scale organization, a development with which many new legal problems are associated; and (3) "the ascendance of social interests over parochial interests" with increased attention to the "socialization of law" (in Roscoe Pound's phrase), subordinating the concept of abstract, individually held rights to considerations of the general welfare.[24]

This last point is particularly well illustrated by major trends in the substance of American law. In an illuminating discussion of developments in the field of labor law, Alfred Blumrosen shows the various stages in which the legal standing and socioeconomic position of labor unions have been shaped. These range from the early treatment of unions as criminal conspiracies, periods in which the labor injunction was used to curtail union activity, and in which the Supreme Court used the "freedom of contract" doctrine to uphold employers' interests, to the gradual judicial realization that unorganized workers did not have the equality of bargaining power necessary for truly free contracting, and eventually (though with occasional setbacks) to the explicit acceptance and extension of the right to organize and bargain collectively and to be protected against the unfair labor practices of the employer. As Blumrosen suggests, this kind of progression is best understood and anticipated if one adopts an "image of a legal system conscious that doctrines represent and reflect policy decisions, that policy decisions require choice among competing values, and that, in making such choices, the social and institutional context is important." [25]

Examination of substantive legal trends concerning such diverse matters as contracts and other commercial transactions, torts (negligence and other breaches of duty), insurance, the family, crime, and the creation and operation of corporations reveals a similar development in all these fields—a development of increasing concern with the public interest and of constant adaptation of the law to changes in social forms and relationships and in general social conditions. Many of these changes in substantive law have occurred not only in the American legal system but in the legal systems of various Western societies.[26] Actually, a good deal of this substantive legal change seems related to all three of Selznick's "master trends." The declining emphasis on fixed status together with the increased attention to furthering the general welfare have tended to develop through the legal system increasingly broad patterns of control over individual behavior. This control is not, however, simply an increase in restriction on individual freedom; on the contrary, the aim has been at least partly to utilize the mechanism of increased legal regulation for the maximization of certain individual freedoms. (Such an aim is clear both in the regulation of economic relations and in the effort to protect and advance the rights and opportunities of racial minorities through legal intervention.) Similarly, the involvement of more and more people in the workings of large-scale organizations has not only led to a tremendous expansion of specific kinds of legal problems, but has highlighted the potential disparity in power as between the individual and the larger organization, hence forcing further regulation in the public interest.

In the recent development of substantive law, legislation obviously has played a most significant role. At the same time, it is highly questionable whether we can arbitrarily segregate the work of the courts (especially the highest appellate tribunals, whose rulings have widespread impact) from such legislative policy-making. It is true that the legislature can more easily and rapidly introduce very broad changes in public policy. The courts are restricted by the adversary procedure to the settlement of the specific disputes before them and to the consideration of only those particular issues raised by the parties to those disputes. Likewise, the appellate judge feels a responsibility to maintain the consistency and integrity of the system of legal rules,[27] whereas the legislator ordinarily feels no such constraint. There is, indeed, under our system of law a continuous tension between legislative and judicial activity, reflected in the constant debate as to whether "judicial policy-making" is legitimate. Yet many observers have come to feel that such policy-making is both inevitable and desirable,[28] and that in fact it is virtually impossible to unearth major judicial holdings that do not embody significant policy implications (indeed, this seems to be true by definition). Changes in substantive law within the American system are also complicated, of course, by the problem of competing jurisdictions established through the federal system of government. This complication is seen most clearly in the frequent conflict between legislation by the states and judicial rulings of the federal government, with the former sometimes being expressly overruled by the latter.

Changing social conditions have been reflected not only in specific areas of substantive law but also in overall changes in the organization and processes of the legal institutions themselves. One of the major changes has been the development of many kinds of specialized tribunals to deal with certain types of claims, and in particular the shifting from the courts to administrative agencies of jurisdiction to "adjudicate" disputes in their areas of special competence. This trend is partly a response to the growing complexity of the relationships between individual citizens on the one hand and large-scale organizations and government on the other. It also reflects the desire to overcome supposed limitations of the adversary procedure dominating the courts, and to develop expert tribunals to handle disputes in areas where specialized knowledge is believed to be particularly relevant (a matter considered further in Chapter Five). At the same time, administrative proceedings often are advocated in order to expedite justice for the individual claimant and in order partially to relieve existing court congestion.[29] A good example of this substitution of administrative for judicial action is seen in the administration of workmen's compensation laws, where nonadversary procedure, investigation by agency staff, and disinterested expert opinion (for example, testimony of the agency's own medical staff) are utilized in the processing of claims relating to work-sustained injuries. While such procedures, in which the agency may even act as a complainant, relieve the injured party of certain tasks and demonstrate public interest in the claim, the fusion of investigative and adjudicative functions may be a ground for criticism. Furthermore, the expectations of inexpensive, quick, and effective proceedings have usually not been realized. It is interesting, for example, that "Under the constant pressure from the legal profession, administrative agencies have tended to follow courtroom procedures more and more closely. Delay has been one of the consequences." [30] And other criticisms of workmen's compensation programs, such as lack of standardization from state to state and the general inadequacy of awards, are often mentioned. There is, then, a continuing disagreement, evident here as in other settings to be discussed later, as to the relative merits of nonadversary settling of disputes by specialized administrators and adherence to the more traditional adversary procedures of the courts. In any event, it is highly significant that a tremendous volume of "litigation," which otherwise would require court action, is being processed by administrative agencies. If it is true, as Selznick suggests, that the "administrative agency is the great modern vehicle of social change," [31] then certainly the workings of such agencies are of great sociological importance and merit further attention from empirical researchers.

Another crucial trend is the incorporation, outside of the legal institutions proper, of procedural norms and mechanisms usually associated with due process and legality. In various writings, Selznick has pointed to the development in large-scale organizations of institutionalized restraints on arbitrary decision, a utilization of mechanisms aimed at impersonal and consistent fair-dealing that may signal the growth of "corporate conscience." [32] Examples of such "private legal systems" would be grievance procedures in industrial concerns, appellate review systems within labor unions, internal systems of labor arbitration accepted as binding by both union and management, procedures for dealing with alleged infringements of academic freedom and tenure in academic institutions, and norms and procedures relating to violations of ethical standards within a profession.

Adopting Selznick's idea that such systems represent "incipient law," we may agree with Jerome Skolnick's suggestion that the sociological study of law should "be concerned with the existence of legal orders where these may not ordinarily have been thought to be, and . . . undertake comparative study of the development of legality in different settings." [33] Not only are these systems worthy of study in their own right, as at least "quasi-legal" phenomena, but also there appear to be various significant interconnections between such private and public legal orders. For example, as William Evan has noted, there is an

increasing tendency for the norms of private legal systems to be judicially recognized, as . . . in a medical malpractice suit in which the code of ethics of the American Medical Association is

> invoked; in a suit involving the internal relations of a trade
> union in which the union's constitutional provisions are ac-
> corded legal status by the court; or in a suit by a student against
> a college or university in which the institution's disciplinary
> rules are judicially recognized.[34]

As Evan points out, not only does such explicit recognition of
private law norms occur, but there may also be a gradual and
unintended diffusion of norms from private to public systems.
There also tends to be a certain amount of interchange of personnel between the two types of systems. Finally, it appears that
certain administrative agencies actually have emerged in response
to the development of private legal orders. Of course the patterns
of influence between private and public law do not flow in only
one direction. To realize this fact, it is only necessary to recall
the basic meaning of private legal system—the adoption within
institutions other than those usually thought of as legal of norms
and procedures that characterize the clearly legal institutions.

The study of legal systems, then, may take us beyond the
courts and legislatures. Weber's definition of law, which referred
to orders upheld through sanctioning by a specialized staff, recognized the possibility that such extension might be necessary. How
far beyond the courts and legislatures we may go in finding legal
mechanisms is not entirely clear. One can conceive, for example,
of a judicial system developed for settling disputes within a large
family. But to consider such a system a legal order may simply
be diversionary. As Evan states, in such situations we do not
ordinarily find a functional specification of statuses relative to
the basic processes of legislation, adjudication, and enforcement.[35] At the same time, in realms lying between such groupings
as the family on the one hand and the officially recognized legal
institutions on the other, we do indeed find definite areas of
actual or potential legal significance.

THE LIMITS OF LAW

While there is little doubt that a legal system responds to broader patterns of normative and structural change, there is a great deal of controversy as to whether law can induce, rather than simply reflect, such change. In this connection frequent mention is made of the inherent limits of law—a point emphasized, in one way or another, by Bentham, Ehrlich, and Pound. This theme was also central to the theories of sociologists of the Social Darwinism school, such as Spencer and Sumner, though, as we have seen, an opposing perspective on the role of law was taken by Sumner's sociological critic Ward. For Sumner, the mores always precede and take precedence over mere laws. He asserted that it is not possible to change the mores "by any artifice or device, to a great extent, or suddenly, or in any essential element; it is possible to modify them by slow and long-continued effort if the ritual is changed by minute variations." [36] If few sociologists today would accept the social-evolutionist belief in the "survival of the fittest folkways" or agree completely that "stateways cannot change folkways," the assertion that law is primarily a dependent variable (an effect, and not a cause) has nonetheless persisted. Modern, empirically oriented sociologists tend to find the mainsprings of social control in internalized group norms and interpersonal pressures much more than in the provisions of formal regulatory codes. At the same time, they usually recognize that legal codes do exert some guidance, influence, and reinforcement effect; the question is, How much?

One area in which we see the extreme difficulty of maintaining control through law alone is that of international relations. As Bohannan's diagram in Figure 2 makes clear, the problem of using law to promote international order is plagued by both the diversity of underlying (national) cultures and the existence of multiple centers of power. In discussing the prospects for international law, or in seeking to answer the question "Is international law, law?", some specialists emphasize the lack of an underlying consensus on norms, while others focus on the multiplicity of conflicting sovereignties and the absence of a system of centrally organized sanctions. Without doubt, both sets of conditions constitute very real obstacles to the creation of a viable system of international law.[37] The conclusion seems inevitable that whereas international law is a great deal more than a figment of the imagination, it is a good deal less secure and smooth-running than the established systems of law within most modern nation-states. Efforts to provide acceptable mechanisms for the adjudication of international disputes, such as the International Court of Justice, are perpetually undermined by the absence of legitimate authority and the lack of a basic normative consensus. As one analyst of such efforts notes, "There are cases when no conclusion reached by the court will settle the issue between the disputant states." [38] On the other hand, this condition often prevails within a nation's legal system, too; it is extremely rare for both sides to a dispute to be fully satisfied with a decision. The crucial point seems to be the development of sanctions or motivation to accept whatever decisions are reached, or both. A consensus on numerous specific norms may not be essential, but recognition of an international tribunal's legitimate authority to render decisions certainly seems an overriding necessity.

On the other hand, the difficulties and limitations of international law should not be allowed to overshadow its actual and potential accomplishments. International agreements have been reached and maintained; to a certain extent even "rules of war" have, at least in the past, prevailed; various instances of accepted adjudication of international disputes can be cited. On many matters in international relations, considerable bodies of "customary law" have been developed and are widely accepted. It is true that the binding nature of all such "law" is, to an extent unparalleled in national systems of law, dependent on the willingness of the parties in any specific case to comply. At the same time, a range of common interests often secures such compliance, and it is hoped today that in the face of nuclear weaponry the overriding common interest of all nations in mutual survival may foster new and creative steps toward a more effective international legal order. This major change in the conditions underlying international relations may have the effect of making more imperative than ever before the development of *preventive* mechanisms of international law. Such a goal implies the need for legislative and enforcement mechanisms as well as judicial ones and is reflected in the numerous proposals for comprehensive or limited world government, strengthening of the United Nations, and development of international peace-keeping or police forces.[39] While advocates of such schemes continue to recognize the critical problems of sovereignty and consensus, at the same time a counter-argument has long been advanced—that more fully developed international legal institutions could actually play a major role in the development of such a consensus and the breaking down of nationalistic resistance to international authority. Thus Robert Hutchins asserted some years ago that "We are so used to thinking of law as repressive and constitutions as the embodiment of pre-existing agreement that we neglect the tremendous force which any constitution and any system of law exerts in behalf of its own acceptance and perpetuation." [40] On the whole, however, the picture that emerges from our actual experience with attempts to develop and strengthen international legal institutions is probably, for most observers, a discouraging one.

Turning to a quite different area of law, that of commercial contracts, one finds some interesting evidence that even where a generally acceptable legal framework exists, parties to a transaction may often consider it preferable to reach agreement through other means. (This preference may be evident in the international sphere too, where nation-states will often evince a preference for informal diplomacy over the processing of an issue through more formal legal institutions.) In interviews with sixty-eight businessmen and lawyers representing forty-three manufacturing concerns and six law firms, Stewart Macauley sought to determine the extent to which business transactions were contractual in nature —that is, the extent to which they involved precise specification of obligations and provision for future contingencies and relied on actual or potential use of legal sanctions to induce performance or compensate for nonperformance. Macauley found that in fact many transactions are not precisely planned and neatly rationalized. Indeed, particularly in the area of adjustment of terms and settlement of disputes, an informal approach tended to prevail. Thus he quotes one lawyer with many large industrial clients as follows:

> Often businessmen do not feel that they have "a contract"— rather they have "an order." They speak of "cancelling the order" rather than "breaching our contract." When I began practice I referred to order cancellations as breaches of contract, but my clients objected since they do not think of cancellation as wrong. Most clients, in heavy industry at least, believe that there is a right to cancel as part of the buyer-seller relationship. There is a widespread attitude that one can back out of any deal within some very vague limits. Lawyers are often surprised by this attitude.[41]

Macauley also found that when disputes do arise, they are often settled without reference to potential or actual legal sanctions. Although the legal positions of the parties (where evident) might influence the course of negotiations, the businessmen studied were reluctant to mention legal rights or to threaten litigation. He quotes one businessman as saying, "You can settle any dispute if you keep the lawyers and accountants out of it. They just do not understand the give-and-take needed in business." As Macauley notes, the essentials of many of these transactions are fully understood by the parties without formal elaboration of all precise terms and contingencies. Furthermore, many effective non-legal sanctions, such as the ability to undermine a business reputation, if necessary, are available to support negotiations and ensure adequate performance. Various other factors, including the internal organization of the concerns involved, also seem to influence the extent to which the transactions are couched in legal form and sanctioned by threat of legal action.[42]

Of course, such findings do not refer to the express failure of legal norms but rather to the limitations of legal control and the tendency for nonlegal norms to complement and perhaps buttress legal ones. Some striking illustrations of the more direct failure of legal norms are found in the area of criminal law. In a sense all criminal laws must, almost by definition, fall short of complete effectiveness. As Edwin Sutherland stated, "When the mores are adequate, laws are unnecessary; when the mores are inadequate, the laws are ineffective." [43] Furthermore, whereas much of our criminal law is based on the assumptions of a rather simplistic pleasure-pain psychology (spell out the punishments precisely, then the potential offender will think twice before committing the crime), such concentration on hedonistic calculation does justice to neither the unconscious nor the situational and subcultural-learning processes that may be involved in crime. It is now widely recognized that relatively little criminal behavior is embarked upon, or deterred, through such simple rational choice processes. In particular, systematic studies have undermined the belief that the death penalty is a significant deterrent to homicide. Comparative analyses of otherwise comparable jurisdictions, some of which employ capital punishment and others of which do not, have found no significant differences in homicide rates.[44] Although this particular example cannot really be said to point up the inadequacy of law in the face of widely held and conflicting social "norms," nevertheless, the body of research on capital punishment has probably had a significant impact on the overall views of sociologists toward the efficacy of legal control.

A good illustration of the systematic ineffectiveness of unsupported law is provided by the utter failure of legislation designed to enforce private morality. Recent interest in this matter has been heightened by the controversy that arose as a result of the report issued in 1957 by a British governmental Committee on Homosexual Offences and Prostitution (usually known as The Wolfenden Report, after the Committee's chairman).[45] At the root of this controversy was the Committee's recommendation that homosexual acts between consenting adults and in private should no longer be considered a criminal offense (a similar provision has also been proposed in this country by the American Law Institute in its Model Penal Code). The Committee took the position that the criminal law is intended to preserve public order and decency, to protect the citizenry from offensive and injurious behavior, and to guard against exploitation and corruption, particularly of those who might have some special vulnerability. Beyond carrying out those purposes, it should not intrude into the private lives of citizens. Furthermore: "Unless a deliberate attempt is to be made by society, acting through the agency of the law, to equate the sphere of crime with that of sin, there must remain a realm of private morality and immorality which is, in brief and crude terms, not the law's business. To say this is not to condone or encourage private immorality." [46]

The Wolfenden Report provoked many critical responses, perhaps the most notable being that of an eminent British jurist, Patrick Devlin, who insisted that "the criminal law as we know it is based upon moral principle. In a number of crimes its function is simply to enforce a moral principle and nothing else." Likewise, Devlin stated, "The suppression of vice is as much the law's business as the suppression of subversive activities; it is no more possible to define a sphere of private morality than it is to define one of private subversive activity." [47] Such criticism, in turn, led to a learned and spirited defense of the Committee's stand by the renowned legal philosopher H. L. A. Hart. Arguing that immorality as such ought not be a crime, Hart noted that "there is very little evidence to support the idea that morality is best taught by fear of legal punishment." [48] Noting the considerable human suffering that laws against private homosexuality cause, Hart found insufficient social gain from legal proscription to justify such an invasion of individual liberty.

As can be seen from these statements, much of the debate surrounding the Wolfenden proposals has been couched in terms of somewhat abstract principles, such as individual freedom and public decency. Actually, the laws at issue here represent but one example of a more general type of situation, which has much interested both legal and social analysts. Legal specialists have noted the special problems of enforcement in areas on the "borderland of the criminal law," [49] and sociologists have been intrigued by situations of "patterned evasion" of norms, in which deviation from expressed rules is so extensive as to render impotent the formal attempt at control and to create a situation of institutionalized ambivalence regarding the offending behavior.[50] The catastrophic experiment with Prohibition alerted sociologists to such situations, which they continue to research and analyze.

The present writer has used the term "crimes without victims" in analyzing a particular type of unenforceable criminal law, that in which society attempts legally to proscribe the willing exchange of socially disapproved but widely demanded goods or services.[51] This term may be useful in highlighting several features of these situations that are of special sociological significance. Especially noteworthy is the fact that a fairly direct transaction or exchange is involved and that ordinarily there is no complainant to initiate enforcement action. Also significant (and these points have been noted in the jurisprudential literature too) are the elements of harm (if any) to self rather than to others and the lack of a public consensus concerning the law. While the study *Crimes Without Victims* deals directly with only three such "offenses"— abortion, homosexuality, and drug addiction—clearly there are additional situations that fall into this same category, including prostitution, gambling, and a variety of other sexual offenses.

While there may be dispute as to whether any of the individuals involved in these situations are being "victimized," from the standpoint of law-enforcement consequences the fact that the offense consists of a consensual transaction, so that there is no complaining victim in the ordinary sense of the term, is crucial. Because of the absence of citizen-complainants (and the fact that the proscribed behavior usually has very low visibility), the police are hamstrung for lack of evidence. This situation forces them to rely on questionable investigative techniques, such as use of decoys and informers; and even with such tactics, they are unable significantly to curb the offending behavior. The strong demand for the goods and services in question is simply shifted into illegal channels, and economic incentives provide for an entrenched illicit traffic.[52] Police corruption and demoralization may result. Furthermore, the "criminalization" of these forms of deviant behavior may also have a pronounced impact on the deviant individuals engaged in them—in some instances driving them into secondary deviation (for example, the addict's need to commit crimes to obtain funds for black-market drugs); nurturing a defensive, deviant subculture (some aspects of the homosexual community may be attributable to such pressures); and promoting the development of criminal self-images (even the woman obtaining a single abortion may conceive of herself as a criminal, while the addict who must continuously steal and who is hounded by the police almost inevitably comes to view himself in this way).

In the next chapter we shall note some aspects of these and other criminal-law situations that are now being subjected to intensive empirical investigation. For present purposes, it should be noted that in one sense (that of their almost complete failure to deter and control the disapproved behavior) these laws provide a significant illustration of the limits of legal action. At the same

time, analysis of the social consequences of such laws points up
the error in assuming that because the laws do not deter they
are without any effect whatsoever. As just noted, these laws seem
peculiarly incapable of inhibiting the banned behavior, yet they
may exert a profound influence on the shaping of the overall,
social-problem situations toward which they were initially directed.

LAW AS AN INSTRUMENT OF CHANGE

The argument that law's effectiveness depends upon substantial support in the mores and that therefore one cannot simply
legislate morality, or dictate it by judicial ruling, is frequently
heard in connection with efforts to develop legal means of reduc-
ing racial discrimination in the United States. In particular, the
U.S. Supreme Court's 1954 ruling that racial segregation in the
public schools is unconstitutional has been criticized on this
ground. (We shall have occasion below to consider the use of evidence from the social sciences in such litigation; for the moment
we are concerned merely with the likely effects of antidiscrimination rulings and legislation.)

There is little doubt that laws and judicial holdings concerning the treatment of Negroes and other minority group members
cannot be expected to eradicate racial prejudice completely and at
once. At the same time, it is very important to distinguish between
prejudice (that is, biased attitudes and the tendency to "prejudge")
and discrimination (overt action that unfairly disadvantages the
minority group member, that denies him equal opportunity, due
process, and so on). Effective reduction of prejudice is not necessarily required for the control of overt discrimination. People
often comply with laws they dislike. Thus, even if legislation and
judicial holdings relating to the rights of Negroes fail, in the first
instance, to reduce personal prejudices, they must be considered
effective if in fact they lead to a wider public implementation of

individual rights—for example, the right to vote, to obtain employment, to enjoy the use of public accommodations, to obtain adequate education and decent housing, and so on. That federal (and, in some instances, state) laws and court decisions have in recent years enunciated an ever widening acknowledgment of such rights is hardly a matter for dispute. Presumably some observers might claim that such "new law" simply incorporates an already developed pattern of general social change and is without any independent effect of its own. Yet probably few sophisticated analysts would be willing to go quite this far in denying the influence of law. In this area, as in others, the truth seems to be that law both reflects and in turn influences the course of social change.

In a number of extremely vital areas of social life, legal recognition and sanction of minority rights have led to the enjoyment of such rights where such enjoyment had not previously been possible.[53] Pronounced change undoubtedly *followed* such legal recognition, and to quibble about whether it was really caused by the legal steps seems unnecessary. Admittedly, some atmosphere or activity had to be created that would lead to such legal measures in the first place. At the same time, these forces alone could not exert the power in shaping general behavior that became possible through legal action. Actually the argument that law is relatively impotent in the area of race relations because of strongly held attitudes is a gross oversimplification in many respects. As various writers have noted, this situation does not really involve an attempt to impose law that runs counter to monolithic, society-wide mores. On the contrary, there are within the community widely divergent attitudes toward minority groups and their rights, and indeed many individuals will tend to be neutral on such issues.[54] Nor is positive approval of legal measures necessary; compliance is all that is required. In this regard, the habit of obedience to law and a belief in preserving the integrity of the legal system may play significant roles. One commentator suggests:

> Compliance without the prod of directly enforceable decrees points up a strong strain of lawabidingness. For some it may indicate agreement (or lack of strong disagreement) with desegregation; for others it does not necessarily mean that their pro-segregation feeling has disappeared or that law has transformed biased attitudes. In a number of newly desegregated communities the change has not been popular. Still, enough citizens uphold it to make the rule a reality.[55]

While the short-run effects of the legal enlargement of minority rights will be felt primarily in a reduction of discrimination and not of prejudice, there is considerable reason to believe that in the long run attitudes are also affected. For one thing, the law may serve a general educative function, reinforcing the norm of equality. It may indeed itself become a "self-fulfilling prophecy," promoting a general atmosphere in which its own enforcement is facilitated. Then too, concrete conditions produced through the laws' implementation may, over time, lead to changes in personal attitudes. There is a good deal of evidence from the social sciences, for example, that increased contact between previously prejudiced whites and Negroes, under conditions of general equality (as in integrated housing projects and in the Armed Forces), may lead to a diminishing of prejudice.[56]

The situation regarding antidiscrimination law in the United States is, obviously, most complicated in those states where deeply engrained norms pronounce the Negro as inferior and where culture patterns of long standing have placed him in a position of constant subservience. Here the potential conflicts built into the federal system of government spring into actuality. But it is noteworthy that even in these situations legal measures have appreciable impact, at least on behavior, if in this case not on attitudes. Even within the segregationist South, there are variations in behavioral and attitudinal resistance to the enforcement of Negro rights. Furthermore, diehard resistance may imperil other cherished values, such as belief in law and order and the desire to maintain a system of public education, with the result that a reluctant accommodation to change may be the preferred solution.[57] It is also noteworthy that a legal event, such as a single court decision in a particular jurisdiction, may result in the marshaling of forces favoring moderation, as well as those favoring resistance. In one Southern community, a desegregation ruling was found to produce a "shift in the structure of the community from a nonpluralistic to a pluralistic one. As a consequence, public discussion became more rational, although much irrationality remained." [58]

Whatever the conclusion as to the force and extent of effects produced by legal measures relating to race relations, it is extremely important to keep in mind that the legal changes did not simply "happen" in any supposedly natural course of events. On the contrary, they were initiated by individuals who filed suits seeking certain legal judgments, and who sought particular kinds of legislation, and they were given substance by judges and legislators who acknowledged such claims to be valid. The organized educational and legal efforts of major pressure groups played a significant role in the process. Similar statements could be made about many if not most striking changes in the domain of public, or legal, policy.

Legal mechanisms, then, are not completely ineffective in promoting or reinforcing social change. The extent to which such impact is felt, however, undoubtedly varies according to the conditions present in a particular situation. As William Evan suggests, the following conditions may have great bearing on the effectiveness of law as an instrument of change: (1) whether the source of the new law is authoritative and prestigeful; (2) whether the law is adequately clarified and justified in legal, as well as sociohistorical terms; (3) whether existing models for compliance

can be identified and publicized; (4) whether proper consideration is given to the amount of time required for the transition;
(5) whether enforcement agents demonstrate their commitment
to the new norms; (6) whether positive, as well as negative sanctions, can be employed to support the law; and (7) whether effective protection is provided to those individuals who would suffer
from the law's violation.[59]

Order, Conflict, and Law

In the light of the foregoing discussion, we may now reconsider
the idea, central to many sociological analyses of law, that the
legal system is best understood as a major integrative mechanism
in society. We have seen that while law may significantly promote
social stability, legal rules and institutions themselves are not
static phenomena. A legal system may embody the wisdom of the
ages relevant to a particular culture, but it does much more than
that. It is a constantly shifting complex of substance and procedure, ever responsive to the continuous changes in general social
conditions. And it represents an institutionalization of conflict,
for it provides social means of resolving the specified disputes and
in some sense reconciling the more general conflicts of interests
and values within a society. As such, it cannot help but reflect
changes in the structure of power relations in the society. We
have seen that law and a society's stratification order are inevitably interrelated. While we may not wish to accept the Marxist
emphasis reflected in his last sentence, the following statement
by Harold Laski reflects a quite cogent general perspective on the
legal order:

> Law . . . is never impartial in the sense of being above the
> battle, or indifferent to the results which may emerge. The
> courts, on the contrary, are a fundamental instrument in that
> battle. They shape the contours of the society, more interstitially,

perhaps, because less directly, than either the legislature or the executive; but they are bound to the same purpose. They give effect to the result of the conflicting class antagonisms which pervade the atmosphere in which they have to work.[60]

Legal institutions can be used to promote conscious ends. This is not to say that they may not incorporate normative ideals and basic processes that transcend particular political goals. But legal rulings exert power. In legal situations there are winners and losers. Some interests are maintained and advanced, while others are set back or repudiated. This is true on the level of specific lawsuits, and it is also true on the level of broad public policy. Again there may be an overriding interest in preserving the integrity of the entire legal system; and as we have seen, a willingness to abide by its rulings, a legitimation of authority is essential if such a system is to survive. Nonetheless, the elements of power, conflict, and change appear to be central to legal phenomena.

Views of the legal system may reflect views of society in general. Those who see societal integration resulting primarily through socialization to, and through consensus about, a system of common values will view the legal system as an embodiment of such values, primarily integrative in function. On the other hand, those who emphasize that society is held together primarily by an uneasy balance or reconciliation of continuously conflicting forces and interests, and that the equilibrium of a social system is but a representation of a continuous process artificially stopped at a given point in time, will tend similarly to assess the legal system in terms of conflict and change.[61] Actually, neither the "order" nor the "conflict" perspective can by itself provide a fully adequate basis for understanding legal phenomena. Just as society in general is a combination of stability and change, of consensus and conflict, so too are these (very likely complementary) forces found within all legal systems.

Chapter Four

❈❈

Law in Action: Selected Areas for Research

A study of the law in action obviously encompasses an enormous array of potential topics for investigation, which vary in terms of legal substance, legal procedure and setting, and general questions of interest to the sociologist. There is almost no end to the empirical studies that might be undertaken with a view to further understanding the real workings of any modern legal system. A number of areas for such research and specific projects have already been mentioned. Studies of the legal needs of the poor and the extent to which these needs are met represent a good example of concentration on the actualities, rather than on the doctrines and formal organization, of the legal order. Similarly, the issue of the effects of law—as a deterrent, as an instrument of social change, and so forth—is another subject falling into this category and is one on which undoubtedly a great deal more research will be done. Furthermore, some research that we might not immediately associate with the phrase "law in action" nonetheless has relevance to a general empirical orientation to legal systems. Thus, historical and comparative perspectives, which cannot be considered further here, may be very useful

141

in throwing additional light on present content and procedures in a particular legal order.[1] Likewise, patterns of legal education, admittedly somewhat removed from the actual processes involved in lawsuits and other legal "events," may indirectly shape a legal system, through their influence (the nature and extent of which require empirical investigation) on the perspectives of lawyers and judges and on their approaches to their work.

Clearly, then, it is beyond the scope of this necessarily brief chapter to explore all the possibilities for research on the "law in action." Instead, we shall consider four areas which have not been directly discussed in earlier sections of this study and which seem particularly important to the development of a comprehensive sociology of law. It should be noted too that in this and the next chapter, the focus will be almost entirely on the present-day American legal system, although many of the specific issues and findings very likely have wider relevance.

Courts, Judges, and Juries

The legal realists and sociological jurists, in writings both theoretical and concerned with policy, drew attention to the very real social action that constitutes the life of the courts. Jerome Frank, in particular, emphasized the key roles of judge and jury at the trial-court level. In recent years, social scientists have begun to explore systematically the court as an arena of legal behavior.

Without doubt, the most impressive effort at an empirical analysis of the courts in action has been the extensive and continuous research of the Chicago Jury Project. This study, by a team of social scientists working closely with legal experts (and maintained as an ongoing research unit of the University of Chicago Law School), has focused mainly on the behavior of jurors; but it has also produced numerous findings illuminating other aspects of court process and organization. The early history of this project is interesting because it suggests some of the problems of interrelationship between sociologists on the one hand and lawyers and the public on the other, which may be activated by the sociological study of legal phenomena.

In 1954, five jury deliberations in a federal court in Kansas were recorded by microphones concealed in the jury room. This research technique was adopted with the permission of the judges and attorneys involved in the cases, but without informing individual jurors. The recordings were edited in such a way that neither the specific case nor the identities of the jurors could be recognized. Over a year after the recordings were made, they were played (at the request of one of the judges) at an official conference of judges in Colorado, so that those present could have a more accurate picture of how juries really deliberate and of whether the judges' instructions to juries are properly understood. This event was picked up by the national press; there followed expressions of editorial outrage at such invasion of the sanctity of the jury room. Eventually there were hearings by a U.S. Senate subcommittee, at which leaders in the Association of American Law Schools supported carefully controlled research using concealed microphones, while the American Civil Liberties Union completely disapproved of the practice. The controversy culminated in the passage of a federal law making any attempt to record, observe, or listen to jury deliberations in any court of the United States a criminal offense.[2] While certainly the matter of jury secrecy raises important policy issues, there is some evidence that in this instance legislators may have partially miscalculated the nature of informed opinion concerning the research practices in question. Although there are no data on reactions of the general public, one sociologist did survey samples of lawyers, sociologists, and political scientists. As might have been predicted, the social scientists overwhelmingly approved of recording jury deliberations for research purposes. What is more surprising is that the lawyers, while much more critical, showed surprisingly strong support for the practice.[3] It is quite likely, therefore, that the clamor in the news about "jury bugging" blew the incident completely out of proportion, with the result that an important research effort received a serious setback.

Subsequent work by the project reveals an ingenious adaptation to this curb on their investigations. A decision was reached to record mock jury deliberations, but the problem presented itself of ensuring that this artificial research situation be as similar as possible to the real thing. The following procedure was adopted.[4] Transcripts of actual cases that had been decided by the courts were edited, condensed, and recorded—with law-school faculty usually playing the principal parts of attorneys, witnesses, judge, and so on. Through the cooperation of presiding judges and bar associations (in Chicago, St. Louis, and Minneapolis), jurors for the study were drawn by lot from regular jury lists and assigned, as part of regular jury duty, to hear these recorded cases. After the jury received an explanation of the study, from a judge, and before listening to the trial, each juror completed a questionnaire (similar to a lawyer's examining of prospective jurors) on which various social-background data were recorded. Jurors then listened to the recorded trial after which, but prior to group deliberation, they completed another short questionnaire stating how they would then have decided the case. The jury then retired to its deliberations (including selection of a foreman, as well as reaching a verdict), all of which were recorded for subsequent analysis. After having reached the verdict, the jurors were again questioned, as to their reactions to the experiment, among other things. The jury was then taken back to the judge to report its verdict and to receive the thanks of the court for its service.

Through this technique, the Chicago researchers have produced a wealth of data concerning the behavior of juries. Social-status factors, for example, have been found to exert a considerable influence on jury deliberations: "Men, in contrast with women, and persons of higher in contrast with lower status occupations have higher participation, influence, satisfaction, and perceived competence for the jury task." Likewise, "it appears that the foreman is expected to be a male, preferably, a male of higher educational status." [5] The project has also examined jury behavior on a wide variety of specific substantive and procedural legal issues, ranging from whether or not the jury takes into account probable attorneys' fees in determining the amount of damages to award in personal injury suits to how the jury evaluates expert psychiatric testimony in criminal trials.[6] Much attention has been devoted to determining which factors weigh most heavily with jurors in reaching decisions and how well they understand the proceedings and in particular the instructions they receive from the court. According to one recent report, the general nature of these findings is such as to allay many of the fears concerning the prejudice and incompetence of the typical jury. Simon writes that "when a group of laymen of diverse backgrounds are brought together as a jury, they function and arrive at verdicts in a manner unexpected by many persons. . . . the law imposes a universalistic and impersonal set of expectations which the jurors internalize, even within as short a period of time as their first trial." While juries do not always proceed with their deliberations in the most "efficient" manner, and while emotional factors certainly influence such deliberations, "Our data suggest that these feelings become socialized. They are redefined so as to be functionally responsive to the expectations of the judicial system and of popular sentiments." [7] If these data do not necessarily provide a complete and definite picture of all aspects of jury behavior, they certainly constitute the closest approximation available at this time. Any subsequent evaluation of the jury system (and debate as to whether it advances or impedes "legality") must surely take these findings into account.

Recognition that jury deliberations must be placed in a larger institutional context has led the Chicago researchers also to inquire more broadly into the workings of the trial courts. Thus the project's first book-length publication, *Delay in the Court,*[8] reports on an extensive survey of the work of the Supreme Court of New York County—analyzing the distribution of types of cases making up the court's workload, the extent of delay and the apparent reasons for it, and the likely consequences of various proposed remedies. The authors also provide cross-jurisdictional data corroborating the existence of variations in "claims consciousness," "in the sense that a comparable series of accidents will give rise to a greater number of claims in some areas or communities than in others."[9] In view of the heavy component of personal-injury suits in the work of the trial courts, such matters are of the utmost policy importance, as indeed are all the aspects of workload and delay considered in this study.[10] Sociologists elsewhere have studied the work patterns of the trial courts, as in the California Civil Justice Project. Preliminary findings there revealed not only that the workload is likely to be excessive, but furthermore that only a small proportion of the judges' time is indeed spent deciding contested cases, and that judges (because of differences in prestige, time and energy required, legal issues posed, and procedures employed) would rather handle certain types of cases in preference to others.[11] Such findings may be extremely important for the light they throw on the role conceptions of judges and on the types of tribunals and staffs most likely to handle specific kinds of judicial work expeditiously and conscientiously.

A rather different body of knowledge about courts and judges is being developed through so-called behavioral studies of judicial decision-making.[12] This mode of research, which has appealed particularly to political scientists, draws heavily on the legal realists' conception of the nature of the judging process. Although some formulations of the realists undoubtedly exaggerated the arbitrary element in decision-making (as seen in apocryphal references to "gastronomical jurisprudence," according to which the quality of the judge's breakfast might be the key determinant of his decisions), the belief that environmental and predispositional factors have importance has strongly persisted. Efforts to discern "voting patterns" among appellate judges, especially those of the United States Supreme Court, have focused on the influence of some of these factors.

This research has taken a variety of forms. Some investigations have centered on the social-background characteristics of judges.[13] Studies have documented these characteristics (one historical analysis found a disproportionate representation of white Anglo-Saxon Protestants among U.S. Supreme Court justices; another survey reached similar findings concerning state-court judges), and some have gone on to test interrelationships between personal background and affiliations and patterns of decision-making. Thus, it has been found (perhaps not surprisingly, though such data at least systematically confirm what one might suspect) that Democratic and Republican judges differ in the tendencies of their decisions across a wide range of legal situations. Democratic judges are more likely (and Republicans less likely) to decide in favor of defendants in criminal cases, unions in labor-management disputes, claimants in unemployment compensation cases, the libertarian position in free-speech cases, the government in tax matters, the claimant in personal-injury suits, and so on. While such findings may be interesting, refined statistical analyses make clear the difficulty of definitely attributing decision patterns to particular factors of background or affiliation. Many variables seem to be involved, and the weighting of each relative to the others is uncertain.

Another approach has been to concentrate on the composition of particular courts as small groups containing coalitions in the form of "voting blocs," a conception developed originally by C. Herman Pritchett in pioneering analyses of the work of the U.S. Supreme Court.[14] This focus, which has interested sociologists as well as political scientists, has produced useful further documentation of the "bloc" tendency, as well as suggestive data concerning possible factors in changing alignments. It also may increase our understanding of judicial leadership,[15] although this quality is particularly difficult to assess through available sources of data. Direct observation of the decision-reaching processes is rarely possible. At the same time, secondary evidence, such as the personal papers of justices, may sometimes usefully supplement analysis of recorded judicial voting behavior.

Out of this recognition of voting blocs and patterns has come the development of efforts to predict the voting behavior of particular judges (and hence the decisions of particular courts) on the basis of past decisions and through varied methods including cumulative scaling, "games theory," and refined mathematical and computer techniques.[16] If it is true that the responses of Judge A to situations of types X, Y, and Z recurrently fall into a neat cumulative ordering ("scale"), then we may be in a good position to predict future responses to similar situations (or to situations related to these in a clearly defined way). Likewise, if a specific judge clearly favors one side on a particular legal issue, then a games-theory analysis based on the steps he is likely to take to maximize desired outcomes may also help us to predict his future judicial behavior.

Such analyses have, however, been subjected to some rather intense criticism. According to the critics, while research of this sort may apply methodological techniques of great sophistication, it may incorporate oversimplified or incorrect assumptions about the nature of the judicial process.[17] Thus, it has been argued that often the behaviorists' categorizations of decisions and justices are artificial or misguided. Judicial votes and the justices themselves are arbitrarily forced into one or the other of the categories established by the researcher. A judge's vote in a particular case is determined to be pro or con civil liberties, for example, even though he might in fact have reached his decision on completely different grounds. As Fuller notes:

A judge votes to declare invalid or unlawful some exercise of power by a labor union. Does this prove he is "against" labor unions? It is quite possible that he has a deep faith in the labor movement, but is convinced that the greatest threat to it lies in irresponsible actions by unions. It may even be that his friendliness toward labor has enabled him to obtain an understanding of such problems denied to those who stand at a greater distance from the battle.[18]

Because the researchers have been interested in judicial voting differences, unanimous decisions have been left out of their analyses, and this omission may distort the overall patterns that emerge. Likewise, they have scored or ranked judges according to votes, not opinions. Sometimes a judge may "vote" a particular way because of a procedural technicality, whereas a written opinion reveals (or would reveal, if he were to write one) a strong and opposing tendency in making decisions, with reference to the substantive issues in the case. Nor is there any definite way of classifying the possible outcomes in a dispute. Thus, it may not always be clear which outcome is pro and which con civil liberties, or even that a civil-liberties issue is necessarily involved in the first place. This sort of problem is best seen in cases in which two liberal causes are competing with each other—as, for example, in disputes concerning pretrial newspaper publicity alleged to prejudice a criminal defendant's case, where the libertarian beliefs in a free press and fair trial are set off one against the other.

Behavioral research, in other words, may oversimplify what is at stake in a legal case. It is not simply a matter of voting pro or con on a single dimension. And as Fuller notes with reference to games theory, such approaches are "concerned with the 'payoff' and not with the rewards of the game itself. . . . judges may derive rewards from collaborative efforts that transcend individual 'pay-offs.'" Indeed, "what a judge may want (some of us are naive enough to hope that this is what he will always want) is a decision that is just, proper, and workable."[19] The behaviorists may thus slight the judge's conception of his professional role, and his interest in preserving the consistency and integrity of the overall legal order as he sees it. Decisions are attributed solely to political predilection; "contradictory" votes reflect shifting attitudes. Behaviorists have been charged with following the legal realists at their most extreme, with taking the position that the law as a developing body of rules is more or less a myth: "Indeed, it appears that a major burden of their studies of the judicial process is to demonstrate that law is not an important element in court decisions." [20]

At any rate, it should be emphasized that these studies have focused largely on the content of decisions and on the work of appellate courts. This focus is not surprising, given the interest of political scientists in constitutional development and in general issues of public policy. Nor is there any question that research of this sort may produce interesting data, which are relevant to a full understanding of the judicial system. Nonetheless, it is likely that the work of sociologists will center mainly on the trial courts and on general processes rather than on specific doctrinal outcomes and trends.

A somewhat different area altogether, and one that should be of mutual interest to political scientists and sociologists, is that of the organization and staffing of the courts. As we have already seen, sociologists have examined the workload of courts and problems of delay, matters that have obvious relevance for the organization of the court system. Thus far the matter of judicial recruitment has not been of central interest to sociologists. An example of research in this area, which is of sociological as well as political relevance, is the study by Joel Grossman, a political scientist, of the workings of the American Bar Association's Standing Committee on Federal Judiciary.[21] Grossman provides a comprehensive, empirically grounded analysis of this influential committee (which advises on appointments to the federal bench) —including its history, its composition, the general nature of its activities, its relationships with the Attorney General's office and the Senate Committee on the Judiciary, and the extent to which its work has affected judicial recruitment patterns. Noting that "for the first time a private group of national scope has become an integral part of the federal recruitment process," Grossman's study concludes that the Committee has achieved some effectiveness in maintaining minimum standards of qualification, but has not gained the power completely to control specific nominations. Although it "operates on the sufferance of both the Attorney General and the Senate Judiciary Committee . . . it has nonetheless altered the previously existing distribution of recruitment power." [22]

Patterns of judicial selection at the state-court level are also of sociological significance, in particular as a revealing indicator of the intersection between our society's legal order and the political system (in the specific party-politics sense). The qualifications of state judges have long concerned analysts of the American judicial system, including such astute observers as James Bryce, who found that in at least some states,

> A place on the bench of the superior courts carries little honour, and commands but slight social consideration. It is lower than that of an English county court judge or [stipendiary] magistrate, or of a Scotch sheriff-substitute. It raises no presumption that its holder is able or cultivated or trusted by his fellow-citizens. . . . Often he stands below the leading members of the State or city bar in all these points and does not move in the best society. . . . a judge is not expected to set an example of conformity to the conventional standards of decorum. [23]

To Bryce, as to subsequent students of the courts, the method of appointment, invariably operating through "the agency of party wirepullers," was seen as a crucial factor in lowering the quality of state judges. As a recent analysis of New York politics has indicated, there is indeed a close functional interdependence between the judicial system and the political party system. Control over court staffing provides the parties with a means of rewarding party workers (and therefore indirectly promoting the incentives to working for the party), of securing party revenues (through the "purchase" of judgeships), of satisfying the demands of religious and ethnic elements in the party, and of protecting its general interests through the recruitment of favorably disposed judges. At the same time, the parties provide the court system with a workable, if somewhat corrupt, means of recruitment, machinery for supporting candidates for electoral judicial posts, and an organized base from which may emanate pressure for higher judicial salaries.[24] The belief that such systems of "mutual accommodation" are detrimental to the soundness of the judiciary has created, at least among lawyers, much discussion of schemes for the "merit selection" of judges.[25] These schemes should be of interest to the sociologist, for clearly the mode of selection employed may have far-reaching implications for the norms and patterns emerging in the work of the courts, as well as for the place of the courts in relation to outside forces in society.

These political aspects of the judicial system also suggest the importance of placing the work of the courts within a general context of competing pressures from opposed interest groups within the society. This point was made above, in connection with power elements in the legal order, and can be seen to be particularly relevant to the question of law as an instrument of conscious social change. The concept of "pressure group" is not one that has been much in vogue with sociologists, but it is difficult to see how the influence of such groups on court action can be ignored. Similarly, while the point is well made that judges seek to develop their rulings without open reference to outside pressures, the opposing positions between which they must choose have to come from somewhere. Interest groups shape these positions in a number of ways, including direct backing or representation of individual litigants and sometimes the filing of *amicus curiae* ("friend of the court") briefs. And these are not the only possibilities. Peltason nicely summarizes the role of groups as follows:

> . . . following certain established procedures, groups enter the judicial forum. Represented by formal litigants, interests seek the support of judges. Part of the action centers in the courtroom where arguments are addressed to the judges and facts are brought to their attention in order to persuade the judges to decide that the "law" is on a particular side. But groups do not limit their action to the courtroom. They seek to influence opinion generally, to secure the support of law writers, and the other agencies of government.[26]

Administration of Criminal Justice

There is, of course, a long tradition of sociological research in the areas of criminology and penology. Sophisticated criminologists have recognized that in a sense, since crimes are "established" through laws, the legal aspect of crime is central. Thus Sutherland and Cressey hold criminology to include within its scope, "the processes of making laws, of breaking laws, and of reacting toward the breaking of laws. These processes are three aspects of a somewhat unified sequence of interactions." [27] Yet American research on crime has until very recently been almost totally preoccupied with studying only the breaking of laws (and more specifically the individuals who break laws). Studies of prisons represented the primary effort to assess the processes of "reacting toward the breaking of laws." The notion that the law itself was a significant indicator of society's reaction to particular forms of behavior was generally slighted. As Hermann Mannheim stated:

> We have made considerable efforts to discover what sort of person the offender is and why he has broken the law, and we rack our brains to find out what to do with him. . . . Hardly

ever do we pause for a moment to examine critically the contents of that very law the existence of which alone makes it possible for the individual to offend against it.[28]

Nor was there much direct interest in enforcement processes, as such.

DEVIANCE AND SOCIETAL REACTIONS

There is a developing reaction, in deviance studies, against the earlier and almost exclusive concentration on the personal and social characteristics of individual offenders. For a long time, the major research method in criminology involved comparing a "sample" of institutionalized or otherwise readily identifiable "offenders," with a matched sample of supposed "nonoffenders." Not only are sociologists becoming more alert to the methodological deficiencies of this procedure (it is now pretty well accepted that such samples are not in fact representative of *actual* offenders and nonoffenders), but increasingly they are also questioning the theoretical assumptions underlying the earlier work. In particular, there is now a greater willingness than before to abandon what has been termed the "assumption of differentiation" [29]—the belief that deviating individuals (apart from their deviance) significantly differ in their personal characteristics from nondeviating individuals, and that such differentness somehow accounts for their deviance. On the contrary, it is now being maintained that the distinguishing characteristic of deviating individuals is the very fact of their having been socially defined as deviant. In this view, deviance is essentially characterized not by "causal factors" but by processes of social definition. As Howard S. Becker puts it:

> Deviance is *not* a quality of the act the person commits, but rather a consequence of the application by others of rules and sanctions to an "offender." The deviant is one to whom that label has successfully been applied; deviant behavior is behavior that people so label.[30]

If one adopts this approach, then the "audience" of reactors, rather than the deviating individual, becomes the crucial object of research.[31] While this perspective is being given renewed emphasis today, it has in fact a substantial heritage in sociological theory—both in such general formulations as the "self-fulfilling prophecy" and in more specific analyses of the social functions of deviance and conflict, alluded to above.[32] In any event, focus on the labeling process is bound to direct increased attention to the ongoing behavior that indeed constitutes the administration of criminal justice. Just as societal reactions "cause" deviance, so also sociolegal reactions (or the "criminalization of deviance," as this writer put it in *Crimes Without Victims*) in a sense cause "criminal" behavior or at least shape problems of crime. Whereas the key research question used to be, "Why does A commit crimes, while B does not?" today sociologists are more and more asking, "Why does society label X behavior a crime?" "What specific processes and reacting agencies are involved in this labeling?" and "What are the social consequences, particularly in terms of the development of criminal self-images and role commitment, of attaching this label to X behavior?"

The consequences of imposing criminal sanctions may be considerable, quite apart from the specific and intended punishments that may be inflicted at any stage in the sanctioning process. Prosecution for a criminal offense constitutes a "status-degradation ceremony," which has the capacity to produce significant modifications of personal identity. As Harold Garfinkel notes:

> The work of the denunciation effects the recasting of the objective character of the perceived other: The other person becomes in the eyes of his condemners literally a different and new person . . . the former identity stands as accidental; the new identity is the "basic reality." What he is now is what, "after all," he was all along.[33]

Likewise, research on prisons, and on other "total institutions" such as mental hospitals, indicates that a severe process of "mortification" and stripping persons of their identity is one of the most significant features of life in such an environment.[34] Sometimes the adverse consequences of labeling deeds as crimes may even be felt by individuals who have no direct contact with official agencies of law enforcement. Thus, in *Crimes Without Victims,* the present writer suggests that the mere knowledge that one's behavior has been socially defined as criminal may have important effects on an individual's self-conceptions and behavior.

That the ramifications of this labeling extend well beyond the law-enforcement processes themselves was documented in a field experiment testing the responses of potential employers to an individual's past prosecution for crime.[35] A researcher, purporting to be an employment agent, presented to one hundred prospective employers at resort hotels information concerning an applicant for an unskilled job. Similar information was given in all instances except with respect to the applicant's involvement with the law: twenty-five employers were shown a record indicating no such involvement; twenty-five others saw a record indicating trial and acquittal on an assault charge and including a letter from the judge certifying acquittal and reminding readers of the presumption of innocence; in another twenty-five instances, trial and acquittal for assault were similarly revealed but without a judge's letter; and finally twenty-five employers were confronted with a record of trial and conviction on the assault charge. Nine of the employers receiving the "no record" folder responded positively to the applicant; among employers shown the folder containing the acquittal plus the judge's letter, there were six positive reactions. Only three of the employers learning of acquittal without the judge's letter indicated they would consider the applicant, and but a single employer among those receiving the "conviction" folder expressed any interest in him. On the other hand, in a related inquiry reported by the same authors, doctors who had been sued for malpractice did not (at least as inferred from interviews with them) experience serious occupational curtailment or harm. While recognizing that the two studies were not strictly comparable, Schwartz and Skolnick concluded that the difference in status (including professional group support) might account for the contrasting sets of consequences in the two situations. On the other hand, as a critic noted, the different kinds of proceedings involved in the two inquiries (criminal prosecution for an act of violence in the one case, and civil suit for professional misconduct in the other) may well have influenced the results.[36] At any rate, the research seems to indicate that the formal legal distinctions between accusation and conviction, and the presumption of innocence that supposedly applies in the absence of the latter, are considerably less potent as shapers of real social action than as abstract legal principles.

ENFORCEMENT DISCRETION

A matter that has been of special interest to legal analysts of the criminal process is the discretion accorded officials at various stages of enforcement as to which procedures shall be followed from that point on, and even as to whether further proceedings of any sort shall occur.[37] In the past, sociologists were concerned with this discretion primarily because of the effect it had on official criminal statistics, leading to "case mortality" at each stage and hence rendering statistics about conviction and especially about prisoners quite misleading. There was also some interest in the fact that informal deals were made in the administration of criminal justice, with the result that a "bargain" model of criminal justice might be applicable.[38] Recently there has been a significant increase in intensive research on these informal social processes underlying the formal structure of criminal-law administration.

A good illustration of this work is provided by a recent report

of observational research into the nature of police officers' contacts with juveniles.[39] Because of the philosophy and practice of
our juvenile court system (discussed further in the next chapter),
the extent of discretionary power resting with officials at almost
every stage is even greater in juvenile cases than in those dealing
with adult offenders. In an intensive study of police work with
juveniles, Piliavin and Briar noted the officer's discretion to invoke a variety of alternative dispositions, ranging from outright
release to arrest and confinement in a juvenile detention center.
Their study revealed that both the decision as to whether to
bring a boy into the police station in the first place, and the subsequent decision as to which particular disposition to invoke,
were based largely on:

> . . . cues which emerged from the interaction between the officer
> and the youth, cues from which the officer inferred the youth's
> character. These cues included the youth's group affiliations, age,
> race, grooming, dress, and demeanor. Older juveniles, members
> of known delinquent gangs, Negroes, youths with well-oiled hair,
> black jackets, and soiled denims or jeans (the presumed uniform
> of "tough" boys), and boys who in their interactions with officers
> did not manifest what were considered to be appropriate signs
> of respect tended to receive the more severe dispositions.
>
> Other than prior record, the most important of the above
> clues was a youth's *demeanor*.[40]

As the authors point out, such reliance on stereotypes may have
self-fulfilling consequences, leading not only to closer surveillance
of Negro and other supposedly "tough" youths (with consequent
higher rates of apprehension and disposition of them), but also
to increased hostility of entire social categories of juveniles toward law and law enforcers with the likelihood of real increases
in offending behavior.

There are signs that the growing interest in the sociology of
law, together with the societal-reactions emphasis in deviance
studies, are combining to generate a comprehensive body of sociological knowledge about police and other enforcement prac-

tices. To such important but somewhat isolated early studies as William Westley's analysis of the police use of violence,[41] are being added new theoretical contributions, such as Stinchcombe's recent treatment of the relation between police practice and institutions of privacy in a society,[42] as well as increasingly systematic and long-term observational and survey research. Jerome Skolnick's book *Justice Without Trial*,[43] based on intensive observational studies, provides a wealth of valuable data about the police, with special attention to practices in the area of the enforcement of laws against "vice." Attempting to sketch the policeman's "working personality," the author considers the general position of the police within the social structure, the pressures and exigencies of the police role, and the values and situational factors that determine patterns of everyday police activity. Emphasizing elements of discretion in the enforcement process, Skolnick goes on to discuss thoroughly police behavior relating to such matters as processing of traffic violations, narcotics control, burglary, and prostitution. He considers in some detail the use of informers and police decoys and the issues surrounding search-and-seizure—matters that should be of sociological as well as legal interest, since behavior of this sort is central to enforcement activity in certain areas of the criminal law. In his general discussion, Skolnick illuminates the ways in which the values of public order and the rule of law may come into conflict and the mechanisms through which the police attempt to reconcile such conflict and at the same time act in a way that is consistent with their own professional values and social perspectives. Also noteworthy in Skolnick's work is the concept of a "criminal law community"—a fairly close-knit, interacting network of judges, lawyers, police, and other officials involved in the enforcement and adjudication process—which must be examined in its entirety by the researcher if the constituent elements are to be fully understood.

The workings of such a community are further revealed in a

recent report on extended observation of the work of a public defender's office.[44] Notwithstanding the ostensible role of the public defender as the protector of the indigent in their dealings with the apparatus of prosecution, it may well be that the relationship between the defender and the prosecutor is much closer than that between the defender and his client. Noting, in line with the concept of "bargain justice" mentioned above, that most cases are settled by a plea of guilty, Sudnow discloses that the public defender rarely prepares to try cases in the conventionally-understood sense of seeking to win. Rather, his efforts are concentrated on securing an appropriate "deal," the possibilities for which are more or less routinely established through past dealings with the cooperating prosecutors. In this connection, his contact with the client need be only extremely limited and is largely aimed at placing the particular offense within one of a variety of categories through which he has come to conceptualize "typical" offense patterns. Such "normal crimes" represent "knowledge of the typical manner in which offenses of given classes are committed, the social characteristic of the persons who regularly commit them, the features of the settings in which they occur, the types of victims often involved, and the like."[45]

Significantly, in this study the public defender was found to share with the prosecutor the presumption that individuals coming before the courts are in fact guilty of the offenses charged. Rather than "defending the interests" of such persons, as the ideal legal norms would have it, the defender's office essentially represents one cog in the machinery by which charged individuals are "processed." The defender is part of the team that accomplishes this processing and is not particularly interested in challenging the system:

> . . . the district attorney, and the county which employs them both, can rely on the P.D. not to attempt to morally degrade police officers in cross examination; not to impeach the state's witnesses by trickery; not to attempt an exposition of the entrap-

ment methods of narcotics agents; not to condemn the community for the "racial prejudice that produces our criminals"
(the phrase of a private attorney during closing argument); not
to challenge the prosecution of "these women who are trying to
raise a family without a husband" (the statement of another
private attorney during closing argument on a welfare fraud
case); in sum, not to make an issue of the moral character of
the administrative machinery of the local courts, the community
or the police. He will not cause any serious trouble for the
routine motion of the court conviction process.[46]

Clearly these recent intensive researches into underlying processes in criminal justice are highly relevant for our understanding
of the legal system in action. No examination of substance and
procedure in the field of criminal law can be completely satisfactory, unless it takes into account the emergence (largely
through informal interaction between individuals occupying the
related roles that constitute the system of criminal justice) of
working patterns of accommodation to situational imperatives
and of routinized modes of everyday operation. Such developing
patterns reflect or even generate a significant amount of strain
between ideal and actual legal norms. They reveal, in particular,
that it is difficult for the legal system to do all things for all people (no matter how contradictory the desired functions of the
system may be) at the same time. This difficulty is most clearly
brought out in Skolnick's discussion of the tremendous strain
imposed on the system by the effort to institutionalize both
"law" (in the sense of adherence to high standards of procedural
legality) and "order" (in the sense of protection of the public
from direct harm and outrage) through police activities.

Also glaringly evident in these patterns is the intersection between the legal order and the general system of social stratification, partly discussed earlier. Wherever informal "justice" domi-
nates the proceedings, the widening of official discretion provides
room for social stereotypes and even prejudices to come into play.
We have seen this tendency quite clearly in police encounters

with juveniles, and it is an element of serious risk attaching to all discretionary police activity. The stratification factor itself has, in certain ways, been institutionalized as an impediment to evenly dispensed criminal justice. Apart from the systematic "legal" discrimination against Negroes in some American jurisdictions, the most blatant example of this process may be the continuing inequities built into the administration of bail. As Ronald Goldfarb has noted:

> Millions of men and women are, through the American bail system, held each year in "ransom" in American jails, committed to prison cells often for prolonged periods before trial. Because they are poor or friendless, they may spend days, weeks, or months in confinement, often to be acquitted of wrongdoing in the end. A man is accused of stealing a few dollars from a subway change-booth, spends six months in jail before trial, and is finally acquitted. . . . His only crime is poverty—he could not afford the $105 fee for a bondsman to put up the $2,500 bond set by the judge. . . . Yet a man with means, accused of far more serious crimes and eventually to be found guilty, may have to spend no time in jail before trial; his only virtue the fact that he could pay his way out of jail and wait comfortably at home for his trial to begin.[47]

As Goldfarb also points out, in the discretion to set bail lies the power to punish (before trial) individuals or groups that are particularly troublesome or unpalatable to the social establishment (civil-rights demonstrators and pacifists may be two examples). In actual practice, the manifest function of bail, to secure the subsequent appearance of the defendant, often has been lost sight of, with a resulting increase in social pain to individuals, which is often completely unjustified, and an unnecessary expense to society. Alternatives to the bail system—such as the Manhattan Bail Project, in which intensive interviews with detainees are used to establish those individuals who constitute good risks, and under which many who would previously have been held are now released on their own recognizance[48]—are bound to influence the patterns of criminal justice in action, and should therefore be of interest to the sociologist.

Styles of Legal Work

Another avenue to an understanding of the law in action involves studying the organization and routine work patterns of the legal profession. As was mentioned earlier, some of the current sociological interest in the legal system developed out of research focused on the general analysis of occupations and professions. From this standpoint a broad array of sociological concepts may be applicable to analyzing the positions and work of the individuals who man the legal order—ranging from "professional self-image" to occupational "role set," from "recruitment" and "socialization" to colleague relationships and possible "role conflicts." Similarly, at least for other than lone practitioners, organization theory may be relevant, with such concepts as "bureaucracy," organizational "commitment," and organizational "goals" coming into play.

It has been suggested, by at least one legal critic, that research along these lines may produce an overly narrow concentration on certain small-scale and mundane aspects of the realm of law. Thus, it is argued that law is much more than simply what lawyers do and further that the lawyer's role is, in some essential aspects, not at all like other occupational and professional roles. Hazard states that "the term 'lawyer' refers less to a social function than to a type of training, a type which in fact is shared by people doing a bewildering variety of tasks." The same writer also insists that for full understanding of legal work one must recognize that with respect to any important legal problem "there is a long, a rich and a demanding intellectual culture." [49] Certainly it is true, and most sociologists accept the fact, that lawyers operate in a great many different settings, that any conception of *the* lawyer (believed to apply to the entire profession) would be misleading. Likewise, sophisticated social analysts are aware of both the relevant heritage of legal philosophy and the significant technical formulations embodied in the legal system. Yet these factors do not vitiate an investigation of law as a profession. Such research represents one of a number of complementary, rather than mutually exclusive, approaches to the study of legal institutions. Nor is it an absolute prerequisite for such research that the sociologist have extensive training in the law. Clearly, some familiarity with legal substance and procedure will be of great help to the investigator. At the same time, it should be kept in mind that to require of the researcher lengthy formal and technical training in the discipline or occupational field to be investigated would greatly hamper sociological research in any number of fields, such as the sociology of science, of medicine, of religion, and indeed the social analysis of any occupation or profession. There is no greater need for specialized knowledge in studying the legal profession than in these other instances. Of course, a very good argument can be made for better communication and more cooperative interaction between sociologists and lawyers; cross-disciplinary team research will often provide a useful means of averting some of the problems just mentioned.

We have already seen that there is a very real social stratification within the legal profession, and that the lawyer's general standing and specific work patterns may be partly determined by his social background and type of legal education. The interplay between the numerous variables involved here is complex, but the overall relationship between recruitment and professional role is well summarized in the following statement: "Social background prescribes two major career contingencies: level of technical skill and access to clients." [50] Whereas all lawyers theoretically share a common body of technical knowledge and special skills, as well as a dual commitment to serve the client (in a personal and confidential relationship) and the public (as "servant of the court"), in practice there is an enormous amount of variation not only in what particular types of lawyers do but also in how they relate to their clients and other individuals and agencies and in how they view their professional roles. If we examine actual work situations, a few dominant patterns emerge.

THE LARGE LAW FIRM

The major law firms maintain a position of considerable power in modern American society. They wield a substantial influence in the business community and on public policy in general. Members of such firms tend to be held in high social esteem. Under these circumstances, it is probably not surprising that the large, well-established firms tend to recruit as new members individuals of relatively high socioeconomic status. Members of large firms are much more likely than are members of small firms or individual practitioners to be Protestant; to have fathers who were in business, managerial or professional positions; to have attended an Ivy League or other high-quality college; and to have attended (and done well at) one of the major, nationally known law schools or at least some other full-time, university-connected law school (as compared with nonuniversity-connected and night law schools).[51] In particular, a man who obtains top grades (and is on the "law review," the prestigeful and influential student-edited journal) at the top, nationally known schools (primarily Harvard, Yale, and Columbia) may be "ticketed for life as a first-class passenger on the escalator for talent." As David Riesman goes on to comment, there is a "self-confirming myth" in legal education, in which the law-review men get the top jobs, make the contacts, and gain the experience necessary for advancement, and hence attain a success that "proves" that the law-school marking system (which, in the first year, determines law-review membership) is an accurate indicator of talent. At an early point in their training, such men gain a high level of confidence and the conviction that they are destined for important jobs.[52]

This conviction is usually upheld through their work experience in the large firms. As one observer puts it, "What the Wall Street lawyers do in their professional capacity is nothing less than to provide prudential and technical assistance in the management of the private sector of the world economy."[53] Surveys reveal significant differences in work patterns and clientele between large-firm lawyers on the one hand and small-firm members and individual practitioners on the other. The former are more likely than the latter to serve business clients (mainly large corporations in the field of heavy industry and finance) and wealthy, Protestant, individual clients, to have an overwhelming concentration of work in the areas of business and probate law, to spend much less time in court, and to deal with federal and appellate courts (rather than local ones) when such contact does occur. There is also a pronounced pattern of higher income for lawyers in the larger firms.[54]

At the very top of the bar's status hierarchy, in the major New York firms described in Smigel's *The Wall Street Lawyer*, the lawyer deals almost exclusively with the corporate and financial problems of big business. Here too, the incoming lawyer gains membership in a substantial organization, which is impressive in its own right. He finds himself part of an establishment that may occupy three or four floors of a downtown office building and that may comprise as many as 50 to 150 lawyers and up to 250 nonprofessional staff. The firm is likely to have a long and renowned history, an atmosphere all its own, and an almost tangible aura of importance. Lawyers in the firm hold positions within a well-elaborated hierarchy—as reflected in the distribution of income and general prestige and in the allocation of status symbols, such as office space, secretaries, and so forth, and of professional tasks and responsibilities. Although the young lawyer's initial work may be of a segmental or highly specialized variety, not involving direct contact with clients and perhaps dealing with only one small facet of a broader matter, he is likely at once to be impressed by the wealth and power of the clients and the sizable nature of their business transactions. Nor is he dealt with as a mere underling. He has been hired for his demonstrated competence and his potential for leadership in the profession, and in many respects he is treated as a colleague, albeit a junior one.[55]

Work in such a setting is not, of course, without its difficulties. Some lawyers feel that the firms engender too early and too great specialization; most of the large firms have separate departments, officially or unofficially, to deal with such areas of work as corporate law, tax law, litigation, and so on. Others find troublesome the very keen competition for advancement to full partnership. Then too, some lawyers may be concerned that the work in the impersonal, bureaucratic setting seems to have little relation to the ideal of the lawyer as a "free professional," as a free-wheeling and confidential advisor to trusting clients. A few of the lawyers may even be defensive about the close ties between the Wall Street firms and big business and conscious of the fact that the bulk of their work contributes little to protecting the underdog, an important theme in popular conceptions of the lawyer's role. And notwithstanding the firms' attempts to maintain a spirit of colleagueship, the fact that they are salaried employees who must in the last analysis take orders is disturbing to some. Finally, the pervasive pressures to conform—personally, socially, and even politically—may cause irritation.[56]

For most of its members most of the time, however, the large law firm provides good earnings, excellent experience, and satisfying work. The prospect of a partnership holds out the possibility of a really sizable income combined with enormous prestige and entrée to the inner circles of the corporate and financial worlds. And for those not destined to achieve partnership, or for those who may be dissatisfied with the firm for one reason or another, there is the possibility of using their positions in the large firm as a stepping stone to other favorable situations—in industry, government, teaching, or in somewhat smaller but still very successful law firms.

INDIVIDUAL PRACTICE

Sharply contrasting with the situation of the elite, large-firm lawyer is that of the typical individual practitioner in a large city. As we have already seen, there are significant differences between lawyers in the two types of practice, both in social background and in the kinds of work they do and the success they achieve. The lone practitioner is likely to be the son of an immigrant, who has worked his way up; he is likely to have attended either a "proprietary" or a Catholic night law school and not to have completed college, which at one time was not always a requirement for admission to such law schools. At least at the lower levels of individual practice, he is earning a precarious living, and his clientele tends to be a transient one of lower-income individuals. His legal work involves mainly small-scale and routine business matters and litigation between individuals. His contact with agencies and courts (the latter being particularly frequent) tends to be at the local level. As Jerome Carlin points out in *Lawyers on Their Own,* an important study of individual practice in Chicago, these men constitute something like a "lower class" of the metropolitan bar. Their practice consists largely of "those residual matters (and clients) that the large firms have not pre-empted" —such as matters too inconsequential (financially or otherwise) for such firms to handle, and "the undesirable cases, the dirty work, those areas of practice that have associated with them an aura of influencing and fixing and that involve arrangements with clients and others that are felt by the large firms to be professionally damaging. The latter category includes local tax, municipal, personal injury, divorce, and criminal matters." [57]

Carlin distinguishes between upper-level and lower-level individual practitioners; the former may have a more stable and secure small-business clientele for whom they perform a wider range of less routine services. It is primarily the lower-level, solo practitioners who are bogged down in the dirty work of the law, whose financial circumstances are perilous, and for whom getting business represents a continuous battle.

At the outset, many lawyers trying to establish practices of their own are closely tied to the local neighborhood, a situation that few find satisfactory. As a fairly successful neighborhood practitioner told Carlin:

> "People don't look at the neighborhood lawyer as on the same professional level as the lawyer in the Loop—but on the same level as service people, real estate and insurance brokers, and similar types of nonprofessional categories. He's looked at more as a neighborhood businessman rather than as a professional. Doctors don't have that problem; you don't consider Loop doctors to be on a completely different level." [58]

Going beyond the neighborhood, the solo lawyer seeks contact with potential clients through membership in a range of communal organizations, which usually have an ethnic or religious basis. Politics is also seen as a useful means of extending one's clientele, as well as developing helpful court and other official contacts. But often these methods are insufficient, and it becomes necessary to rely on individuals who, for one reason or another, may be in a position to channel legal business in his direction. As Carlin notes, such a "broker" (between lawyer and client) may be "another lawyer, an accountant, a real estate or insurance broker or agent, a building contractor, a doctor, a policeman, bondsman, precinct captain, garage mechanic, minister, undertaker, plant personnel director, foreman, etc." [59] Personal injury cases often are referred by a variety of individuals who may serve as "runners"; waitresses and bar girls may refer divorce matters, policemen criminal matters. At the same time, and especially in connection with wills, business, and real-estate matters, these lawyers face continuous and increasingly strong competition from nonlegal sources, such as banks, real-estate brokers, and accountants. These competitors often have the edge both in specialized skill and visibility; and as Carlin points out, the lawyer cannot today claim exclusive access to the agencies that process the matters in question.

Apart from the sheer difficulty of earning a decent living under these circumstances, the less successful of the individual practitioners experience a generalized and severe status dilemma. Whereas "law appeared to provide the easiest and cheapest avenue to professional status . . . they find that access to the higher status positions is all but closed to them and that the positions they do manage to achieve are often marginal, their practice residual, and their foothold in the profession precarious." [60] Not only is much of their work relatively insignificant by the dominant standards of the profession, but they have very little contact (and virtually no sense of real colleagueship) with the more successful, large-firm lawyers. Individual practitioners rarely attain positions of leadership in the bar, and in fact they are not even as likely as large-firm lawyers to maintain membership in the leading professional associations, often finding it more valuable to be active in the smaller, ethnic bar associations. While solo lawyers can at least pride themselves on being their own boss, most seem to recognize that this independence is a very mixed blessing.[61]

Of course it must be kept in mind that the "Wall Street lawyer" and the lower-level individual practitioner represent the extreme points of a continuum along which legal practices vary. In between are numerous gradations involving membership in a variety of middle-sized and small firms, many of which are very successful and handle a considerable range of interesting legal work. Also, it should be noted that there certainly are some individuals who practice on their own and attain a high degree of success, both financially and in terms of professional standing. This attainment may occur particularly when a lawyer develops a reputation for great skill in a highly specialized field, such as patent law, literary property, civil liberties, or even matrimonial or criminal law. Indeed, all of the comments made thus far concerning stratification within the metropolitan bar must be recognized as reflecting statistical regularities only. They refer to large classes of individual instances, and to each generalization there are undoubtedly specific exceptions.

Furthermore, the major studies of legal practice have concentrated almost exclusively on lawyers in the largest metropolitan centers. As Carlin mentions, "In comparison with the highly stratified metropolitan bar, the smaller city bar has over the years remained a fairly homogeneous professional community." Attributing this homogeneity partly to the absence of huge "law factories," he noted that (in 1958) there were no firms with as many as fifteen lawyers in American cities of less than 200,000 population, and very few with more than five or six lawyers.[62] Similarly, there has been virtually no sociological analysis of the position and functions of the small-town lawyer. Legal practice in such a setting undoubtedly varies a good deal from that of the lone practitioner in the metropolis. It is quite possible that some lawyers in small towns may be able satisfactorily to combine the independence of individual practice with a considerable measure of financial success and professional and social standing within the local community.[63] Other varieties of legal work—including positions in government agencies, in prosecutor's and legal-aid offices, and as "house counsel" on corporation staffs—also deserve further attention from researchers. Undoubtedly each type of legal practice has its peculiar recruitment and work patterns, compensations, drawbacks, strains, and dilemmas.

LEGAL ETHICS AND ROLE STRAIN

Within any profession, just as within society in general, there is always a problem of social control. While dominant norms regulating behavior may provide a workable amount of stability, there is never complete consensus about them nor full adherence to them. Considering the various and sometimes conflicting personal and societal expectations of the lawyer, it is not surprising that there are, as Parsons has noted, certain strains in his professional role that may lead to deviant behavior.[64] Conflicts of interest, and hence a built-in likelihood of committing some impropriety, seem to stalk the lawyer wherever he goes. He is supposed to act in a cool, dignified manner befitting a professional man, yet he is called upon to deal with human problems often baffling in their complexity and sometimes heavily freighted with conflict, irrationality, exploitation, cruelty, or greed. His reasonable interest in earning a good living is perpetually challenged by his fiduciary role as a trusted agent. Often he is privy to information about his clients or their business that he could easily turn to his own financial advantage, yet the interest of the client must always override his own.

Sometimes conflicting too will be the lawyer's obligation to the client and his role as a public servant. In the criminal law, the possibilities for such conflict are ever present. A criminal court seeks the facts and aims at judgments designed to maximize societal interests; yet under our adversary system the proceeding cannot go beyond those facts brought forth by the parties, and each party is committed to presenting the best possible case for its side. To what extent, under these circumstances, is the defense lawyer obligated to provide full disclosure of all facts in his possession? What are the ethics governing the lawyer's intentionally conveying a misleading or false impression in a criminal trial?

These are questions that have yet to be answered definitely and to the satisfaction of all legal experts.[65] Conflict between obligation to the client and to the public may also arise in connection with business matters and other noncriminal legal work. The lawyer advising a corporation in the preparation of a securities prospectus is not only supposed to be safeguarding the interests of his client, but also to be indirectly helping to ensure that the securities-buying public is protected against misrepresentation. Without doubt, the strain on the lawyer imposed by this sort of situation is most glaringly evident in the field of tax law. There is in our present legal system but a tenuous line between the more or less institutionalized game of "tax avoidance" and the socially and legally proscribed behavior known as "tax evasion." In one sense, tax evasion may sometimes be little more than an effort at avoidance that doesn't work. Of course this is a bit of an oversimplification; the sensible (and secure) lawyer advises prudence and follows the many specific legal guidelines that are available to him. But as Parsons points out, the lawyer is expected to be "both permissive and supportive in his relation with his clients," and yet at the same time he must often "resist their pressures and get them to realize some of the hard facts of their situations." [66] It should be clear that such a complex undertaking, even for a lawyer who is unusually skillful and subtle in interpersonal relations and in legal craftsmanship, can generate serious ethical dilemmas and produce a great deal of tension and strain.

Having in mind the dual concept of the lawyer as a "free professional" and a public servant, and in line with that independence of the legal profession that is often considered a key feature of a system grounded in the rule of law, the profession has long sought to regulate conduct within its own ranks through a formal system of social control embodying stated ethical norms (Canons of Legal Ethics) and machinery for their enforcement. The operation of this system is now coming under empirical investigation by sociologists. As mentioned earlier, an important study by Jerome Carlin, based on a survey of the New York City bar, has revealed a "moral division of labor" in which patterns of adherence to and deviation from these stated norms relate closely to stratification within the profession.[67] Asked how they had behaved or would behave in a variety of situations of ethical conflict, most lawyers in large firms (fifteen or more lawyers) turned out to be high conformers to the ethical canons. There was decreasing conformity among members of medium-sized firms (five to fourteen lawyers), small firms (fewer than five lawyers) and individual practitioners. (Carlin also found that the formal grievance machinery of the bar association was not the effective control mechanism; rather, a combination of inner disposition, client pressure, court and agency atmosphere, and colleague controls operated to permit or deter violations.)

Although the large-firm lawyer may encounter substantial temptation to deviate, his financial security and the relative stability of his clientele enable him to sustain a cultural pattern in which serious ethical violations may be considered out of the question. The individual practitioner, on the other hand, has both opportunity to transgress and little motivation to conform. Not only is he subjected to severe economic problems but he has no stable clientele on which to rely. Since he must constantly be concerned with attracting business, he is heavily dependent on the activities of nonprofessional intermediaries. And the clientele he does attract often requires that he act in manipulative and ethically questionable ways in order to secure compliance or even mere action on the part of minor officials. It is hardly surprising, under these circumstances, that individual practitioners often tend to view law as a business rather than as a profession. Carlin found, in his Chicago study, that "Close to half the respondents were unable to say without hesitation that the practice of law is a profession and a little over a fourth, including practically all the lawyers in the personal injury field, were clearly convinced that it is not." [68]

As this last point suggests, the substance and administration of particular fields of law may crucially affect the propensity to violate ethical norms. Personal-injury suits—in which the client is typically a one-shot proposition and in which a "contingent fee" arrangement (the lawyer gets a percentage of the verdict) usually prevails—breed not only improper solicitation of legal business and the stirring up of litigation (both proscribed by the canons of ethics) but also active efforts to misrepresent evidence, and other types of ethical violation.[69] Recognition of these tendencies, along with the desire to reduce court congestion and delay for the litigant, has led to proposals for new methods of processing automobile accident claims, including schemes modeled on workmen's-compensation procedures.

Matrimonial work also introduces ethical dilemmas and imposes considerable strain on the lawyer's image of himself as a dignified professional. In a study of New York lawyers who specialized in matrimonial practice,[70] O'Gorman found widespread criticism of that state's divorce laws, which at that time provided only one ground for divorce, adultery. These laws were held to be unrealistic, to be discriminatory (since the wealthy could go out of state and the poor could not), and systematically to generate deviant behavior. As O'Gorman points out, the need to engage in collusion and perjury in order to establish the necessary evidence of "fault" in such cases (and thus satisfy the client's wish to dissolve the marriage) is a potent source of role conflict and strain for the lawyer. Some of his respondents indicated this strain:

> Ninety percent of the undefended matrimonials are based on perjury. They are all arranged. The raids are made with the consent of the defendant. We all know this. The judges know it. *It's embarrassing to go [to court].*

[The laws] are a farce. . . . I have in mind especially the un-
defended matters before official referees. You have these black
nightgown routines with the man in the blue shorts. *I tell you
it's insulting to a lawyer.*[71]

The lawyer's situation in matrimonial cases is further complicated by the need to deal with clients many of whom are in an
extremely emotional state and tend to demand extravagant settlements. As in the personal-injury field, these conditions have led
to proposals for reform of both the substance and procedures of
the law. Likewise (and again, a similar situation holds true for
personal-injury work) many lawyers avoid divorce matters completely or wherever possible. Since O'Gorman's study was conducted, the New York statutes have been revised to allow a
number of grounds for divorce rather than the single one that
previously existed. A follow-up investigation, after enough time
had elapsed for any impact of the change to be felt, might produce some interesting results.

These comments may point up the inadequacy of a sociology
of law that either considers legislation outside its realm or determines that the substance of law shall never be considered
worthy of social investigation. Clearly, there is a reciprocal relationship between the substantive law (including statutes) and the
way lawyers go about and react to their work. Just as unworkable
criminal legislation puts special pressures on the police, which
may significantly influence enforcement behavior and the policeman's professional self-image, substantive law of any sort with
which he must deal affects the lawyer's activities and self-conceptions. Thus, in assessing the factors that shape the lawyer's
situation, we must add to training, stratification of the bar, and
the organization of legal practice, the institutionalized legal arrangements within which he must operate.

The Public and the Law

Although the desirability of specific legislation, or judicial rulings, is not a direct professional concern of sociology, the somewhat elusive interplay between public opinion and the law must be taken into account in any analysis of the legal order.[72] The importance of this relationship is evident in those discussions that stress the "living law" as a necessary grounding for effective legislation, and such importance would more generally seem central to any conception of legal institutions in which the law is seen (at least partly) as a means for achieving identifiable social ends. If research on the effectiveness of specific laws is to have an adequate focus, it is necessary first to know the goals toward which such laws are directed. Thus to the analysis of actual social effects of laws and legal procedures, the sociologist should add research into the relevant public attitudes and understandings. Such research may also have an indirect benefit for policymakers, some of whom, for example, might agree that "the question, What sorts of behavior should be declared criminal? is one to which the behavioral sciences might contribute vital insights. This they have largely failed to do, and we are the poorer for it." [73] Notwithstanding his recognition that he cannot, as scientist, *answer* basic questions of policy, the sociologist may provide useful data and analysis that will facilitate the process of reaching intelligent answers.

Two recent instances of official and quasi-official decision-making on controversial legal issues illustrate the potential relevance of sociological research of this sort. In connection with a naturalization proceeding, the question was raised whether the individual seeking citizenship (who had deliberately put to death his thirteen-year-old son—blind, mute, and horribly deformed since birth through brain injury—and who for this offense was found guilty of second-degree manslaughter and given a five- to ten-year suspended sentence) could be said to be of "good moral character" as required by the Nationality Act.[74] Asserting that the conduct in question had to be tested against "the generally accepted moral conventions current at the time," Judge Learned Hand, speaking for the court, concluded: ". . . quite independently of what may be the current moral feeling as to legally administered euthanasia, we feel reasonably secure in holding that only a minority of virtuous persons would deem the practice morally justifiable, while it remains in private hands, even when the provocation is as overwhelming as it was in this instance." He therefore ruled that the petition for naturalization be dismissed, without prejudice to the filing of a new petition, which would, because of the later filing date, avoid consideration of this offense, since the statute only insisted on good moral character for five years prior to the date of petition. Judge Jerome Frank, dissenting, stated his belief that "the attitude of our ethical leaders" would be the most appropriate test in such matters. If, as the governing precedents indicated, general public opinion should be the guide, then, Frank argued, the case should have been remanded to the lower court so the litigants could "bring to the judge's attention reliable information on the subject, which he may supplement in any appropriate way. All the data so obtained should be put on record. On the basis thereof, the judge should reconsider his decision and arrive at a conclusion." [75] Clearly, a systematic survey of opinion might have been of assistance in this situation.

The same kind of problem arose in connection with the deliberations of the American Law Institute concerning a draft provision in its Model Penal Code under which homosexual offenses between consenting adults would not be held criminal. As it turned out, this issue, which was hotly debated within the

Institute, was finally resolved by a vote of its members, who upheld the view that such behavior should be removed from the list of criminal offenses. In subsequent publications, various observers examined this procedure—some insisting that a survey by social scientists would have provided a valuable guide to action, others arguing either that the behavior in question was clearly a violation of moral standards about which no research was necessary, or that in any case public opinion would not necessarily provide a sound basis for formulating principles of criminal law.[76]

A major attempt at "ascertaining the moral sense of the community" by scientific means was made by an interdisciplinary research team at the University of Nebraska. Through interviews with a large sampling of the adult population of that state, the researchers sought public reactions to a variety of issues bearing on the law as it related to the allocation of authority and responsibility between parent and child. While there was not a clear-cut consensus among the respondents on all of the issues, the findings did suggest the existence of a considerable discrepancy between the general tendency of opinion and some of the prevailing legal norms. Above all, this study provides an example (imperfect as it may be in some methodological details) that could suggest to lawmakers some of the ways in which social scientists may assist them.[77]

Several other investigations have focused on public attitudes toward specific provisions of the criminal law. In a 1955 study, a sample of university students was asked to rank in seriousness various hypothetical behaviors that constituted violations of the penal code (of California).[78] In a Michigan study, reported in 1958, a sample composed of three subgroups—a group from the general population, a group of convicts in a Michigan prison, and male students in two criminology classes—ranked in seriousness some nineteen felonies, and imposed hypothetical sentences for the various offenses.[79] Such research may be quite useful in pointing up possible discrepancies between stated norms and public sentiments, particularly with respect to borderline criminal offenses. A recent inquiry, in which the present author's study *Crimes Without Victims* was taken as a point of departure, explored social reactions to such borderline behavior. A sample of adults in the San Francisco Bay Area was questioned regarding information and attitudes relating to abortion, homosexuality, and drug addiction. By concentrating on a few specific types of behavior, this survey was able to elicit considerable information on attitudes toward each. The data also suggested a likely relationship between misconceptions and stereotypes and low tolerance of the deviating behaviors, and they showed an interesting comparison of tolerance levels for the three "offenses." Thus: ". . . citizens appear to be most tolerant or permissive regarding abortion, less tolerant of proposed changes in laws and practices regarding homosexuals, and least accepting of changes in the handling of drug addicts. This rank order of tolerance for victimless crimes holds for all of the subgroups compared. . . ." [80] The study of public information about, and conceptions of, behavior subject to the criminal law takes us one step beyond mere expressions of agreement or disagreement with specific legal provisions. Growing interest in research on attitudes toward, and stereotypes concerning, deviant behavior should indirectly enhance our understanding of some important aspects of our legal system.[81]

So far, most of these investigations have been limited in scope. While they may contribute to policymaking, it should certainly be emphasized that in no sense can they be expected to eliminate the final value assessments that must go into determining whether or not certain behavior should be legally proscribed. At the same time, systematic study of this sort provides a useful antidote to glib statements concerning the state of public opinion on such matters. It is often claimed, without any empirical substantiation, that public opinion simply will not accept a proposed reform, or that "all right-thinking people" condemn a particular form of behavior. Often the law lags behind changes in public opinion, and this lag can be revealed through the social survey. (Of course, the very concept of "lag" here really suggests a value judgment, for we could decide, alternatively, that the law in such situations is preserving worthwhile values that the public is misguidedly abandoning.) On the other hand, social reformists may insist that at certain times the law must move ahead even if it is in advance of public opinion. In any event, it must be recognized that the social scientist has not yet fully convinced the legislator that systematic surveys are a major adjunct to the policymaking process. Sophisticated legal analysts are alert to the technical limitations of such research,[82] while less sophisticated lawyers may still view the social analyst as a perhaps well-meaning but probably misguided interloper in the policy realm.

In addition to surveying public opinion relating to specific laws or legal proposals, sociology could usefully explore public understandings and attitudes regarding the legal system in general. Such research would probably reveal considerable ignorance or misunderstanding of legal procedures and substance. Attitudes toward, and feelings about, the overall legal order, and the role of the legal profession, would very likely show variation between different groups and strata in society. We have already seen the value of exploring the distribution within the social system of objective legal needs and of legal services available for meeting those needs. An important and related dimension consists of attitudes and values. Do people believe that lawyers are helping them or exploiting them? Do they think that the legal order is there for their benefit and that it really dispenses justice? What goals do they believe the legal system, and the legal profession, should advance?

We have touched on such issues from time to time throughout this study. It seems evident that conceptions of the legal system will vary according to a person's position in the social structure. For the Negro American, justice all too often appears to be "white man's justice," with the entire legal order being seen as a systematic mechanism for racial oppression. For the lower-class consumer, legal procedure may frequently represent a source of bureaucratic entanglement making an already precarious financial situation even more trying, or a clever device through which unscrupulous dealers take advantage of him. Most likely it is only within the upper socioeconomic strata that there develops the notion of a continuing relationship with a lawyer who serves as a trusted advisor. In the realm of attitudes toward the law and lawyers, we can expect to find a reflection of the "moral division of labor" within the bar itself, which, as we saw, shapes lawyers' attitudes toward their work and their clients. It is interesting that when a middle-class white man literally puts himself in the position of a lower-class Negro, as lawyer-writer William Stringfellow tried to do when he went to live and work in Harlem, he finds it exceedingly difficult to maintain the positive conceptions of the legal system that he previously accepted without reservation.[83] Undoubtedly the nature of actual encounters with legal practitioners, or with their nonprofessional surrogates, and procedures has important bearing on the development of attitudes toward law. Further research concerning such encounters, and the "definitions of the situation" of parties to them, will contribute greatly to our total understanding of the law in action. In this connection, it should be noted that sometimes the individual's impressions of law may actually develop through contacts with nonlawyer intermediaries, as when an insurance-claims adjustor seeks to settle an automobile-accident case prior to actual "legal" intervention.[84]

It has often been said that American attitudes toward law and the lawyer are ambivalent. The lawyer is respected as an important and powerful figure, yet at the same time regarded with great suspicion and even fear. Systematic research on the "images of law" will make clear whether, and if so, to what extent and under what conditions, these stereotyped notions are grounded in empirical reality.

Chapter Five

✶✶✶

Scientific Justice and Legality

Jurists have long hoped, though largely in vain, for some means of making justice "scientific." To this end, the specialist in a field other than law is often looked to as a possible means of ensuring "correct" decisions. The use of opinion surveys as a potential aid in formulating legislation has just been noted. Presumably the findings from such surveys and other "evidence" from the social sciences should be useful in the judicial setting as well. In an era increasingly dominated by scientific and technical specialists, it is not surprising that the courts, as well as other social institutions, reflect the quest for specialization and expertise. Recently, for example, great interest has been shown in the use of computers as a means of facilitating the judicial process. Although few observers foresee the day when the computer might replace the judge and jury, there is a growing recognition that through its use in the organization, storing, and retrieval of legal literature and other data, we may be able to ensure more complete and accurate legal research and hence reduce the possibility of logical and careless errors in the arguing and deciding of cases.[1]

Evidence from the Social Sciences

Another effort to bring science to bear on judicial proceedings involves reliance on the social scientist as an expert witness in specific legal cases. An interesting example of this reliance involved an attempt to introduce opinion-survey findings as evidence in support of a motion for change of venue (that is, place of trial) in the retrial of a Negro for the rape of a white woman in Marion County, Florida, in 1952.[2] At the request of the National Association for the Advancement of Colored People, which had undertaken the defense in that case, the Roper public-opinion research organization conducted a sample survey in Marion County, the adjoining county in which the original trial (which had been invalidated by the U.S. Supreme Court, on other grounds) had been held, and in two other Florida counties further north. When respondents were asked specifically how they felt about the case, the amount of prejudgment among the white population was greatest in the county where the original trial was held (63 percent), but was also substantial (43 percent) in Marion county where the retrial was to be held; in the counties further away, the percentages were 17 and 25. It was also found that 84 percent of Negro respondents (but only 16 percent of the whites) in Marion County expressed the belief that "something might happen" to any juror who voted "not guilty" in the case. Although a social scientist was permitted to testify regarding the techniques used in opinion surveys generally and in this particular one, the district attorney's objections to introducing any of the specific findings were upheld by the court, and the survey data were ruled out as hearsay evidence. By contrast, the prosecution was allowed to present individual lay witnesses who testified that the state of opinion in the county would permit a fair trial. The motion for change of venue was denied, and the defendant was retried and convicted. Of course, even if the findings had been allowed as evidence, they could hardly have provided a scientific answer to the question posed, preferable as they undoubtedly would have been to the nonrepresentative statements of partisan witnesses. As the researcher himself recognized, the scientist could not establish "whether 43 percent for Marion County is such a degree of pre-judgment as to preclude the possibility of a fair trial or not. That is for the court to decide. He can only point to the contrast between this county and the two in the north of the state." Nonetheless, the case illustrates well both the potential value of survey data in court and the continuing legal resistance to its introduction as evidence.[3]

Another, more celebrated, example was provided by the uses of evidence from the social sciences in the school desegregation cases. In the major U.S. Supreme Court decision of *Brown v. Bd. of Education*,[4] the court's opinion cited (in a footnote) reports based on studies by social scientists supporting its conclusion that racial segregation in elementary schools is psychologically harmful. Likewise, as an appendix to their briefs in the cases, appellants had included a comprehensive statement signed by numerous eminent social scientists, summarizing evidence on this matter.[5] These references to scientific studies enabled political critics of the decision to charge that it embodied "sociology not law," and that the judges had allowed their personal value preferences to determine the ruling. (Such critics evaded the point that prior decisions, in which segregation had not been as fully invalidated, also embodied personal judgments even if they were different ones. Few segregationists had complained that the earlier "separate but equal" doctrine reflected values and policy.) But even among sophisticated legal analysts who supported the ruling as a just one, there was considerable criticism of the way in which the decision had been reached. In an important essay calling for "neutral principles of constitutional law," Professor Herbert Wechsler charged that the court had been too much concerned with the immediate outcome of particular cases. He asserted that "the main constituent of the judicial process is precisely that it must be genuinely principled, resting with respect to every step that is involved in reaching judgment on analysis and reasons quite transcending the immediate result that is achieved. . . ." [6]

Also subjected to criticism was the actual (lower-) court testimony provided by social scientists in several of the desegregation suits, testimony that was designed to show the adverse psychological effects of segregation. Psychologist Kenneth Clark testified as to the findings in so-called doll tests, in which children in the segregated schools were shown and questioned about "white" and "Negro" dolls, and which found that Negro as well as white children showed a decided preference for the white dolls. Critics claimed that Clark's testimony had been incomplete (he failed to note other findings indicating even greater preference for the white dolls among Negro children in northern schools) and based on a very small sample (sixteen children in the study on which testimony was given), and that the findings did not constitute a satisfactory demonstration that school segregation was psychologically harmful (indeed, it was charged that such findings indicated nothing directly about school segregation as such). Professor Edmond Cahn expressed some of the reasons for concern in the following statement:

> . . . since the behavioral sciences are so very young, imprecise, and changeful, their findings have an uncertain expectancy of life. Today's sanguine asseveration may be cancelled by tomorrow's new revelation—or technical fad. It is one thing to use the current scientific findings, however ephemeral they may be, in order to ascertain whether the legislature has acted reasonably in adopting some scheme of social or economic revaluation. . . . It would be quite another thing to have our fundamental rights rise, fall, or change along with the latest fashions of psychological literature. Today the social psychologists—at least the leaders of

the discipline—are liberal and egalitarian in basic approach. Suppose, a generation hence, some of their successors were to revert to the ethnic mysticism of the very recent past; suppose they were to present us with a collection of racist notions and label them "science." What then would be the state of our constitutional rights?[7]

That such conjecture was not entirely fanciful is seen in the fact that even at present some social scientists (a minority) refuse to accept the dominant thinking on race of anthropologists and social psychologists. Thus, in the lower-court opinion in a Mississippi desegregation suit, reference is made to the testimony of "seven distinguished scientists" each of whom testified to "the existence of such differences between the two groups [whites and Negroes] to constitute a rational basis for separate schooling." The opinion further stated that through such testimony "the 'Cultural Hypothesis' [that Negro-white I.Q. score differences reflect varying environmental conditions rather than differences in innate intelligence] was shown to be both unsupported and negated by the facts." [8] (Of course, even if group differences in intelligence could be scientifically established, such findings would not have any necessary and direct relevance to the essentially *political* decision concerning segregation of public schools.) It seems clear, then, that on many matters considered by the social sciences there are, at present, a number of differing professional opinions and interpretations of "fact"; hence the nature of the scientific evidence to be received in court may sometimes depend upon *which* scientists testify.

This problem is but one of the difficult problems posed in connection with evidence from the social sciences. As a scientist, the sociologist is supposed to conduct objective, value-free research; yet when he enters a court case he must ordinarily represent one side. As a scientist, he should always note the basis for, and the limitations of, his findings—which he also acknowledges to be tentative, subject to revision or refutation through subsequent investigation. When he takes on the quite different role of participant in an adversary proceeding, what principles govern his behavior? Furthermore, at what point have sufficient scientific data emerged to permit their use in a legal context? If he were to wait until "all the evidence is in," the social scientist might feel inhibited from ever stating any findings in such a setting. On the other hand, if he has at hand evidence relevant to the legal cause (and perhaps the "best" evidence currently available), might he not even have a social if not a professional responsibility to bring it to the attention of the relevant legal functionaries? Thus, not only is there a crucial issue for the legal system concerning its acceptance of scientific evidence, but also there are some very real ethical and professional dilemmas for the sociologist in deciding whether or not to enter the legal forum.

Specialized Tribunals

As we have already seen, a major trend in the American legal system (and in Western legal systems generally) has involved increased reliance on administrative agencies and other specialized tribunals, which often exercise judicial or quasi-judicial functions. The example was cited of workmen's compensation boards, which process an enormous volume of potential litigation. Similarly, the development of "private legal systems" within large-scale organizations has served an important preventive function by providing mechanisms through which important areas of dispute are dealt with outside of the formal legal institutions.

One area in which this general trend, and the associated desire to incorporate specialized knowledge in the legal process, have been strongly felt is that of criminal justice. Unfortunately, the effort to mate reliance on expertise and adversary procedure has not been a happy one. This point is well illustrated by the insanity-as-a-defense problem in criminal trials, where the typical outcome has usually been a battle of the experts. The defense introduces psychiatric testimony indicating that the defendant was not legally sane at the time of his act (according to prevailing tests of legal sanity) and therefore cannot be held responsible for such act, while the prosecution offers the testimony of other psychiatrists who have concluded that the defendant was sane at the time and hence can be held criminally responsible. Schemes involving a single panel of court-appointed and supposedly impartial psychiatrists may partially eliminate this perplexing state of affairs, but even under such conditions the adversary nature of the trial may subtly adulterate or compromise the expert's disinterestedness.[9]

THE JUVENILE COURT

Widespread dissatisfaction with adversary procedure has provided a significant impetus to the development of special procedures in which the adversary element is minimized. An important example of this development is the American juvenile court. There were complex historical and philosophical forces underlying the juvenile court movement. Prior to the development of the specialized juvenile court procedures, the common-law principles of responsibility were invoked in criminal cases involving children. A child under seven years of age was presumed incapable of harboring the "intent" necessary for criminality; between seven and fourteen there was the possibility of this intent being present (its presence would be determined in each particular case); and children over fourteen were definitely capable of criminality. Under this system, children held responsible were tried and punished in much the same way as adults. Reaction to the harshness of this approach led to an entirely new mode of procedure, beginning with the first juvenile court, established in Chicago in 1899. One of the initial aims of the reformers was to "get the children out of the jails"; but as it developed, the juvenile court movement went way beyond that limited reform. As various commentators have noted, juvenile court statutes created an entirely new category of persons, "juvenile delinquents." The jurisdiction of the newly established juvenile courts extended to all youngsters beneath a specified age (in most states now sixteen or higher) who committed what for an adult would be an ordinary criminal offense, or who otherwise (under a variety of statutory provisions) were held to need state care, protection, or treatment.

Under the strong influence of humanitarian reformers, the new courts were to constitute an embodiment in concrete legal institutions of what Francis Allen has termed "the rehabilitative ideal." [10] The aim was to help the child, rather than to punish him. As another interpreter of the juvenile court stated:

> The juvenile court was to act for the state according to the legal philosophy of *parens patriae*. It was not to be a court of "an eye for an eye." The court, acting for the state as a parent, was to recognize the individuality of the child and adapt its orders accordingly. There was legal precedent for this basic idea in the English tradition of the court of equity. A duty of such court was (and always should be) to see that neglected and abused children were given a chance under protection of the court to grow into useful citizenship.[11]

In line with this philosophy, the procedures, terminology, and sanctions of the juvenile court are sharply differentiated from those of the adult criminal court.[12] An informal (and usually private) hearing is substituted for the formal and public criminal trial, with few of the technical legal restrictions (such as rules of evidence) that apply in the latter and with an emphasis on garnering as scientifically as possible a maximum amount of information about the individual "in whose behalf" the hearing is held. Whereas in a criminal trial detailed psychological- and social-background information usually is presented only after determination of guilt (in a probation officer's "presentence investigation" report to assist the judge in sentencing), in the juvenile court system a similar investigation usually is made prior to, and indeed as a partial basis for, the individual's "adjudication as a delinquent" (terminology which is often contrasted with "conviction" as a "criminal").

An important aim of the system is "individualized" or "personalized" justice, and the actual commission of a particular delinquent act is only one concern of the court. Equally important is its overall assessment of the past, present, and potential psychological makeup and social situation of the child. Rather than mete out set penalties for specified offenses, the court seeks to provide whatever protection and care is called for by the child's general condition. Such situations and behavior as "neglect," "ungovernability," "immoral or indecent conduct," "habitual truancy," "incorrigibility," "growing up in idleness and crime," and "knowingly associating with vicious or immoral persons" often are included in the omnibus delinquency statutes.[13] Since the court is providing protection and care, rather than imposing punishment, it is considered reasonable that treatment shall be for as long as "necessary." Therefore, those individuals whose conduct comes within its purview are usually subject to the juvenile court's jurisdiction for an indeterminate period, often until the age of twenty-one. Thus, an individual adjudicated a delinquent at the age of fourteen might, in a jurisdiction having such a provision, face institutionalization for a period of up to seven years. (In practice, reasonable interpretation combined with the exigency of badly overcrowded institutions usually precludes holding the youth for the maximum period; nonetheless, the characteristic of indeterminacy is a usual feature of commitments by a juvenile court.)

Both legal and sociological observers have strongly criticized juvenile court procedures. Few of these commentators would quarrel with the underlying humanitarian goals of avoiding formal stigmatization of the child as a "criminal," emphasizing his rehabilitation rather than mere punishment (although there is considerable debate about the success of particular rehabilitative schemes), and segregating institutionalized youths from more hardened adult offenders. At the same time, however, many express grave reservations concerning the vagueness of the grounds for adjudication, the laxity of the courtroom procedures, the vast discretion of the court, and the indeterminacy of the sanctions. Paul Tappan, a lawyer-sociologist who was a major critic of the juvenile court system, stated of its procedures:

> . . . their greatest fault is in failing to give to the defendant some of the most basic protections of due process which inhere in our modern legal system. Under our constitutions and laws the defendant deserves at very least (1) a definite charge of a particular offense, (2) the right to be confronted by the witnesses from whom is derived the evidence on which he is convicted, (3) a (real) right to counsel and appeal, and (4) conviction only upon a preponderance of credible, competent, relevant evidence. . . . These rights are assured even in the administrative tribunals of today; their disappearance from our criminal and quasi-criminal courts should not be tolerated.[14]

Technically, of course, the child is not a defendant, and ostensibly he is neither convicted nor punished. Yet numerous analysts insist that we must distinguish between this euphemistic terminology and the law-in-action of the juvenile court. As Allen has emphasized, "We shall escape much confusion here if we are willing to give candid recognition to the fact that the business of the juvenile court inevitably consists, to a considerable degree, in dispensing punishment." [15] Thus, it is widely recognized that adjudication as a delinquent, and perhaps even an appearance in juvenile court that does not result in adjudication, is bound to be stigmatizing. Likewise, commitment to a juvenile institution, even if it be called a training school rather than a prison, does constitute punishment for the child. In fact, given the indeterminate nature of juvenile commitments, the child may even receive more severe punishment (or at least he will view it that way) than he might have received for the same offense under adult criminal law.[16] Considering these circumstances, the demand for additional procedural safeguards in the juvenile court is not surprising.

In his recent book *Delinquency and Drift*,[17] David Matza has carried analysis of the juvenile court system one step further; not merely does he note the danger that constitutional safeguards may be bypassed or infringed, but he also examines the impact the court's procedures may have on the juvenile's outlooks, both toward the legal system and toward his position in the social order generally. Describing the system as one of "rampant discretion" (he goes so far as to equate it with Moslem *kadi* justice), Matza asserts that the vagueness, variability, and euphemistic labeling of the court's procedures and outcomes strike the juvenile as somewhat mystifying but at the same time patently unfair. Confronted with the court's social-work-oriented and professedly benevolent procedures, the juvenile is likely to ask himself just what is going on:

> Why should persons so important and influential as the judge and his helpers lie to him regarding the true bases of disposition? Why should they insist, as they frequently do, that it is not what he did—which strikes delinquents and others as a sensible reason for legal intervention—but his underlying problems and difficulties that guide court action? Why do they say they are helping him when patently they are limiting his freedom of action and movement by putting him on probation or in prison? What on earth could they possibly be hiding that would lead them to such heights of deception?[18]

Matza suggests that only by assuming that the system embodies favoritism, arbitrariness, and incompetence can juveniles find any sensible meaning in it. Hence their feelings of injustice, both legal and social, are greatly heightened; and the rationalizations and forces that may cause or permit them to drift into delinquency are further activated or abetted.

PSYCHIATRIC COMMITMENT

Similar problems reflecting a tension between expert decision-making and legality arise in connection with procedures for involuntary confinement of the mentally ill.[19] Here too implementation of the rehabilitative ideal has led to an informal procedure, ostensibly because it serves the "patient's" best interests, although whether it necessarily does so may be open to question. Specific legal procedures governing involuntary commitment to mental hospitals vary greatly between the different American jurisdictions. Ordinarily, such persons as relatives, spouses, guardians, and physicians may submit a petition calling for an individual's hospitalization, which, if supported by the specified psychiatric certifications and upheld by the court, will result in the individual's confinement. Hospitalization through such judicial proceeding is usually for an indeterminate period, with release to be determined by hospital authorities. Although a court hearing is part of such procedure, in some jurisdictions the patient's appearance may be waived if the court is convinced that his appearance would be "detrimental to his health." At any rate, the hearing tends to be informal and brief, typically involving little more than court perusal (and, invariably, acceptance) of the psychiatric recommendations. Since mental commitment is not a criminal proceeding, rigorous procedural safeguards such as are found in a trial do not apply. Indeed, psychiatrists are at great pains to divest the proceedings of any vestiges of criminal procedure; they insist on the sharp distinction between hospitalization, which is for the individual's benefit, and imprisonment. Many states also permit nonjudicial commitment for a limited time for observation or in apparent psychiatric emergency situations, with the opportunity for court review of the confinement at the end of a stipulated period. Invariably there are judicial procedures through which the confined person may, at various stages, challenge his commitment to or retention in an institution. Many committed mental patients, however, are unaware of these possibilities or of the technical means of implementing them, and often there is nobody on the outside with sufficient personal concern or legal awareness to look after their interests. Furthermore, in practice, release, like confinement, is determined almost entirely by the decisions of hospital authorities. Here again, the confined individual is at a pronounced legal disadvantage, whatever his actual mental condition might be; for the rationale underlying the entire proceeding is that only the psychiatric specialists really know what action will be in his best interests.

For some time, thoughtful legal observers have been alert to the need for greater protection of the civil liberties of prospective and actual inmates of mental hospitals. While many psychiatrists continue to argue for the least formal sort of procedure (that is, that which emphasizes the noncriminal nature of psychiatric commitment), various legal analyses and the reports of special commissions investigating the topic have urged a tightening up of confinement procedures. Typical proposals include automatic review after a specified period of time, so that hospitalization is never formally without time limit; better provision to the patient of full notice of his legal right to a judicial hearing and to representation by counsel; and the creation of independent review boards that would review all cases of involuntary admission and retention of mental patients and that could not only provide general assistance to individuals so committed but could also, on their behalf, initiate legal proceedings for hearing or release.[20]

Although most psychiatrists appear convinced that relatively few individuals are hospitalized without proper medical cause, there is wide professional and lay recognition that it is much easier to be placed in a mental hospital than to be released from one. The specter of "false commitment" has been raised forcefully in the various writings of psychiatrist Thomas S. Szasz.[21] Of particular concern to Szasz is the use of psychiatric commitment as an alternative to criminal process. In his book *Psychiatric Justice,* he relates various cases in which persons charged with criminal offenses were denied the right to a trial through court-ordered, pretrial psychiatric examination. When such persons are declared mentally unfit to stand trial, they may be incarcerated in a mental hospital more or less indefinitely, even though their criminal guilt has never been established. Szasz comments that "The individual subjected to such an examination is [in effect] imprisoned first and tried later, if at all," [22] and notes that the sentence prescribed in this procedure may often greatly exceed that which could have been legally declared upon criminal conviction. While he would agree that there are some individuals who may, temporarily, be incompetent to stand trial because of their mental condition, Szasz feels that this category has been unscientifically and improperly expanded.

Indeed, Szasz argues that our whole approach to the question of confinement for mental illness, is entirely too casual. He insists that we have been too ready to define mental illness narrowly as a medical problem calling for medical solutions. Furthermore, unlike many of his professional colleagues, Szasz stresses that involuntary psychiatric diagnosis and commitment are not merely scientific processes. They are efforts at social control, in which troublesome people are dealt with forcibly. He argues that notwithstanding declarations of humane motivation, the psychiatrist who arranges an involuntary confinement is helping to affix a socially discrediting and stigmatizing label on the individual, and is in reality prescribing punishment for him (given the self-destructive effects of incarceration and the deplorable conditions and inadequate treatment facilities in most public mental hospitals).[23] While Szasz would go so far as to argue for a complete abolition of involuntary mental hospitalization (with an increased reliance on criminal trials, where required by overt antisocial conduct), short of that unlikely development he urges a tightening up of all relevant legal procedures so as to heighten the protection of individuals "charged" with, and facing commitment for, mental illness.

Some of the dangers implicit in current methods of confinement are illustrated in the findings of an observational study of screening procedures in four courts handling large numbers of mental-commitment cases in a Midwestern state, reported by the sociologist Thomas Scheff.[24] This research suggests that even a formal court hearing may afford the patient little real protection. In one court, for example, "we observed twenty-two judicial hearings, all of which were conducted perfunctorily and with lightning rapidity. (The mean time of these hearings was 1.6 minutes.) The judge asked each patient two or three routine questions. Whatever the patient answered, however, the judge always ended the hearings and retained the patient in the hospital." Likewise, in discussing the screening procedures with judges and other court officials, the researchers were told "that although the statutes give the court the responsibility for the decision to confine or release persons alleged to be mentally ill, they would rarely if ever take the responsibility for releasing a mental patient without a medical recommendation to that effect." [25] Clearly, the crucial step in the commitment process, in this jurisdiction, was the examination of each patient by a court-appointed psychiatrist. Since observation of over a hundred judicial hearings had led to a conclusion that in many cases the basis for retaining the patient seemed weak, more intensive study of these examinations seemed desirable. The researchers managed to arrange direct observation of twenty-six such psychiatric examinations, as well as interviewing other psychiatrists used by the courts for this purpose.

The results of this further investigation were similarly disturbing. Psychiatric interviews were quite brief (the mean time was 10.2 minutes) and revealed inadequate reliance on consistent and meaningful criteria for determining mental illness. The researchers uncovered a large proportion of cases in which they felt uncertain about whether or not the statutory criteria for hospitalization were met but in which the examiner made an unqualified recommendation for hospitalization. There was an apparent and quite strong presumption of illness held by the examiners, who went to considerable extremes in finding indications of mental disturbance. Thus in one case, an examiner even "stated he thought the patient was suspicious and distrustful, because he had asked about the possibility of being represented by counsel at the judicial hearing." [26] Although the courts in this state drew on a panel of physicians, who were mostly but not all psychiatrists, for its medical examiners, and paid a flat fee of only 10 dollars per examination—a factor that might well influence the nature and extent of the screening process—at the same time Scheff noted that the state in question was noted for its progressive psychiatric policies. Therefore, it may be assumed that the findings in this study do not reflect simply the bad practices of a single jurisdiction. In complementary research on release procedures, Scheff found that factors other than the patient's apparent medical condition (as reflected in ratings by hospital authorities of his likelihood of harming himself or others and of his degree of mental impairment) do in part determine release prospects. These other factors are "social, rather than psychiatric contingencies" such as type of hospital in which retained, age of patient, and present length of confinement.[27]

THE LEGALITY ISSUE

Juvenile court and mental-commitment proceedings represent but two examples of the revision of traditional adjudicatory mechanisms in the direction of a nonadversary and expert-administered process. To a certain extent, this drift from conventional judicial process to administration may, as Skolnick suggests, reflect the fact that America has become a "mass society." [28] Without doubt the need to cope with an enormous volume of claims has helped to sustain the workmen's compensation system. Similar considerations now lie behind proposals for the processing of automobile-accident claims by administrative means. But there are at least three additional, and related, factors underpinning the increased reliance on administration.

First of all, there has been a profound shift in the extent to which it is felt that the legal system must be grounded in special concepts of individual "intent" and "fault." Liability without fault ("strict" or "absolute" liability, as the lawyers call it) has become a significant aspect of Anglo-American law. This concept lies at the core of the workmen's compensation law and is also evident in the proliferation of regulatory crimes such as violations of food and drug laws and other white-collar offenses. Dissatisfaction with the requirement of proving fault and with the consequences of reliance on fault doctrines increasingly pervades the realm of tort law, and especially enters into the debate about how best to handle personal-injury cases. The fault requirement is similarly seen to lead to subterfuge and inequities in the area of divorce law. And in the proceedings just examined, we see the traditional notion of inferring a particular state of mind from a specific act undergoing change. Both the juvenile and the prospective mental patient are not being held responsible for "the likely consequences" of a concrete act so much as they are being assessed in general and supposedly scientific terms. Throughout all these areas of the law there now runs the idea that justice should somehow be socialized, that the law should be actively doing things *for* people (although this process may sometimes mean doing things *to* them that they won't like), that the legal system should increasingly incorporate active, state-administered processes of social control and regulation. In this connection, administrative rather than conventionally judicial process is seen as being better able to cope flexibly with a variety of factual situations and changing social conditions. Court adjudication is viewed as being hamstrung by legalistic formality and a tendency toward the inflexible application of (sometimes unworkable) general rules.

Related to this idea is a strong distrust of adversary procedure, a distrust that undoubtedly stems in large measure from the teachings of the legal realists. Here, substantive justice is seen as often being sacrificed in the interests of formalism. Particularly because adversary procedure places the burden of going forward on the litigants themselves, there is a strong potential for injustice, especially for impecunious or ignorant claimants. This danger is evident in various spheres of civil law, such as personal injury, landlord-tenant relations, matrimonial law, and welfare law. Furthermore, awareness of all the stratagems and evasions that may characterize the "combat" of the court trial has led to considerable disenchantment concerning the ability of the judicial process to effect an accurate and complete finding of the facts. An administrative agency, which can conduct its own independent and objective investigation, often seems preferable from this standpoint. Finally, there is the desire to take advantage of technical skills and knowledge. The specialized proceeding or agency can be manned by experts in the particular field, who through their processing of a large number of similar cases can build up substantial experience with the specific problem area in question, thereby enhancing the possibilities for reaching scientific judgments.

The adversary procedure, however, has its staunch defenders as well as its critics. As noted earlier, some attempts to formulate a conception of "the distinctively legal" have indeed found the hallmark of the legal in those very qualities of adversariness that characterize the conventional court trial in our society. Lon Fuller, for example, finds such adversariness to lie at the center of what he deems crucial to the moral integrity of the "enterprise" of law. Similarly, Selznick, in his discussion of conditions that enhance legality, emphasizes the role of a system of institutionalized criticism, in which, as he notes, the adversary principle has a special place.[29] Furthermore, it is asserted that in court adjudication an element of institutionalized restraint usefully controls the judge's performance to limit arbitrariness, whereas this element is not present in administrative agencies. According to this view then, the court trial combines the give-and-take necessary to permit all sides of a question to be raised in a public forum with a mechanism for decision-making that is guided by such limits on arbitrariness as procedural standards and substantive rules. The jury trial adds to these important features a supposed recourse to standards of community judgment that may be considered a vital component of democracy.

It has also been suggested that somehow those very elements of fault and intent that the nonadversary procedures slight may be essential for democratic legal order. Thus Fuller states that the legal enterprise "involves of necessity a commitment to the view that man is, or can become, a responsible agent, capable of understanding and following rules, and answerable for his defaults." [30] Thomas Szasz similarly insists on the importance of holding individuals responsible for their actions and suggests that to shift the burden for judging social behavior to the psychiatric specialist is to substitute a rule of men for the rule of law.[31] While these arguments have some merit, and while a "therapeutic state" could certainly have a strong totalitarian potential, they do not entirely come to grips with the recognition (underlying welfare law and many of the new procedures) that individuals vary in their resources and capacities and hence in the degree to which they can shoulder various responsibilities. We may wish, wherever possible, to view man as a freely choosing and acting being, but it is wise to recognize that some men are freer than others. Very likely the tension between providing necessary services (partly through the application of specialized knowledge) on the one hand, and maintaining the personal integrity and civil liberties of the individual on the other, will continue to plague the legal system of democratic society.

Conclusion

✳✳

The legal system is at once an embodiment of high ideals and a means by which men can deal with the quite mundane and often messy conflicts and problems that arise in everyday living. Especially in modern industrial society, legal norms and procedures pervade virtually all aspects of social interaction. As a result, the study of society cannot be complete unless it takes into account the legal element. Yet if modern sociology has been remiss in neglecting law, lawyers have also been mistaken in believing that their own technical modes of analysis and conceptualizations are fully adequate for an understanding of the legal order. Not only is law integral to society, but as part of society, law is inherently social. Sociological perspectives and inquiries are necessary if we are to appreciate the social nature of law.

The sources, organization, and development of legal systems, and the more specific ongoing patterns of legal behavior within such systems, all merit further sociological attention. In this endeavor, it is unlikely that any one theoretical model or research technique will suffice. Moreover, although the sociologist may tend to focus on forms and procedures, he cannot ignore the substance of law. "Rights" and "duties" are not abstract entities, but rather attain their significance in relation to specific patterns of behavior and to socially meaningful entitlements and obligations. While substantive legal norms may at first seem almost infinitely variable, closer scrutiny will often reveal underlying patterns. The cross-institutional nature of legal norms means that even substantive legal concepts and perspectives may appear in seemingly diverse areas of the law. The pervasive development of "strict-liability" approaches, discussed in the last chapter, is a good example of this fact. No analysis that focused *solely* on organization and procedure (although there are indeed important procedural aspects of this development) could really come to grips with such phenomena, which clearly are of major *social* as well as legal significance.

Sociological perspectives make clear that the legal order reflects underlying social values and the constantly changing status of numerous conflicts of interest within the social system. That the effectiveness of enacted legal norms will be hampered by the absence of substantive social grounding and public support now seems to be well established. At the same time, many sociologists have exaggerated the inadequacies of formal social control mechanisms. We are now beginning to discard an exclusively negative conception of law and to see its potential as a positive influence upon social situations and human behavior. A further interesting outcome of the new sociological attention to law may be a heightened recognition that informal and formal social control are in fact not mutually exclusive. Only in the most homogeneous and stable close-knit collectivities can we expect to find social order maintained exclusively by informal means. Likewise, as the study of law in action makes clear, to consider legal phenomena as entirely formal in nature is highly misleading. Just as in the study of large-scale organizations we have become alert to "bureaucracy's other face," which always seems to be present, so too in the study of legal institutions do we find informal mechanisms and organization to be of great significance. Such phenomena as the "criminal-court community," the prestige structure of the large law firm, and the informal negotiation of commercial agreements, represent covert understandings and interactional networks that help oil the machinery of law as an ongoing social enterprise.

At the same time, it is important to keep in mind that through their legal systems men attempt to erect an ordering of social life that attains consistency, reflects overarching principles, and produces justice. There is no guarantee that this endeavor will always be fully successful, or indeed that there will be complete consensus as to the conditions indicating success. Nor is it likely that the sociologist can fully satisfy the lawyer's need for answers to the numerous policy questions continually plaguing the profession and requiring solution within the legal system. As always, the sociologist must essentially content himself with the important business of understanding. The possibility that such increased understanding may indirectly promote the development of a more rational and just legal order is, of course, one that appeals greatly to sociologists and lawyers alike.

Notes

✳✳✳

Introduction: Sociology and the Law

1. For an attempt to organize the sociology of law in terms of these categories see William M. Evan, Introduction, to William M. Evan, ed., *Law and Sociology: Exploratory Essays* (New York: Free Press, 1962).
2. Richard D. Schwartz, "Introduction," to "Law and Society," supplement to *Social Problems*, Vol. 13 (Summer 1965), p. 1.
3. This is particularly true of Weber and Durkheim, some of whose writings on law will be mentioned below.
4. David Riesman, "Law and Sociology: Recruitment, Training, and Colleagueship," in Evan, ed., *op. cit.*, p. 14.
5. Karl Mannheim, "American Sociology," in Karl Mannheim, *Essays in Sociology and Social Psychology* (London: Routledge & Kegan Paul, 1953).
6. Robert MacIver and Charles H. Page, *Society: An Introductory Analysis* (London: Macmillan, 1950), p. 179.
7. Philip Selznick, "Legal Institutions and Social Controls," *Vanderbilt Law Review*, Vol. 17 (1963), p. 83.
8. Henry Sumner Maine, *Ancient Law* (London: J. Murray, 1863), p. 170.
9. See Max Rheinstein, ed., *Max Weber on Law in Economy and Society*, trans. by E. Shils and M. Rheinstein (Cambridge: Harvard Univ. Press, 1954), especially Ch. XI.
10. Reinhard Bendix, *Max Weber: An Intellectual Portrait* (Garden City, N.Y.: Doubleday, 1960), p. 395.
11. Gilbert Geis, "The Social Sciences and the Law," *Washburn Law Journal*, Vol. 1 (1962), p. 574.
12. A good example may be the findings concerning lawyers' violations of professional ethics in a recent study of social control within the legal profession. See Jerome Carlin, *Lawyers' Ethics* (New York: Russell Sage Foundation, 1966).

13. See for example Henry J. Abraham, *The Judicial Process* (New York: Oxford Univ. Press, 1962); John P. Roche, *Courts and Rights: The American Judiciary in Action* (New York: Random House, 1961); and C. G. Post, *An Introduction to the Law* (Englewood Cliffs, N.J.: Prentice-Hall, 1963). For a somewhat more technical treatment consult Harold J. Berman, *The Nature and Functions of Law* (Brooklyn, N.Y.: Foundation Press, 1958); and Charles G. Howard and Robert S. Summers, *Law: Its Nature, Function, and Limits* (Englewood Cliffs, N.J.: Prentice-Hall, 1965).

Chapter One: Jurisprudence and Sociology

1. See "The Problem of the Grudge Informer," in Lon L. Fuller, *The Morality of Law* (New Haven: Yale Univ. Press, 1964), pp. 187–195.
2. Lon L. Fuller, "The Case of the Speluncean Explorers," *Harvard Law Review*, Vol. 62 (1949); reprinted in Ray D. Henson, ed., *Landmarks of Law* (Boston: Beacon Press, 1963), paperback ed.
3. See for example Carl Friedrich, *The Philosophy of Law in Historical Perspective*, 2nd ed. (Chicago: Univ. of Chicago Press, 1963); George H. Sabine, *A History of Political Theory*, rev. ed. (New York: Holt, 1950); Wolfgang Friedmann, *Legal Theory*, 2nd ed. (London: Stevens, 1949); Julius Stone, *The Province and Function of Law* (Cambridge: Harvard Univ. Press, 1961); Morris R. and Felix S. Cohen, eds., *Readings in Jurisprudence and Legal Philosophy* (Englewood Cliffs, N.J.: Prentice-Hall, 1951).
4. See Graham Hughes, review of Samuel Schuman, "Legal Positivism," in *Natural Law Forum*, Vol. 9 (1964), pp. 164–171.
5. John Austin's major work is *Lectures on Jurisprudence* (1832), 3rd ed. rev. (London: J. Murray, 1869).
6. Stone, *op. cit.*, p. 62.
7. Judith Shklar, *Legalism* (Cambridge: Harvard Univ. Press, 1964), p. 34.
8. For a statement of Hans Kelsen's basic ideas see his "The Pure Theory of Law: Its Methods and Fundamental Concepts," *The Law Quarterly Review*, Vol. 50 (October 1934), pp. 474–535.
9. *Ibid.*, p. 482.
10. *Ibid.*, p. 535.
11. John H. Hallowell, *Main Currents in Modern Political Theory* (New York: Holt, 1950), p. 349.
12. Kelsen, *op. cit.*, pp. 517–518.
13. Friedrich Karl von Savigny, *Of the Vocation of Our Age for Legislation and Jurisprudence* (1814, 1831); reprinted in Cohen and Cohen, *op. cit.*, p. 388.
14. John Chipman Gray, *Nature and Sources of the Law* (1909) (Boston: Beacon Press, 1963), paperback ed., pp. 90–91.
15. Henry Sumner Maine, *Ancient Law* (London: J. Murray, 1863).

16. *Ibid.*, p. 3.
17. *Ibid.*, p. 170.
18. Friedrich, *op. cit.*, p. 141.
19. Jeremy Bentham, *An Introduction to the Principles of Morals and Legislation* (1789) (New York: Hafner, 1948), p. 1.
20. *Ibid.*, pp. 170, 171.
21. On these points see the discussion by Andrew Hacker, *Political Theory: Philosophy, Ideology, Science* (New York: Macmillan, 1961), pp. 395–415.
22. Bentham, *op. cit.*, p. 320.
23. Rudolph von Ihering, *Der Zweck im Recht* (1877–1883), Vol. I trans. by I. Husik as *Law as a Means to an End* (1913). For a comprehensive discussion of Ihering's work see Stone, *op. cit.*, Ch. XI.
24. Von Ihering, as quoted by Stone, *op. cit.*, p. 301.
25. Stone, *op. cit.*, pp. 311–312.
26. E. Ehrlich, *The Fundamental Principles of the Sociology of Law* (1913), trans. by W. Moll (Cambridge: Harvard Univ. Press, 1936).
27. F. S. C. Northrop, *The Complexity of Legal and Ethical Experience* (Boston: Little Brown, 1959), pp. 248–249.
28. E. Ehrlich, *op. cit.*, Foreword.
29. *Ibid.*, pp. 192–193, as quoted by Stone, *op. cit.*, p. 651.
30. See the discussion by Northrop, *op. cit.*, especially Chs. III and V.
31. *Ibid.*, Ch. VIII.
32. Roscoe Pound's major works included *Outlines of Lectures on Jurisprudence* (1903); *The Spirit of the Common Law* (1921); *An Introduction to the Philosophy of Law* (1922); and *Interpretations of Legal History* (1923). Some of Pound's most sociological writings were in the form of numerous influential law-journal articles, some of which are cited below.
33. Pound, *An Introduction to the Philosophy of Law* (1922) (New Haven: Yale Univ. Press, 1959), paperback ed., p. 47.
34. Stone, *op. cit.*, pp. 406–408.
35. Gilbert Geis, "Sociology and Sociological Jurisprudence: Admixture of Lore and Law," *Kentucky Law Journal,* Vol. 52 (Winter 1964), pp. 267–293.
36. Edward A. Ross, *Social Control* (New York: Macmillan, 1922), p. 106. See also the discussion of Ross in Charles H. Page, *Class and American Sociology* (New York: Octagon Books, 1964), Ch. VII.
37. Geis, *op. cit.*, p. 273.
38. Lester F. Ward, *Applied Sociology* (Boston: Ginn, 1906), p. 339. See also Page, *op. cit.*, Ch. II.
39. Albion Small as quoted by Geis, *op. cit.*, p. 276. See also Page, *op. cit.*, Ch. IV.
40. See Geis, *op. cit.*, p. 279.
41. American Bar Association Reports, Vol. 29, Pt. 1 (1906), pp. 395–417; reprinted in Henson, *op. cit.*
42. *International Journal of Ethics,* Vol. 27 (January 1917), pp. 150–167.
43. Roscoe Pound, "The Need of a Sociological Jurisprudence," *Green Bag* (1907), pp. 607, 608, as quoted in Geis, *op. cit.*, p. 280.
44. Edmond Cahn, "A Dangerous Myth in the School Segregation Cases," *New York University Law Review,* Vol. 30 (January 1955), p. 154.

45. See Wilfrid E. Rumble, Jr., "Legal Realism, Sociological Jurisprudence and Mr. Justice Holmes," *Journal of the History of Ideas*, Vol. XXVI (October–December 1965), pp. 547–566.

46. *Southern Pacific Co. v. Jensen*, 244 U.S. 205, 222 (1901).

47. *Harvard Law Review*, Vol. 10 (March 1897), pp. 457–478.

48. *Ibid.*, p. 458.

49. *Ibid.*, pp. 460–461.

50. *Ibid.*, p. 462.

51. *Ibid.*, pp. 465–466.

52. *Ibid.*, p. 476.

53. K. N. Llewellyn and E. Adamson Hoebel, *The Cheyenne Way: Conflict and Case Law in Primitive Jurisprudence* (Norman, Okla.: Univ. of Oklahoma Press, 1941).

54. *Ibid.*, Ch. XI. See also K. N. Llewellyn, "The Normative, the Legal and the Law Jobs," *Yale Law Journal*, Vol. 49 (1940), pp. 1355–1400.

55. K. N. Llewellyn, "A Realistic Jurisprudence: The Next Step," *Columbia Law Review*, Vol. 30 (1930), as quoted in Cohen and Cohen, *op. cit.*, p. 473.

56. K. N. Llewellyn, "Remarks on the Theory of Appellate Decision and the Rules or Canons About How Statutes Are to Be Construed," *Vanderbilt Law Review*, Vol. 3 (1950); reprinted in C. Auerbach, *et al.*, eds., *The Legal Process*. (San Francisco: Chandler, 1961), p. 497.

57. Jerome Frank, *Courts on Trial* (New York: Atheneum, 1963), Ch. III, "Facts Are Guesses."

58. *Ibid.*, p. 85.

59. See Edwin M. Schur, "Scientific Method and the Criminal Trial Decision," *Social Research*, Vol. 25 (Summer 1958), pp. 173–190.

60. Morton G. White, *Social Thought in America: The Revolt Against Formalism* (New York: Viking, 1949).

61. Jerome Frank, *Law and the Modern Mind* (Garden City, N.Y.: Anchor Books, 1963), p. 22.

62. For some of Arnold's views on law and social reform, see Thurman W. Arnold, *The Symbols of Government* (New Haven: Yale Univ. Press, 1935).

63. Wilfrid E. Rumble, Jr., "The Paradox of American Legal Realism," *Ethics*, Vol. LXXV (April 1965), pp. 166–178.

64. Friedrich Kessler, "Theoretic Bases of Law," *University of Chicago Law Review*, Vol. 9 (1942); reprinted in Henson, *op. cit.*, pp. 3–16.

65. Philip Selznick, "Sociology and Natural Law," *Natural Law Forum*, Vol. 6 (1961), p. 84; reprinted in John Cogley, *et al.*, *Natural Law and Modern Society* (Cleveland: Meridian, 1966).

66. Kessler, *op. cit.*, p. 4.

67. The relevant sources are as follows: Aristotle, *Politics*, Bk. i; Cicero, *de republica*, Bk. iii; Aquinas, *Summa Theologica*, Pt. II, First Part, Quest. 90; and Grotius, *De jure belli ac pacis*, Bk. i, c. 1.

68. Erich Fromm, *The Sane Society*. (New York: Holt, Rinehart & Winston, 1955). I am grateful to Judy Schur for perceptive comments concerning Fromm's relevance in this context.

69. Robert Hutchins, "Natural Law and Jurisprudence," in Cogley, *et al.*, *op. cit.*, p. 33.

70. H. L. A. Hart, *The Concept of Law* (London: Oxford Univ. Press, 1961), especially pp. 189–195. For a sociological view compare D. F. Aberle, *et al.*, "The Functional Prerequisites of a Society," *Ethics*, Vol. LX (1950), pp. 100–111.

71. Kai Nielsen, "The Myth of Natural Law," in Sidney Hook, ed., *Law and Philosophy* (New York: New York Univ. Press, 1964), p. 133.

72. Felix Oppenheim, "The Metaethics of Natural Law," *ibid.*, p. 245.

73. John Cogley, Introduction to Cogley, *et al., op. cit.*, p. 21.

74. Robert Gordis, "Natural Law and Religion," *ibid.*, p. 248.

75. Selznick, *op. cit.*

76. *Ibid.*, p. 95.

77. Philip Selznick, "Sociology of Law," paper prepared for the *International Encyclopedia of the Social Sciences,* Berkeley, Cal., April 1965, mimeographed, p. 11.

78. Fuller, *The Morality of Law,* p. 97.

79. *Ibid.*, p. 39. On the "internal morality of law" generally, see Ch. II.

80. Selznick, "Sociology and Natural Law," p. 93.

81. *Ibid.*, p. 102.

82. See Edwin M. Schur, "Normative and Functional Models of the Legal System," paper presented at annual meeting of the American Sociological Association, Miami Beach, Fla., August 1966, duplicated.

83. Gordis, *op. cit.*, p. 257.

84. Hart, *op. cit.*, Ch. V.

85. Selznick, "Sociology of Law," pp. 9, 10.

86. See for example Max Gluckman, "Natural Justice in Africa," *Natural Law Forum,* Vol. 9 (1964), pp. 25–44.

87. The trend toward greater "legality" in Soviet law is often referred to in this connection. See Harold J. Berman, *Justice in the U.S.S.R.*, rev. ed. (New York: Vintage Books, 1963).

88. In general see Hook, *op. cit.*, Pt. I; Harrop A. Freeman, *et al., Civil Disobedience* (Santa Barbara, Cal.: Center for the Study of Democratic Institutions [The Fund for the Republic], 1966); Richard Wasserstrom, "Disobeying the Law," *The Journal of Philosophy*, LVIII, 21 (October 12, 1961), 641–653; Hugo A. Bedau, "On Civil Disobedience," *ibid.*, 653–665; Stuart M. Brown, Jr., "Civil Disobedience," *ibid.*, LVIII, 22 (October 26, 1961), 669–681; Carl Cohen, "Essence and Ethics of Civil Disobedience," *The Nation* (March 16, 1964); and Charles Frankel, "Is Breaking Law Ever Right?" *The New York Times,* Western ed. (January 14, 1964), p. 7.

89. See for example, Franz Neumann, *The Democratic and the Authoritarian State* (New York: Free Press, 1957), especially Ch. V, "On the Limits of Justifiable Disobedience."

90. As quoted by Wolfgang Friedman, "An Analysis of 'In Defense of Natural Law,'" in Hook, *op. cit.*, p. 152.

91. Freeman, in Freeman, *et al., op. cit.*, pp. 2–10.

92. Frankel, *op. cit.*

93. In preparing this section I have benefited from an unpublished paper by Jan Novack, "Nuremberg; Eichmann—Judicial Aspects of the War Crime Trials."

94. See George A. Finch, "The Nuremberg Trial and International Law,"

American Journal of International Law, Vol. 41 (January 1947), pp. 20–37; Quincy Wright, "The Law of the Nuremberg Trial," *ibid.,* pp. 38–72; Herbert Wechsler, "The Issues of the Nuremberg Trial," *Political Science Quarterly,* Vol. 62 (1947), pp. 11–26; Otto Kirchheimer, *Political Justice* (Princeton: Princeton Univ. Press, 1961), Ch. VIII.

95. Charles E. Wyzanski, Jr., "Nuremberg—A Fair Trial?" *Atlantic Monthly,* Vol. 177 (April 1946); reprinted in Charles E. Wyzanski, *The New Meaning of Justice* (Boston: Little Brown, 1965) (New York: Bantam, 1966), p. 134. See also his second thoughts in "Nuremberg in Retrospect," *Atlantic Monthly,* Vol. 178 (December 1946); reprinted in *The New Meaning of Justice,* pp. 137–145.

96. Shklar, *op. cit.,* p. 156.

97. See Yosal Rogat, *The Eichmann Trial and the Rule of Law* (Santa Barbara, Cal.: Center for the Study of Democratic Institutions [The Fund for the Republic], 1961). See also Hannah Arendt, *Eichmann in Jerusalem* (New York: Viking, 1965); and Gideon Hausner, *Justice in Jerusalem* (New York: Harper & Row, 1966).

98. Kirchheimer, *op. cit.,* p. 341.

Chapter Two: Law and Order

1. Jack P. Gibbs, "The Sociology of Law and Normative Phenomena," *American Sociological Review,* Vol. 31 (June 1966), p. 315.

2. See *Soviet Legal Philosophy,* trans. by Hugh W. Babb (Cambridge: Harvard Univ. Press, 1951); Rudolph Schlesinger, *Soviet Legal Theory* (New York: Oxford Univ. Press, 1945); and Harold J. Berman, *Justice in the U.S.S.R.,* rev. ed. enlarged (New York: Vintage Books, 1963), Ch. I.

3. On the need for formal control mechanisms in urban society, see Louis Wirth, "Urbanism as a Way of Life," *American Journal of Sociology,* Vol. 44 (July 1938); reprinted in Paul K. Hatt and Albert J. Reiss, Jr., *Cities and Society* (New York: Free Press, 1957).

4. Richard D. Schwartz, "Social Factors in the Development of Legal Control: A Case Study of Two Israeli Settlements," *Yale Law Journal,* Vol. 63 (February 1954), pp. 471–491.

5. K. N. Llewellyn and E. Adamson Hoebel, *The Cheyenne Way: Conflict and Case Law in Primitive Jurisprudence* (Norman, Okla.: Univ. of Oklahoma Press, 1941).

6. See Lewis Coser, *The Functions of Social Conflict* (New York: Free Press, 1956); Ralf Dahrendorf, "Out of Utopia: Towards a Re-Orientation of Sociological Analysis," *American Journal of Sociology,* Vol. 64 (September 1958), pp. 115–127; Kai Erikson, "Notes on the Sociology of Deviance," *Social Problems,* Vol. 9 (Spring 1962), pp. 307–314; and Lewis Coser, "Some Functions of Deviance and Normative Flexibility," *American Journal of Sociology,* Vol. 68 (September 1962), pp. 172–181.

7. For a recent symposium on anthropological approaches, see Laura Nader, ed., *The Ethnography of Law*, Special Publication, *American Anthropologist*, Vol. 67, No. 6, Pt. 2 (December 1965). In her lead article, "The Anthropological Study of Law," Nader provides a useful overview of past efforts and more recent research. See also Max Gluckman, *The Judicial Process Among the Barotse of Northern Rhodesia* (Manchester, England: Manchester Univ. Press, 1955); Paul Bohannan, *Justice and Judgment Among the Tiv* (London: Oxford Univ. Press, 1957); and Leopold Pospisil, *Kapauku Papuans and Their Law* (New Haven: Yale Univ. Publications in Anthropology, 1958).

8. A useful discussion of this matter is provided by Lucy Mair, *Primitive Government* (Baltimore: Penguin, 1962). On the general relationship between law and custom see Robert MacIver and Charles H. Page, *Society: An Introductory Analysis* (London: Macmillan, 1950), Ch. 8.

9. Bronislaw Malinowski, *Crime and Custom in Savage Society* (1926) (Paterson, N.J.: Littlefield, 1959), p. 55.

10. *Ibid.*, p. 59.

11. See Claude Levi-Strauss, "The Principle of Reciprocity," in Lewis Coser and Bernard Rosenberg, eds., *Sociological Theory* (New York: Macmillan, 1957); and Alvin W. Gouldner, "The Norm of Reciprocity," *American Sociological Review*, Vol. 25 (April 1960), pp. 161–178.

12. See discussion and critique of E. Adamson Hoebel, *The Law of Primitive Man* (Cambridge: Harvard Univ. Press, 1961), Ch. VIII.

13. As quoted *ibid.*, p. 26.

14. *Ibid.*, p. 28.

15. Max Rheinstein, ed., *Max Weber on Law in Economy and Society*, trans. by E. Shils and M. Rheinstein (Cambridge: Harvard Univ. Press, 1954), p. 5.

16. *Ibid.*, p. lxiv.

17. Philip Selznick, "Sociology of Law," paper prepared for the *International Encyclopedia of the Social Sciences* Berkeley, Cal., April 1965, mimeographed.

18. H. L. A. Hart, *The Concept of Law* (London: Oxford Univ. Press, 1961), Ch. V.

19. Paul Bohannan, "The Differing Realms of Law," in Nader, *op. cit.*, p. 35.

20. *Ibid.*, p. 36.

21. *Ibid.*, p. 41.

22. Hoebel, *The Law of Primitive Man*, Ch. II, "The Functions of Law."

23. Talcott Parsons, "The Law and Social Control," in William M. Evan, ed., *Law and Sociology: Exploratory Essays* (New York: Free Press, 1962), pp. 57, 58. See also Talcott Parsons, "An Outline of the Social System," in Talcott Parsons, *et al.*, *Theories of Society*, Vol. I (New York: Free Press, 1961).

24. Parsons, "The Law and Social Control," pp. 58–64.

25. Harry C. Bredemeier, "Law as an Integrative Mechanism," in Evan, *op. cit.*, pp. 73–90.

26. *Ibid.*; the difficulties are summarized on p. 89.

27. Some of the points that follow are considered in my "Normative and Functional Models of the Legal System," paper presented at annual meet-

ing of the American Sociological Association, Miami Beach, Fla., August 1966, duplicated.

28. Arnold Rose, "Some Suggestions for Research in the Sociology of Law," *Social Problems,* Vol. 9 (Winter 1962), pp. 281–283.

29. Harold J. Berman, *The Nature and Functions of Law* (Brooklyn, N.Y.: Foundation Press, Inc., 1958), p. 33.

30. See Robert K. Merton, *Social Theory and Social Structure,* rev. ed. (New York: Free Press, 1957), Ch. I.

31. For general discussions of power see Bertrand Russell, *Power: A New Social Analysis* (New York: Norton, 1938); Bertrand de Jouvenal, *On Power* (New York: Viking, 1949); Max Weber, *Theory of Social and Economic Organization,* trans. by A. M. Henderson and Talcott Parsons (Glencoe, Ill.: Free Press, 1947); Harold Lasswell and Abraham Kaplan, *Power and Society* (New Haven: Yale Univ. Press, 1950); Richard A. Schermerhorn, *Society and Power* (New York: Random House, 1961); and Robert Bierstedt, "An Analysis of Social Power," *American Sociological Review,* Vol. 15 (December 1950), pp. 730–738.

32. Coser and Rosenberg, eds., *Sociological Theory,* p. 123.

33. Schermerhorn, *op. cit.,* p. 14.

34. Robert MacIver, *The Web of Government* (New York: Macmillan, 1947), p. 66. See also MacIver and Page, *op. cit.,* pp. 154–161; and Schermerhorn, *op. cit.,* pp. 36–40.

35. See Kurt H. Wolff, ed. and tr., *The Sociology of Georg Simmel* (Glencoe, Ill.: Free Press, 1950), Pt. III, "Superordination and Subordination."

36. Charles E. Merriam, *Political Power* (New York: McGraw-Hill, 1934), p. 254.

37. De Jouvenal, *op. cit.,* p. 316, and see generally Ch. XVI, "Power and Law." See also my comments on Kelsen's "pure theory of law" in Chapter One, pp. 27–28, of this book.

38. Bierstedt, *op. cit.*

39. Hans Gerth and C. Wright Mills, *Character and Social Structure* (New York: Harbinger Books, 1964), p. 260.

40. Robert MacIver, *Power Transformed* (New York: Macmillan, 1964), p. 207.

41. Franz Neumann, *The Democratic and the Authoritarian State* (New York: Free Press, 1957), Ch. IX, "Notes on the Theory of Dictatorship."

42. See for example Franz Neumann, *Behemoth,* 2nd ed. (New York: Oxford Univ. Press. 1944); G. F. Kramer, "The Influence of National-Socialism on the Courts of Justice and the Police," in M. Baumont, *et al.,* eds., *The Third Reich* (New York: Praeger, 1955); and Edith Roper and Clara Leiser, *Skeleton of Justice* (New York: Dutton, 1941).

43. This is the subtitle of Otto Kirchheimer's *Political Justice* (Princeton: Princeton Univ. Press, 1961).

44. See Neumann, *Behemoth,* pp. 111–120.

45. Gwendolyn M. Carter, *The Politics of Inequality* (New York: Praeger, 1958, particularly Ch. III, "Spelling out Apartheid."

46. *Ibid.,* Ch. XV, "International Reactions." See also International Commission of Jurists, *South Africa and the Rule of Law* (Geneva, 1960).

47. Merle Fainsod, *How Russia Is Ruled* (Cambridge: Harvard Univ. Press, 1954), Ch. XIII, "Terror as a System of Power." Also Harold Berman,

Justice in the U.S.S.R., rev. ed. (New York: Vintage B. ᴏᴋs, 1963) , pp. 46–65; and Kirchheimer, *op. cit.*

48. Alex Inkeles, "Social Stratification and Mobility in the Soviet Union, 1940–1950," *American Sociological Review*, Vol. 15 (August 1950), pp. 465–479; and Robert A. Feldmesser, "Equality and Inequality Under Khrushchev," *Problems of Communism*, Vol. 9 (1960), pp. 31–39; both reprinted in Alex Inkeles and Kent Geiger, eds., *Soviet Society* (Boston: Houghton Mifflin, 1961).

49. See for example Barbara Wooton, *Freedom Under Planning* (Chapel Hill, N.C.: Univ. of North Carolina Press, 1945).

50. Karl Mannheim, *Man and Society in an Age of Reconstruction* (New York: Harcourt Brace, 1940); and Karl Mannheim, *Freedom, Power, and Democratic Planning* (New York: Oxford Univ. Press, 1950).

51. For a good overview see George E. Simpson and J. Milton Yinger, *Racial and Cultural Minorities*, 3rd ed. (New York: Harper & Row, 1965), Chs. XIV and XV. See also Arnold Rose, *The Negro in America* (New York: Harper, 1948), Ch. XI.

52. *Mississippi Black Paper* (New York: Random House, 1965).

53. See Guy B. Johnson, "The Negro and Crime," *The Annals*, Vol. 217 (September 1941), pp. 93–104.

54. The concept of "categoric risk" is developed by Walter C. Reckless, *The Crime Problem*, 3rd ed. (New York: Appleton-Century-Crofts, 1961). See also Marvin Wolfgang, *Crime and Race: Conceptions and Misconceptions* New York: Institute of Human Relations Press, 1964).

55. Fowler V. Harper and Jerome H. Skolnick, *Problems of the Family*, rev. ed. (Indianapolis: Bobbs-Merrill, 1962), pp. 88–105. A U.S. Supreme Court decision, *Loving v. Virginia*, 87 S. Ct. 1817 (1967), delivered as this book was going to press, held unconstitutional one such antimiscegenation statute; this ruling is believed to have generally invalidated such legislation.

56. Leonard Zeitz, "Survey of Negro Attitudes to Law," cited in Jerome E. Carlin and Jan Howard, "Legal Representation and Class Justice," *UCLA Law Review*, Vol. 12 (January 1965), pp. 381–437.

57. James Baldwin, *Nobody Knows My Name* (New York: Dial Press, 1961), pp. 65–66.

58. See G. Franklin Edwards, *The Negro Professional Class* (New York: Free Press, 1959), pp. 133–138. See also William H. Hale, "The Career Development of the Negro Lawyer," unpublished doctoral dissertation, University of Chicago, 1959.

59. Leon Friedman, ed., *Southern Justice* (New York: Pantheon, 1965); *Mississippi Black Paper;* William M. Kunstler and Arthur Kinoy, "Southern Justice: Lawyers Walk in Fear," *The Nation* (June 8, 1964); Louis Lusky, "Justice With a Southern Accent," *Harper's*, Vol. 228 (March 1964); and Daniel H. Pollitt, "Timid Lawyers and Neglected Clients," *Harper's*, Vol. 229 (August 1964).

60. Carlin and Howard, *op. cit.*, p. 407.

61. *Ibid.*, p. 387.

62. Monrad G. Paulsen, "The Legal Needs of the Poor and Family Law," in *The Extension of Legal Services to the Poor*, Conference Proceedings

(Washington: U.S. Govt. Printing Office, 1965); and Justine Wise Polier, "Problems Involving Family and Child," in *Proceedings of National Conference on Law and Poverty* (Washington: U.S. Govt. Printing Office, 1966).

63. Nancy E. LeBlanc, "Landlord-Tenant Problems," in *The Extension of Legal Services to the Poor*; and Julian H. Levi, "Problems Relating to Real Property," in *Proceedings of National Conference on Law and Poverty*.

64. David Caplovitz, *The Poor Pay More* (New York: Free Press, 1963); and David Caplovitz "Consumer Problems," in *The Extension of Legal Services to the Poor*. See also Allison Dunham, "Consumer Credit Problems of the Poor," in *Proceedings of National Conference on Law and Poverty*.

65. Edward V. Sparer, "The New Public Law: The Relation of Indigents to State Administration," and Elizabeth Wickenden, "The Indigent and Welfare Administration," in *The Extension of Legal Services to the Poor*; Charles A. Reich, "The New Property," *Yale Law Journal*, Vol. 73 (April 1964), pp. 733–787; and Richard A. Cloward and Richard M. Elman, "Poverty, Injustice, and the Welfare State," *The Nation* (February 28, 1966 and March 7, 1966).

66. Carlin and Howard, pp. 398–399. See also Cloward and Elman, *op. cit.*

67. Reich, *op. cit.*, p. 786.

68. Caplovitz, *The Poor Pay More*, p. 155.

69. *Ibid.*, pp. 160–161.

70. Caplovitz, "Consumer Problems," pp. 64–65.

71. *Gideon v. Wainwright*, 372 U.S. 335 (1963); Anthony Lewis, *Gideon's Trumpet* (New York: Random House, 1964); and Robert G. Sherrill, "Justice for the Poor: The Banner of Gideon," *The Nation* (April 13, 1964).

72. See for example Charles Grosser, "The Need for a Neighborhood Legal Service and the New York Experience"; William H. Wells, "The Boston Neighborhood House Proposal"; and Charles J. Parker, "The New Haven Model"; all in *The Extension of Legal Services to the Poor*. I have benefited from conversations with William H. Wells concerning these programs and their problems.

73. See the section on "Legal Services to the Rural Poor," in *Proceedings of National Conference on Law and Poverty*.

74. Alexis de Tocqueville, *Democracy in America*, Vol. I (1835, 1840) (New York: Vintage Books, 1945), p. 286.

75. Thorstein Veblen, *The Theory of the Leisure Class* (1899) (New York: Modern Library, 1934), p. 231.

76. C. Wright Mills, *The Power Elite* (New York: Oxford Univ. Press, 1957), p. 289.

77. Suzanne Keller, *Beyond the Ruling Class* (New York: Random House, 1963), p. 325.

78. Erwin O. Smigel, *The Wall Street Lawyer* (New York: Free Press, 1964), Ch. I, "The Large Law Firm in American Society."

79. Jerome Carlin, *Lawyers' Ethics* (New York: Russell Sage Foundation, 1966).

80. *Ibid.*, Jerome Carlin, *Lawyers on Their Own* (New Brunswick, N.J.: Rutgers Univ. Press, 1962); Smigel, *op. cit.*; Hubert J. O'Gorman, *Lawyers and Matrimonial Cases* (New York: Free Press, 1963); Jack Ladinsky, "Careers of Lawyers, Law Practice, and Legal Institutions," *American Sociological Review*, Vol. 28 (February 1963), pp. 47–54; Jack Ladinsky "The Impact of Social Backgrounds of Lawyers on Law Practice and the Law," *Journal of Legal Education*, Vol. 16 (1963), pp. 127–143; and John Young, "The Jewish Law Student and New York Jobs," *Yale Law Journal*, Vol. 73 (March 1964), pp. 626–660.

81. See for example Fred P. Graham, "Shriver Opposed on New Legal Aid," *The New York Times* (June 23, 1966), p. 37. See also Charles J. Parker, "The Relations of Legal Services Programs with Local Bar Associations," in *Proceedings of National Conference on Law and Poverty*.

82. See articles cited in note 59.

83. Albert J. Reiss, Jr., *Occupations and Social Status* (New York: Free Press, 1961).

84. See Riesman, "Law and Sociology: Recruitment, Training, and Colleagueship," in Evan, *op. cit.* On some of the limits of formal socialization see Dan Lortie, "Laymen to Lawmen: Law Schools, Careers, and Professional Socialization," *Harvard Educational Review*, Vol. 29 (Fall 1959), pp. 352–369.

85. Carlin, *Lawyers on Their Own.*

86. Seymour Warkov and Joseph Zelan, *Lawyers in the Making* (Chicago: Aldine, 1965), p. 12.

Chapter Three: Law and Social Change

1. F. James Davis, "Law in Operation," in F. James Davis, *et al.*, *Society and the Law* (New York: Free Press, 1962), p. 77.

2. Max Rheinstein, ed., *Max Weber on Law in Economy and Society*, trans. by E. Shils and M. Rheinstein (Cambridge: Harvard Univ. Press, 1954), p. 303.

3. Reinhard Bendix, *Max Weber: An Intellectual Portrait* (Garden City, N.Y.: Doubleday, 1960), p. 388.

4. See Rheinstein's discussion of this typology in *Max Weber on Law in Economy and Society*, pp. xlvii–lxiii.

5. Max Weber, *The Theory of Social and Economic Organization*, reprinted in Talcott Parsons, *et al.*, *Theories of Society*, Vol. I (New York: Free Press, 1961), pp. 626–32.

6. Emile Durkheim, *The Division of Labor in Society* (1893), trans. by George Simpson (New York: Free Press, 1960).

7. *Ibid.*, p. 111.

8. Richard D. Schwartz and James C. Miller, "Legal Evolution and Societal Complexity," *American Journal of Sociology*, Vol. 70 (September 1964), pp. 159–169.

9. *Ibid.*, p. 166.

10. *Ibid.*, pp. 168–169.

11. See for example George H. Mead, "The Psychology of Punitive Justice," *American Journal of Sociology*, Vol. 23 (1918), pp. 577–602. See also works cited in Chapter Two, note 6, in this book.

12. Geoffrey Sawer, *Law in Society* (London: Oxford Univ. Press, 1965), pp. 65–66.

13. See for example Karl Renner, *The Institutions of Private Law and Their Social Functions*, O. Kahn-Freund, ed., trans. by A. Schwarzchild (London: Routledge & Kegan Paul, 1949); and George Rusche and Otto Kirchheimer, *Punishment and Social Structure* (New York: Columbia Univ. Press, 1939).

14. Pitirim A. Sorokin, *Society, Culture, and Personality* (New York: Harper, 1947), p. 626.

15. Pitirim A. Sorokin, *The Crisis of Our Age* (New York: Dutton, 1941); and Pitirim A. Sorokin, *The American Sex Revolution* (Boston: Porter Sargent, 1956).

16. Harold J. Berman, *Justice in the U.S.S.R.*, rev. ed. enlarged (New York: Vintage Books, 1963), Chs. I and II.

17. *Ibid.*, p. 64.

18. *Ibid.*, Ch. II.

19. A. Sukharev, "Pressing Problems Facing the Legal Profession," *The Soviet Review*, VI, 2 (Summer 1965), 55–64; N. V. Zhogin, "Vyshinsky's Distortions in Soviet Legal Theory and Practice," *ibid.*, VI, 4 (Winter 1965–1966), pp. 44–52.

20. Leon Lipson, "Socialist Legality: The Road Uphill," in Abraham Brumberg, ed., *Russia Under Khrushchev* (New York: Praeger, 1962), p. 469.

21. Berman, *Justice in the U.S.S.R.*, especially Chs. V–IX.

22. Jerome A. Cohen, "The Criminal Process in the People's Republic of China: An Introduction," *Harvard Law Review*, Vol. 79 (January 1966), pp. 469–533.

23. Berman, *Justice in the U.S.S.R.*, Chs. X–XVI.

24. Philip Selznick, "Sociology of Law," paper prepared for the *International Encyclopedia of the Social Sciences*, Berkeley, Cal., April 1965, mimeographed, pp. 24–25.

25. Alfred W. Blumrosen, "Legal Process and Labor Law," in William M. Evan, ed., *Law and Sociology: Exploratory Essays* (New York: Free Press, 1962), p. 186.

26. For excellent discussion of a large number of these trends see Wolfgang Friedmann, *Law in a Changing Society* (London: Stevens, 1959).

27. Herbert Wechsler, "Toward Neutral Principles of Constitutional Law," *Harvard Law Review*, Vol. 73 (November 1959), pp. 1–35.

28. Victor G. Rosenblum, *Law as a Political Instrument* (New York: Random House, 1955).

29. On the development of administrative procedures see Friedmann, *op. cit.*, Chs. XI–XIII; Lewis Mayers, *The American Legal System*, rev. ed. (New

York: Harper & Row, 1964), Chs. XIV–XVIII; and C. Auerbach, *et al.*, eds., *The Legal Process* (San Francisco: Chandler, 1961), Pt. 3.

30. Auerbach, *et. al.*, eds., *op. cit.*, p. 767.

31. Selznick, *op. cit.*, p. 23.

32. *Ibid.;* Philip Selznick, "Legal Institutions and Social Controls," *Vanderbilt Law Review,* Vol. 17 (1963), p. 83, and Philip Selznick, "Private Government and the Corporate Conscience," unpublished paper presented at Symposium on Business Policy, Harvard Business School (April 1963). See also William Evan, "Organization Man and Due Process of Law," *American Sociological Review,* Vol. 26 (August 1961), pp. 540–547.

33. Jerome Skolnick, "The Sociology of Law in America: Overview and Trends," in "Law and Society," supplement to *Social Problems,* Vol. 13 (Summer 1965), p. 29.

34. William M. Evan, "Public and Private Legal Systems," in Evan, ed., *Law and Sociology,* p. 176.

35. *Ibid.*, p. 168.

36. William Graham Sumner, *Folkways* (1906) (New York: Mentor Books, 1960), p. 89. See also Charles H. Page, *Class and American Sociology* (New York: Octagon, 1964), Ch. III; H. V. Ball, George E. Simpson and K. Ikeda, "Law and Social Change: Sumner Reconsidered," *American Journal of Sociology,* Vol. 67 (March 1962), pp. 532–540; and on the limits of law generally, Robert MacIver and Charles H. Page, *Society: An Introductory Analysis* (London: Macmillan, 1950), pp. 457–463.

37. H. L. A. Hart, The Concept of Law (London: Oxford Univ. Press, 1961), Ch. X; and Friedmann, *op. cit.,* Pt. 5. See also Kenneth S. Carlston, *Law and Organization in World Society* (Urbana, Ill.: Univ. of Illinois Press, 1962); Myres S. McDougal and Florentino Feliciano, *Law and Minimum World Public Order* (New Haven: Yale Univ. Press, 1961); and the materials in Richard A. Falk and Saul H. Mendlovitz, eds., *International Law* (New York: World Law Fund, 1966).

38. Julius Stone, *The International Court and the World Crisis,* in *International Conciliation,* No. 536 (New York: Carnegie Endowment for World Peace, 1962), p. 7.

39. See for example Grenville Clark and Louis B. Sohn, *World Peace Through World Law* (Cambridge: Harvard Univ. Press, 1958). See also Richard A. Falk and Saul Mendlovitz, eds., *International Law* and *Toward a Theory of War Prevention* (New York: World Law Fund, 1966).

40. Robert M. Hutchins, "Constitutional Foundations for World Order," in Falk and Mendlovitz, eds., *Toward a Theory of War Prevention,* p. 76.

41. Stewart Macauley, "Non-Contractual Relations in Business: A Preliminary Study," *American Sociological Review,* Vol. 28 (February 1963), p. 61.

42. *Ibid.*, pp. 62–67.

43. Edwin Sutherland and Donald Cressey, *Principles of Criminology,* 7th ed. (Philadelphia: Lippincott, 1966), p. 11.

44. See materials in Hugo A. Bedau, ed., *The Death Penalty in America* (Garden City, N.Y.: Anchor Books, 1964), especially Chs. VI and VII.

45. Committee on Homosexual Offences and Prostitution, *Report,* Home Office, Cmnd. 247 (London: Her Majesty's Stationery Office, 1957).

46. *Ibid.*, pp. 9–10, 24.
47. Patrick Devlin, *The Enforcement of Morals* (London: Oxford Univ. Press, 1965), p. 7, 13–14.
48. H. L. A. Hart, *Law, Liberty and Morality* (Stanford, Cal.: Stanford Univ. Press, 1963), p. 58.
49. Francis A. Allen, *The Borderland of Criminal Justice* (Chicago: Univ. of Chicago Press, 1964), especially pp. 1–24.
50. Robin Williams, *American Society: A Sociological Interpretation*, 2nd ed. (New York: Knopf, 1960), Ch. X.
51. Edwin M. Schur, *Crimes Without Victims* (Englewood Cliffs, N.J.: Prentice-Hall, 1965).
52. Merton noted this point some years ago. See Robert K. Merton, *Social Theory and Social Structure*, rev. ed. (New York: Free Press, 1957), p. 79. See also Herbert Packer, "The Crime Tariff," *American Scholar*, Vol. 33 (1964), pp. 551–557. It will be interesting to see whether public determination to prevent use of "psychedelics" (hallucinatory drugs such as LSD) produces a similar economic spiral and expansion of the "problem."
53. Jack Greenberg, *Race Relations and American Law* (New York: Columbia Univ. Press, 1959); Albert P. Blaustein and Clarence Ferguson, Jr., *Desegregation and the Law* (New Brunswick, N.J.: Rutgers Univ. Press, 1957, 1962); and Morroe Berger, *Equality by Statute* (New York: Columbia Univ. Press, 1948). See also, Robert MacIver, *The More Perfect Union* (New York: Macmillan, 1948), especially Chs. 7 and 10; and Robert K. Merton, "Discrimination and the American Creed," in MacIver, ed., *Discrimination and National Welfare* (New York: Harper, 1949).
54. John P. Roche and Milton M. Gordon, "Can Morality Be Legislated?" *The New York Times Magazine* (May 22, 1955).
55. Greenberg, *op. cit.*, p. 7.
56. Roche and Gordon, *op. cit.* See also the excellent survey of evidence in Simpson and Yinger, *op. cit.*, Ch. XXII.
57. See James Vander Zanden, *Race Relations in Transition* (New York: Random House, 1965), Ch. VII, "Accommodation to Desegregation."
58. Warren Breed, "The Emergence of Pluralistic Public Opinion in a Community Crisis," in Alvin Gouldner and S. M. Miller, eds., *Applied Sociology* (New York: Free Press, 1965), p. 145.
59. William Evan, "Law as an Instrument of Social Change," in Gouldner and Miller, especially pp. 288–292.
60. Harold Laski, *The State in Theory and Practice* (New York: Viking, 1935), p. 160.
61. See John Horton, "Order and Conflict Theories of Social Problems as Competing Ideologies," *American Journal of Sociology*, Vol. 71 (May 1966), pp. 701–713. See also materials cited in Chapter Two, note 6, in this book.

Chapter Four: Law in Action

1. See for example William J. Chambliss, "A Sociological Analysis of the Law of Vagrancy," *Social Problems,* Vol. 12 (Summer 1964), pp. 67–77.
2. For excerpts from the Senate hearings and text of the federal law see R. C. Donnelly, J. Goldstein and R. D. Schwartz, *Criminal Law* (New York: Free Press, 1962), pp. 82–84.
3. Waldo Burchard, "A Study of Attitudes Toward the Use of Concealed Devices in Social Science Research," *Social Forces,* Vol. 36 (December 1957), pp. 111–116; and Waldo Burchard, "Lawyers, Political Scientists, Sociologists—and Concealed Microphones," *American Sociological Review,* Vol. 23 (December 1958), pp. 686–691.
4. As summarized by Rita James Simon, "Trial by Jury: A Critical Assessment," in Alvin Gouldner and S. M. Miller, eds., *Applied Sociology* (New York: Free Press, 1965), p. 306.
5. Fred L. Strodtbeck, Rita M. James, and Charles Hawkins, "Social Status in Jury Deliberations," *American Sociological Review,* Vol. 22 (December 1957), p. 718. See also Fred L. Strodtbeck and R. D. Mann, "Sex Role Differentiation in Jury Deliberations," *Sociometry,* Vol. 19 (March 1956), pp. 3–11; and Rita M. James, "Status and Competence of Jurors," *American Journal of Sociology,* Vol. 64 (May 1959), pp. 563–570.
6. See Hans Zeisel, "Social Research on the Law," in William M. Evan, ed., *Law and Sociology: Exploratory Essays* (New York: Free Press, 1962); Fred L. Strodtbeck, "Social Process, the Law, and Jury Functioning," *ibid.;* and Simon, *op. cit.*
7. Simon, *op. cit.,* p. 304.
8. Hans Zeisel, Harry Kalven, Jr., and Bernard Buckholz, *Delay in the Court* (Boston: Little, Brown, 1959). A second volume based on the project's studies has just been issued. See Kalven and Zeisel, *The American Jury* (Boston: Little, Brown, 1966).
9. *Ibid.,* p. 237.
10. See Maurice Rosenberg, "Court Congestion: Status, Causes, and Proposed Remedies," in Harry W. Jones, ed., *The Courts, the Public, and the Law Explosion* (Englewood Cliffs, N.J.: Prentice-Hall, 1965). See also Maxine Boord Virtue, *Survey of Metropolitan Courts: Final Report* (Ann Arbor, Mich.: Univ. of Michigan Press, 1962).
11. Jerome Carlin, "Preliminary Notes on Adjudication and the Administration of Justice," Center for the Study of Law and Society, University of California, Berkeley, Cal. May 1964, duplicated.
12. See Glendon Schubert, ed., *Judicial Behavior* (Chicago: Rand McNally, 1964); and Glendon Schubert, *Judicial Decision-Making* (New York: Free Press, 1963). See also symposium on "Jurimetrics," *Law and Contemporary Problems,* Vol. XXVIII (Winter 1963); and symposium on "Social Science Approaches to the Judicial Process," *Harvard Law Review,* Vol. 79 (June 1966).

13. For example, John R. Schmidhauser, "The Background Characteristics of United States Supreme Court Justices," in Schubert, *Judicial Behavior*; and Stuart Nagel, "The Relationship Between the Political and Ethnic Affiliation of Judges, and their Decision-Making," *ibid*. See also Joel Grossman, "Social Backgrounds and Judicial Decision-Making," *Harvard Law Review*, Vol. 79 (June 1966), pp. 1551–1564.

14. C. Herman Pritchett, *The Roosevelt Court* (New York: Macmillan, 1948). See also Eloise C. Snyder, "Uncertainty and the Supreme Court," *American Journal of Sociology*, Vol. 65 (November 1959), pp. 241–245; Eloise C. Snyder, "The Supreme Court as a Small Group," *Social Forces*, Vol. XXXVI (March 1958), pp. 232–238; and Walter F. Murphy, "Courts as Small Groups," *Harvard Law Review*, Vol. 79 (June 1966), pp. 1565–1572.

15. S. Sidney Ulmer, "Leadership in the Michigan Supreme Court," in Schubert, *Judicial Decision-Making*; and Walter F. Murphy, "Leadership, Bargaining, and the Judicial Process," in Schubert, ed., *Judicial Behavior*.

16. See Joseph Tannenhaus, "The Cumulative Scaling of Judicial Decisions," *Harvard Law Review*, Vol. 79 (June 1966), pp. 1583–1594; Glendon Schubert, "The Certiorari Game," in Schubert, ed., *Judicial Behavior*; and readings in *ibid*., Ch. V, "Mathematical Prediction of Judicial Behavior."

17. Wallace Mendelson, "The Neo-Behavioral Approach to the Judicial Process: A Critique," *American Political Science Review*, Vol. LVII (September 1963), pp. 593–603; and Lon Fuller, "An Afterword: Science and the Judicial Process," *Harvard Law Review*, Vol. 79 (June 1966), pp. 1604–1628.

18. Fuller, *op. cit.*, p. 1612.

19. *Ibid.*, p. 1607.

20. Mendelson, *op. cit.*, p. 593.

21. Joel B. Grossman, *Lawyers and Judges: The ABA and the Politics of Judicial Selection* (New York: Wiley, 1965). See also Jack Peltason, *Federal Courts in the Political Process* (New York: Random House, 1955), Ch. IV, "Recruiting Judges."

22. *Ibid.*, pp. 208, 209. For a survey of lawyers' opinions of the committee's work see Jack Ladinsky and Joel Grossman, "Occupational Consequences of Professional Consensus: Lawyers and the Selection of Judges," *Administrative Science Quarterly*, Vol. 11 (June 1966), pp. 79–106.

23. James Bryce, *The American Commonwealth*, 2nd ed. rev. (New York and London: Macmillan, 1891), p. 513.

24. Wallace Sayre and Herbert Kaufman, *Governing New York* (New York: Russell Sage Foundation, 1960).

25. Glen R. Winters and Robert E. Allard, "Judicial Selection and Tenure in the United States," in Jones, ed., *op. cit.*

26. Peltason, *op. cit.*, p. 54.

27. Edwin Sutherland and Donald Cressey, *Principles of Criminology*, 7th ed. (Philadelphia: Lippincott, 1966), p. 3. See also Gresham Sykes, *Crime and Society* (New York: Random House, 1956), Ch. I.

28. Hermann Mannheim, *Criminal Justice and Social Reconstruction* (New York: Oxford Univ. Press, 1946), p. 1.

29. David Matza, *Delinquency and Drift* (New York: Wiley, 1964), Ch. I.

30. Howard S. Becker, *Outsiders* (New York: Free Press, 1963), p. 9.

31. Kai T. Erikson, "Notes on the Sociology of Deviance," *Social Problems,* Vol. 9 (Spring 1962), pp. 307–314.

32. See references in Ch. Two, note 6. A classic criminological statement on "labeling" is Frank Tannenbaum's discussion of the "dramatization of evil" (early stigmatization of youngsters as delinquent), in *Crime and the Community* (New York: Columbia Univ. Press, 1957). A major statement of deviance theory in processual terms is Edwin Lemert, *Social Pathology* (New York: McGraw-Hill, 1951).

33. Harold Garfinkel, "Conditions of Successful Degradation Ceremonies," *American Journal of Sociology,* Vol. 61 (March 1956), pp. 421–422.

34. Erving Goffman, *Asylums* (New York: Anchor Books, 1961).

35. Richard D. Schwartz and Jerome H. Skolnick, "Two Studies of Legal Stigma," *Social Problems,* Vol. 10 (Fall 1962), pp. 133–142.

36. See comments of H. Laurence Ross, and rejoinder by Richard D. Schwartz and Jerome H. Skolnick, *Social Problems,* Vol. 10 (Spring 1963), pp. 390–392.

37. Joseph Goldstein, "Police Discretion Not to Invoke the Criminal Process: Low Visibility Decisions in the Administration of Justice," *Yale Law Journal,* Vol. 69 (1960), pp. 543–594; and Sanford Kadish, "Legal Norms and Discretion in the Police and Sentencing Processes," *Harvard Law Review,* Vol. 75 (March 1962), pp. 904–931.

38. Donald J. Newman, "Pleading Guilty for Consideration: A Study of Bargain Justice," *Journal of Criminal Law, Criminology and Police Science,* Vol. 46 (March–April 1956), pp. 780–790.

39. Irving Piliavin and Scott Briar, "Police Encounters with Juveniles," *American Journal of Sociology,* Vol. 70 (September 1964), pp. 206–214.

40. *Ibid.,* p. 210.

41. William A. Westley, "Violence and the Police," *American Journal of Sociology,* Vol. 49 (August 1953), pp. 34–41.

42. Arthur L. Stinchcombe, "Institutions of Privacy in the Determination of Police Administrative Practice," *American Journal of Sociology,* Vol. 69 (September 1963), pp. 150–160.

43. Jerome H. Skolnick, *Justice Without Trial: Law Enforcement in Democratic Society* (New York: Wiley, 1966). See also David J. Bordua, *The Police: Six Sociological Essays* (New York: Wiley, 1967).

44. David Sudnow, "Normal Crimes: Sociological Features of the Penal Code in a Public Defender Office," *Social Problems,* Vol. 12 (Winter 1965), pp. 255–276.

45. *Ibid.,* p. 259.

46. *Ibid.,* p. 273.

47. Ronald Goldfarb, *Ransom: A Critique of the American Bail System* (New York: Harper & Row, 1965), p. 1.

48. *Ibid.,* Ch. V.

49. Geoffrey C. Hazard, Jr., "Reflections on Four Studies of the Legal Profession," in "Law and Society," supplement to *Social Problems,* Vol. 13 (Summer 1965), pp. 50, 51.

50. Jack Ladinsky, "Careers of Lawyers, Law Practice, and Legal Institutions," *American Sociological Review,* Vol. 28 (February 1963), p. 53.

51. Jerome Carlin, *Lawyers' Ethics* (New York: Russell Sage Foundation, 1966), Ch. II, "The Social Structure of the Metropolitan Bar"; and Ladinsky, *op. cit.*

52. David Riesman, "Law and Sociology: Recruitment, Training, and Colleagueship," in Evan, ed., *op. cit.*

53. Hazard, *op. cit.*, p. 53.

54. Carlin, *Lawyers' Ethics;* and Ladinsky, *op. cit.*

55. Erwin O. Smigel, *The Wall Street Lawyer* (New York: Free Press, 1964).

56. *Ibid.*, Ch. X, "Strains and Dilemmas." For excellent fictional accounts of life and work in the large law firm see Louis Auchincloss, *Powers of Attorney* (Boston: Houghton Mifflin, 1963).

57. Jerome E. Carlin, *Lawyers on Their Own* (New Brunswick, N.J.: Rutgers Univ. Press, 1962), pp. 17–18; generally, on the background and work of these lawyers, see Chs. I, II, and III.

58. *Ibid.*, p. 125.

59. *Ibid.*, pp. 135–136.

60. *Ibid.*, p. 173.

61. *Ibid.*, Ch. V, "The Anatomy of Dissatisfaction."

62. *Ibid.*, pp. 23, 39.

63. For an interesting fictional portrayal of the lawyer in a small community see James Gould Cozzens, *The Just and the Unjust* (New York: Harcourt, Brace & World, 1942).

64. Talcott Parsons, "The Law and Social Control," in Evan, ed., *op. cit.*

65. See articles by law professor Monroe H. Freedman and others to appear in a forthcoming issue of the *University of Michigan Law Review,* concerning the question of whether defense lawyers in criminal cases always must be truthful and candid in court. Reported in *Boston Globe* (June 5, 1966), p. A–5. See also Walter F. Murphy and C. Herman Pritchett, *Courts, Judges and Politics* (New York: Random House, 1961), Ch. IX, "The Bar."

66. Parsons, *op. cit.*, p. 69.

67. Carlin, *Lawyers' Ethics.*

68. Jerome Carlin, *Lawyers on Their Own* (New Brunswick, N.J.: Rutgers Univ. Press, 1962), p. 192.

69. Kenneth J. Reichstein, "Ambulance Chasing: A Study of Deviation and Control Within the Legal Profession," *Social Problems,* Vol. 13 (Summer 1965), pp. 3–17; and Carlin, *Lawyers on Their Own*, pp. 71–91.

70. Hubert J. O'Gorman, *Lawyers and Matrimonial Cases* (New York: Free Press, 1963).

71. *Ibid.*, pp. 33, 34. (Italics in original.)

72. See the classic study by A. V. Dicey, *Lectures on the Relation Between Law and Public Opinion in England During the Nineteenth Century* (London: Macmillan, 1905); and more recently Morris Ginsberg, ed., *Law and Opinion in England in the Twentieth Century* (Berkeley, Cal.: Univ. of California Press, 1959).

73. Francis A. Allen, *The Borderland of Criminal Justice* (Chicago: Univ. of Chicago Press, 1964), p. 31.

74. *Repouille v. U.S.*, 165 F.2d. 152 (2d. Cir., 1947); reprinted in Donnelly, Goldstein, and Schwartz, *op. cit.*, pp. 124–126.

75. *Ibid.*
76. See the materials reprinted in Donnelly, Goldstein, and Schwartz, *op. cit.*, pp. 126–132.
77. Julius Cohen, Reginald A. H. Robson, and Alan Bates, *Parental Authority: The Community and the Law* (New Brunswick, N.J.: Rutgers Univ. Press, 1958). For critical comment see Jerome Skolnick, "The Sociology of Law in America: Overview and Trends," in "Law and Society," supplement to *Social Problems*, Vol. 13 (Summer 1965), p. 31.
78. Arnold M. Rose and Arthur Prell, "Does the Punishment Fit the Crime? A Study in Social Valuation," *American Journal of Sociology*, Vol. 61 (November 1955), pp. 247–259.
79. G. M. Gilbert, "Crime and Punishment: An Exploratory Comparison of Public, Criminal, and Penological Attitudes," *Mental Hygiene*, Vol. 42 (1958), pp. 550–557.
80. Elizabeth A. Rooney and Don C. Gibbons, "Social Reactions to 'Crimes Without Victims,'" *Social Problems*, Vol. 13 (Spring 1966), p. 407.
81. See John Kitsuse, "Societal Reaction to Deviance: Problems of Theory and Method," *Social Problems*, Vol. 9 (Winter 1962), pp. 249–256; and J. L. Simmons, "Public Stereotypes of Deviants," *Social Problems*, Vol. 13 (Fall 1965), pp. 223–232.
82. W. J. Blum and Harry Kalven, Jr., "The Art of Public Opinion Research: A Lawyer's Appraisal of an Emerging Science," *University of Chicago Law Review*, Vol. 24 (1956), pp. 1–12; reprinted in Donnelly, Goldstein, and Schwartz, *op. cit.*, pp. 132–136.
83. William Stringfellow, *My People is the Enemy* (New York: Holt, Rinehart, & Winston, 1964).
84. An ongoing study of the role of one such intermediary, the claims adjuster, is described by H. Laurence Ross, "Settled Out of Court: An Interim Report," New York University, New York, 1966, duplicated.

Chapter Five: Scientific Justice and Legality

1. See the symposium on "Jurimetrics," *Law and Contemporary Problems*, Vol. XXVIII (Winter 1963). See also comments by Jerome Skolnick, "The Sociology of Law in America: Overview and Trends," in "Law and Society," supplement to *Social Problems*, Vol. 13 (Summer 1965), pp. 27–28.
2. Julian A. Woodward, "A Scientific Attempt to Provide Evidence for a Decision on Change of Venue," *American Sociological Review*, Vol. 17 (August 1952), pp. 447–452.
3. See Note, "Public Opinion Surveys as Evidence: The Pollsters Go to Court," *Harvard Law Review*, Vol. 66 (1953), pp. 498–512.
4. *Brown v. Bd. of Education of Topeka*, 347 U.S. 483 (1954).

5. "The effects of segregation and the consequences of desegregation: a social science statement," reprinted in C. Auerbach, *et al.*, eds., *The Legal Process* (San Francisco: Chandler, 1961), pp. 105–114.

6. Herbert Wechsler, "Toward Neutral Principles of Constitutional Law," *Harvard Law Review*, Vol. 73 (November 1959), p. 15; but for a contrasting view see Arthur S. Miller and Ronald F. Howell, "The Myth of Neutrality in Constitutional Adjudication," *University of Chicago Law Review*, Vol. 27 (Summer 1960), pp. 661–695.

7. Edmond Cahn, "A Dangerous Myth in the School Segregation Cases," *New York University Law Review*, Vol. 30 (1955); reprinted in Auerbach, *et al.*, eds., *op. cit.*, p. 124. See also Herbert Garfinkel, "Social Science Evidence and the School Segregation Cases," *Journal of Politics*, Vol. 21 (1959), reprinted in Auerbach, *et al.*, eds. *op. cit.*, pp. 125–128; and comment by Skolnick, *op. cit.*, pp. 21–22.

8. *Evers v. Jackson Municipal Separate School District, et al.* (U.S. Dist. Ct. for So. Dist. Mississippi. Civil Action No. 3379, opinion rendered July 1964 by U.S. Dist. Ct. Judge Sidney Mize); reprinted in National Putnam Letters Committee, *The Evers Opinion* (Washington, n.d.), pp. 15, 17.

9. Bernard L. Diamond, "The Fallacy of the Impartial Expert," *Archives of Criminal Psychodynamics*, Vol. III (1959); reprinted in R. C. Donnelly, J. Goldstein, and R. D. Schwartz, *Criminal Law* (New York: Free Press, 1962), pp. 798–800. On the general issue of insanity as a defense see materials in Donnelly, Goldstein and Schwartz, *op. cit.*, pp. 733–847.

10. Francis A. Allen, *The Borderland of Criminal Justice* (Chicago: Univ. of Chicago Press, 1964), especially pp. 25–41.

11. Gustav L. Schramm, "Philosophy of the Juvenile Court," *The Annals*, Vol. 261 (January 1949), p. 101. See also *People v. Lewis*, 260 N.Y. 171 (1932), cert. den. 289 U.S. 709 (1933); reprinted in Sheldon Glueck, *The Problem of Delinquency* (Boston: Houghton Mifflin, 1959), pp. 338–343.

12. See Edwin Sutherland and Donald Cressey, *Principles of Criminology*, 7th ed. (Philadelphia: Lippincott, 1966), Ch. XX. See also Albert K. Cohen and James F. Short, Jr., "Juvenile Delinquency," in Robert Merton and Robert Nisbet, eds., *Contemporary Social Problems*, 2nd ed. (New York: Harcourt, Brace & World, 1966), pp. 84–88.

13. Sol Rubin, "The Legal Character of Juvenile Delinquency," *The Annals*, Vol. 261 (January 1949), pp. 1–8.

14. Paul W. Tappan, "Treatment Without Trial," *Social Forces*, Vol. 24 (March 1946), pp. 306–311. See also Paul W. Tappan, *Delinquent Girls in Court* (New York: Columbia Univ. Press, 1947; and Margaret K. Rosenheim, ed., *Justice for the Child* (New York: Free Press, 1962).

15. Allen, *op. cit.*, p. 18.

16. See *In re: Holmes*, 379 Pa. 589, 109 A.2d. 523 (1954); reprinted in Glueck, *op. cit.*, pp. 422–433, especially the dissent of Justice Musmanno. A decision of the U.S. Supreme Court in May of 1967, *In the Matter of Gault*, 87 S. Ct. 1428 (1967), has held unconstitutional the denial of various procedural safeguards in a juvenile court case arising in Arizona. It is expected that this ruling will have a significant impact on such procedures

in other jurisdictions as well. For excerpts of the decision and commentary, see *The New York Times*, May 16, 1967, p. 1.

17. David Matza, *Delinquency and Drift* (New York: Wiley, 1964).
18. *Ibid.*, pp. 133–134.
19. I am indebted to Stephen Lenn for research assistance in connection with this topic.
20. See *Mental Illness and Due Process, Report and Recommendations on Admission to Mental Hospitals under New York Law, by the Special Committee to Study Commitment Procedures of the Association of the Bar of the City of New York, in Cooperation with the Cornell Law School* (Ithaca, N.Y.: Cornell Univ. Press, 1962. See also F. T. Lindman and D. M. McIntyre, eds., *The Mentally Disabled and the Law, Report of the American Bar Foundation on the Rights of the Mentally Ill* (Chicago: Univ. of Chicago Press, 1961); and materials in Jay Katz, Joseph Goldstein, and Alan M. Dershowitz, *Psychoanalysis, Psychiatry, and Law* (New York: Free Press, 1967).
21. See Edwin M. Schur, "Psychiatrists Under Attack: The Rebellious Dr. Szasz," *Atlantic Monthly* (June 1966), pp. 72–76.
22. Thomas S. Szasz, *Psychiatric Justice* (New York: Macmillan, 1965), p. 13.
23. Thomas S. Szasz, *Law, Liberty and Psychiatry* (New York: Macmillan, 1963). See also Thomas S. Szasz, *The Myth of Mental Illness* (New York: Hoeber, 1961). For a sociologist's somewhat similar view of the hospitalization process see Erving Goffman, *Asylums* (New York: Anchor Books, 1961).
24. Thomas J. Scheff, "The Societal Reaction to Deviance: Ascriptive Elements in the Psychiatric Screening of Mental Patients in a Midwestern State," *Social Problems,* Vol. 11 (Spring 1964), pp. 401–413; also reported in Thomas J. Scheff, *Being Mentally Ill* (Chicago: Aldine, 1966), pp. 128–154.
25. *Ibid., Social Problems,* p. 405.
26. *Ibid.*, p. 409.
27. Scheff, *Being Mentally Ill, op. cit.*, pp. 155–168.
28. Skolnick, *op. cit.*, pp. 15–18.
29. Selznick, "Sociology of Law," paper prepared for the *International Encyclopedia of the Social Sciences,* Berkeley, Cal., April 1965, mimeographed, pp. 15–17.
30. Fuller, *The Morality of Law*, (New Haven: Yale Univ. Press, 1964), p. 162.
31. Szasz, *Law, Liberty, and Psychiatry, op. cit.*

Selected Readings

❖❖❖

Berman, Harold J. *Justice in the U.S.S.R.* rev. ed., enlarged. New York: Vintage Books, 1963. A stimulating and comprehensive analysis of the development and major themes of the Soviet legal system.

Caplovitz, David. *The Poor Pay More.* New York: Free Press, 1963. A survey study of the lower-class citizen as consumer, revealing the inadequate legal knowledge and low access to legal assistance that render such persons prey to exploitation.

Carlin, Jerome 'E. *Lawyers on Their Own.* New Brunswick, N.J.: Rutgers Univ. Press, 1962. An interview study of individual practitioners of law in Chicago, describing career patterns, organization of legal practice, economic strains, and ethical dilemmas.

————. *Lawyers' Ethics.* New York: Russell Sage Foundation, 1966. An analysis of conformity to, and deviation from, norms of professional conduct, based on a large-scale survey of the New York City bar.

Cogley, John, *et al. Natural Law and Modern Society.* Cleveland: Meridian, 1966. Essays on the present-day relevance of natural-law perspectives, including Philip Selznick's important statement, "Sociology and Natural Law."

Evan, William M., ed. *Law and Sociology: Exploratory Essays.* New York: Free Press, 1962. A collection that includes treatment of a number of theoretical, methodological, and substantive areas of cross-disciplinary concern.

Frank, Jerome. *Courts on Trial.* Princeton: Princeton Univ. Press, 1949. A caustic appraisal of the adversary procedure of our courts and an important statement of the legal-realist approach to the judicial process.

Fuller, Lon L. *The Morality of Law.* New Haven: Yale Univ. Press, 1964. A critical study of various approaches to the meaning and essence of law,

228

which develops the author's conception of that "internal morality" basic to a well-developed legal system.

Hart, H. L. A. *The Concept of Law.* London: Oxford Univ. Press, 1961. A critical analysis of the nature and groundings of legal systems in their relation to custom, force, and morals.

————. *Law, Liberty and Morality.* Stanford, Cal.: Stanford Univ. Press, 1963. An elegant statement in defense of limiting the scope of the criminal law so as not to interfere with the realm of private morality. Should be read in conjunction with the opposing Patrick Devlin. *The Enforcement of Morals.* London: Oxford Univ. Press, 1965.

Henson, Ray D., ed. *Landmarks of Law.* Boston: Beacon Press, 1963, paperback ed. Classic legal essays, ranging from Oliver Wendell Holmes, "The Path of the Law" to Lon L. Fuller, "The Case of the Speluncean Explorers."

Hoebel, E. A. *The Law of Primitive Man.* Cambridge: Harvard Univ. Press, 1961. A study of the role of law in preliterate society, with specific description and analysis of the legal norms and institutions of selected societies.

Jones, Harry W., ed. *The Courts, the Public, and the Law Explosion.* Englewood Cliffs, N.J.: Prentice-Hall, 1965. Essays on the organization, procedures, and problems of our civil and criminal courts.

Kalven, Harry, Jr. and Hans Zeisel. *The American Jury.* Boston: Little, Brown, 1966. The second major publication of the Chicago Jury Project. A general analysis of the criminal jury trial based largely on data from a questionnaire study dealing with over 3,500 actual jury trials.

"Law and Society," supplement to *Social Problems,* Vol. 13 (Summer 1965). A collection of essays by sociologists and lawyers, including a lengthy overview of the developing field of the sociology of law by Jerome Skolnick.

Nader, Laura, ed. *The Ethnography of Law.* Special Publication, *American Anthropologist,* Vol. 67, No. 6, Pt. 2 (December 1965). Theoretical essays and empirical reports assessing the present and potential contribution of anthropology to an understanding of legal systems.

O'Gorman, Hubert J. *Lawyers and Matrimonial Cases.* New York: Free Press, 1963. An interview study of New York lawyers specializing in matrimonial practices, indicating how legal norms and procedures can shape law practice and lawyers' self-conceptions.

Rheinstein, Max, ed. *Max Weber on Law in Economy and Society.* trans. by E. Shils and M. Rheinstein. Cambridge: Harvard Univ. Press, 1954. Weber's major writings on law, rich in historical material and major theoretical formulations.

Schubert, Glendon, ed. *Judicial Behavior.* Chicago: Rand McNally, 1964. A reader on the judicial process, including both classic, legal and philosophical analyses and modern empirical studies by the so-called neobehavioral school in political science.

Skolnick, Jerome H. *Justice Without Trial.* New York: Wiley, 1966. A report of an intensive observational study of the police in action with special reference to vice-law enforcement. Also includes general discussion of the place of police activity in the legal system of a democratic society.

Smigel, Erwin O. *The Wall Street Lawyer*. New York: Free Press, 1964. An interview study of lawyers in the top twenty large law firms in New York City. Detailed information on selective recruitment, organization of legal practice, career patterns within the firms, and strains and dilemmas of bureaucratization.

Zeisel, Hans, Harry Kalven, Jr., and Bernard Buckholz, *Delay in the Court*. Boston: Little, Brown, 1959. The first book-length report deriving from the Chicago Jury Project. Intensive empirical analysis of court procedures and congestion (with special attention to personal injury suits) and critical analysis of various proposals for reform.

Index

abortion, law and, 118, 133–134, 180

adjudication, 56, 77, 83, 126, 198

administrative agencies, 4, 124–126, 188, 198–201

adversary procedure, 13, 40–48, 50, 124, 188, 198–201

Africans, legal subordination of, 90

Allen, Francis, 190

American Bar Association, 150

American law, trends in, 121–126; see also law

American Law Institute, 132, 178

amicus curiae briefs, 152

analytical jurisprudence, 26; see also jurisprudence

Ancient Law (Maine), 32

anthropology, law and, 11, 73–75, 77–79

antimiscegenation laws, 94

antiparasite laws, 119

apartheid policy, 90

appellate review systems in labor unions, 125

Aquinas, Saint Thomas, 25, 51, 61

Aristotle, 25, 51

Arnold, Thurman, 50

"assumption of differentiation," 154

Augustine, Saint, 61

Austin, John, on jurisprudence, 25–27, 75

bail, inequities of, 162

Baldwin, James, 94

bar associations, 101, 105, 150, 174, 182

"bargain justice," 160

"basic norm," 27–28; see also norm(s)

Becker, Howard S., 154

behavioral studies of judicial process, 146–150

Bendix, Reinhard, 13, 108

Bentham, Jeremy, 25, 33–36, 42, 127

Berman, Harold, 83, 116–120

Blumrosen, Alfred, 121–122

Bodin, Jean, 26

Bohannan, Paul, 77–78, 127

"borderland of criminal law," 133

Brandeis, Justice Louis D., 42

"Brandeis brief," 42

Bredemeier, Harry C., 81–83

Briar, Scott, 158

Brown v. Bd. of Education, 185

Bryce, James, 151

bureaucracy, 109, 163, 203

Cahn, Edmond, 42, 186

California Civil Justice Project, 146

canons of legal ethics, 173, 175
capital punishment, 7, 119, 131
Caplovitz, David, 98–99
Carlin, Jerome, 95–96, 103–104, 168–171, 174
"case mortality," 157
Catholicism, natural law and, 52, 54
"Causes of Popular Dissatisfaction with the Administration of Criminal Justice" (Pound), 42
"charismatic" authority, 109
Cheka, Russian secret police, 116
Cheyenne Way, The (Llewellyn-Hoebel), 45, 79
Chicago Jury Project, 142–145, 189
China, Communist, 120
Cicero, on natural law, 51
civil disobedience, 60–62
civil liberties, 149, 195, 201
civil rights, 7, 60, 87, 95, 105, 162
Clark, Kenneth, 186
class and law in United States, 92–101
"class enemies," 91
class legislation, 90
coercion, 59; Malinowski on, 74; right of state to, 89; Selznick on, 76
Comrades' Courts in Soviet Union, 119
commercial transactions, 122
commitment, psychiatric, 194–198; false, 195; involuntary, 194, 196; nonjudicial, 194
Communist China, 120
"concept of law," 76
conflict: law and social, 139–140; of lawyer's roles, 172–177
contracts, 96, 122; breaches of, 130; commercial, 129; consumers', 98; freedom of, 114, 121
corporation law, 122
counsel in legal systems, 111–112
courts: American, 69, 83, 89, 123, 126, 197; adjudication in, 201; appellate, 49, 102, 166; behavior of, 46–49; Comrades', in Soviet Union, 119; congestion of, 124; criminal, 190, 204; international, 128; judges and juries in, 142–153; juvenile, 158, 189–193, 198; lower, 49; low-income families and, 99; under National Socialism in Germany, 89; People's, in Soviet Union, 116; physician and psychiatrist in, 197–198; and trials, 49, 146; see also United States Supreme Court
Courts on Trial (Frank), 46
court trials, 47, 90, 142–153, 200–201; see also trial courts; trials
Cressey, Donald, 153
crime: Durkheim on, 110–111, 113; normal, 160; prosecution and, 157; regulatory, 199; self-image in, 134; society and, 113; substantive law and, 122; war, 62–67
Crime and Custom in Savage Society (Malinowski), 73–74
Crimes Without Victims (Schur), 133, 155–156, 180
criminal court versus juvenile court, 190
criminal justice, 96, 100, 110, 188; administration of, 153–163; patterns of, 162–163; processes of, 161
criminal law, analogy doctrine in, 117; "borderland" of, 133; deviant behavior and, 134, 180; failure of legal norms in, 131; indigence and, 100; lawyer conflict in, 172–173; legislation and, 176; Marxist theory and, 115; Negro and, 95; public opinion and, 179–180; sociologists on, 9; Wolfenden Committee on, 132
"criminal law community," 159, 204
cultural relativism, 56–57
cultural schools, 25
"customary international law," 65, 128

death penalty, 7, 119, 131
"degrees of legality," 57; see also legality

Delay in the Court (Chicago Jury Project), 146
Delinquency and Drift (Matza), 193
delinquents, processing of, 158, 189–193; *see also* juvenile delinquent
desegregation suits, 185–187
deviant behavior, 134, 154–157, 180
Devlin, Patrick, 132
discrimination, legal aspect of, 94, 137; Negroes and, 162; *see also* Negro
division of labor, Durkheim on, 110
divorce laws, 175–176, 199, 200
doll tests as evidence, 186
Douglas, William O., 50
drug addiction, 133–134, 180
Durkheim, Emile, 33, 110, 112–113

Ehrlich, Eugen, 25, 37–39, 42, 127
Eichmann, Adolf, 66
enforcement discretion, 157–163
"equality before the law" concept, 14, 94
ethics, legal, 101, 172 177
euthanasia, 178
Evan, William, 125 126, 130
evidence, social sciences and, 42, 184–188

"fact skepticism," 46
fair-housing legislation, 60
"false commitment," 195
family, law and the, 96, 122, 126
food and drug laws, 199
formalistic jurisprudence, 24–30
formal rationality, 13–14, 109–110
Frank, Jerome, 25, 43, 46–50, 142, 178
freedom of contract, 114, 121
Freud, Sigmund, 50
Friedrich, Carl, 33
Fromm, Erich, 52
Fuller, Lon L., 19–20, 22, 55–57, 148, 200–201
functional interdependence, 80, 88

functional theory, 79–85; criticisms of, 82–85
Fundamental Principles of the Sociology of Law (Ehrlich), 37

gambling, 134
games theory, 148
Gandhi, Mohandes K., 60
Garfinkel, Harold, 155
garnishees, 98
"gastronomical jurisprudence," 146
Geis, Gilbert, 40–41
gemeinschaft and *gesellschaft*, 70–71, 114
German law, 30, 89
Germany: Nazi regime in, 62–65, 89; Nuremberg trials in, 63–67
Gerth, Hans, 87
Gideon v. Wainwright, 100
Goldfarb, Ronald, 162
Gordis, Robert, 58
Gray, John Chipman, 31
Great Britain, central planning in, 92
grievance procedures in industry, 125
Grossman, Joel, 150–151
Grotius, Hugo, 25, 52
groups, minority, 135; *see also* minority rights
Grundnorm, 27

Hand, Judge Learned, 178
Hart, H. L. A., 52, 59, 72, 76–77, 80, 132–133
Hazard, Geoffrey C., Jr., 163
historical jurisprudence, 25, 30–33, 107
Hobbes, Thomas, 26
Hoebel, E. A., 45, 72, 75, 79–80
Holmes, Justice Oliver Wendell, 25, 43–45, 50
homosexuality, 132–134, 178, 180
Howard, Jan, 95–96
Hughes, Everett, 103
Human Relations Area Files, 111

human rights, law and, 12
Hutchins, Robert, 52, 129

ideational values, 115
Ihering, Rudolph von, 25, 36
immorality, law and, 132–133
"incipient law," 125
individual freedoms, law and, 12
individual practitioners, 168–172, 174; *see also* lawyer
industrial societies, 109, 113, 125, 202
insanity-as-a-defense problem, 188–189
institutions: international, 78; legal, 77–78, 84, 89–91, 94–95, 108, 111–112, 120, 125–126, 129–130, 140, 188, 190, 203; social, 77, 117
insurance, 122
International Court of Justice, 128
international law, 63, 64, 65, 76, 78, 113, 128–129, 174
International Military Tribunal, 63
Introduction to the Principles of Morals and Legislation, An (Bentham), 34
irrationality, legal, 109

Jouvenal, Bertrand de, 86
judges: appellate, 123, 147; background characteristics of, 147; behavior of, 49; courts and juries in relation to, 142–153; as human beings, 23; in mental commitment process, 197; perspectives of, 142; power wielded by, 101; realists' view of, 47; recruitment of, 150–151; role of in legal system, 48–50; trial court and, 46–47; voting patterns of, 147–149
judicial decision-making, 30, 48, 83, 146–150
judicial policy-making, 102, 123
judicial recruitment, 150–151
"jural postulates," 40
juries, 142–153, 201; behavior of, 142,

145; "bugging" of, 144; deliberations of, 143–145; foreman of, 145; Negroes on, 94; mock, 144–145; qualifications and role of jurors for, 47, 50, 145; scientific justice and, 183
jurisprudence, 17–67; analytical, 26; cultural and historical, 30–33; formalistic approaches in, 24–30, 84; "gastronomical," 146; historical, 107; influences from, 23–24; meaning of, 17–18; natural law, 51–58; positivistic, 24, 26, 29; realist, 43–50; sociological, 37–43; utilitarian, 33–36
justice: criminal, 96, 100, 110, 153–163, 188; "individualized" or "personalized," 191; informal, 161; *kadi* form of, 193; legality and, 55–58; the Negro and, 181–182; obedience and, 58–67; procedural, 97; "scientific," 183–204; substantive, 84, 97, 110, 200
Justice Without Trial (Skolnick), 159
juvenile court, 158, 189–193, 198
juveniles, police encounters with, 158

kadi justice, 193
Kelsen, Hans, 25, 27–28
Kessler, Friedrich, 51
King, Martin Luther, 61
kinship, social control and, 121
Kirchheimer, Otto, 90
Kohler, Josef, 40
kvutza, Israeli, 71

labor law, 121, 125, 129
landlord-tenant relations, 200
Laski, Harold J., 139
law: American trends in, 121–126; attitudes toward, 177–182; basic functions of, 79–82; definitions of, 10, 68–79; as instrument of change, 135–139; limits of, 127–135; research areas in, 141–182;

two-edged nature of, 11–12, 89, 139–140, 202–204
Law and the Modern Mind (Frank), 46, 50
Law as a Means to an End (Ihering), 36
"law as prediction," 48–49
law firms: influence of, 102–103, 165; large, 165–168
"law jobs," 45, 79
law practice, individual, 168–172; *see also* lawyers
"law review," 165
lawyers: as trusted advisors, 182; civil-rights cases and, 105; conflict of roles of, 172–177; dual concept of, 173–174; ethics and, 101, 104, 172–177; Hazard on, 163; as individual practitioners, 168–172; large-firm, 103, 166–168, 174; in legal assistance programs, 105; lower-class need for, 96; matrimonial practice of, 176; "moral division of labor" among, 106, 174; Negro, 105; perspectives of, 142; power positions of, 102; recruitment of, 103, 106; social background of, 104, 164–165, 168–169; specialized individual practice, 171; Wall Street, 104, 166–168, 170; values of future practitioners, 106
Lawyers on Their Own (Carlin), 168
legal action, limits of, 127–135
Legal Aid Society, 99
legal assistance programs, 96, 100–101, 104–105
legal change, 107–141
legal education: in Soviet Union, 118–119; in United States, 29, 47, 50, 142, 165
legal ethics, 101, 104, 172–177
legal functionaries, power of, 85, 101
legal institutions, 4, 77–78, 84, 89–91, 94–95, 108, 111–112, 125–126, 129–130, 140, 188, 190, 203; Bohannan on, 77; changing nature of, 123–126; international, 129; the Ne-

gro and, 94; power and, 87; "rational" quality of, 108; in Soviet Union, 90–91; use of, for political ends, 89–91, 140
legality: ideal of, 55–58; nonadversary procedure and, 198–201; procedural requirements for, 55–56; right to resist and, 61; "scientific" justice and, 183–204; war crimes and, 62–67
legal norms, 28, 81, 131, 160–161, 174, 179, 202–203; *see also* norm(s)
legal policy, sociologist and, 14–15, 177, 187–188, 204
"legal positivism," 24, 26, 29
legal realism and realists, 25, 35–36, 39, 43–50, 142, 146, 200
legal sanity, determination of, 189
legal systems: basic functions of, 79–82; conflict inherent in, 83, 139–140, 202; dysfunctional aspects of, 62, 82–85; evolution of, 73–78, 107–108, 110–116, 121–126; integrative function of, 80–81; interdependence with other subsystems, 4, 81–82; normative aspect of, 18, 54–57, 59, 61, 198–200, 204; stratification and, 85–106; uniformities and diversity in, 11, 73, 111–113
legal work, styles of, 163–177
legislation: antidiscrimination, 135–137; "class," 90; conditions influencing impact of, 138–139; "political system" concerned with, 81; private morality and, 35–36, 132–136; social impact of, 135–139; sociological importance of, 83
legitimacy, coercion and, 59, 75–76
liability, absolute and strict, 199
"Limits of Effective Legal Action, The" (Pound), 42
litigation, administrative agencies and, 125
living law, 37–38, 177
Llewellyn, Karl, 25, 43, 45–46, 72, 79
low-income families or clients, 98–99, 106

Macauley, Stewart, 130
MacIver, Robert, 7, 86–87
Maine, Sir Henry, 13, 25, 32–33, 113–114
Malinowski, Bronislaw, 73–74
management, labor and, 125
Manhattan Bail Project, 162
Mannheim, Hermann, 153
Mannheim, Karl, 6, 92
Marxist theory, law and, 70, 91, 114, 120, 139
mass society, 121, 198
matrimonial law, 175–176, 199, 200
"maturity of a legal order," 57
Matza, David, 193
mechanical solidarity, 110
mediation, 111–112
mental commitment, process of, 194–198
"merit selection," 152
Miller, James C., 111–112
Mills, C. Wright, 87, 102
minority groups, treatment of, 90–94, 135
minority rights, 136–137
Model Penal Code, 132, 178
Moore, Underhill, 38
"moral division of labor" among lawyers, 103, 106, 174, 182
morality: "internal," of law, 55; law and, 17–18, 24, 26, 50, 51–52, 61, 66–67, 69–70; legislation of, 135; private, 35–36, 132–136
Morality of Law, The (Fuller), 19, 55
moral law, 26, 132
mores, 131, 135; Sumner on, 127
moshav, Israeli, 71
"mutual accommodation" of judicial and political systems, 152

natural law, 23, 25, 50–60; civil disobedience and, 61; nontheological, 52; Nuremberg trials and, 65; "minimum content of" (Hart), 72; post-

war period, 63; "procedural," 53; Roman Catholicism and, 52–54
Nazi regime, war crimes and, 62–65, 89
negligence, 78
Negro, the: civil rights for, 7; criminal law and, 95; disenfranchisement of, 94; doll test and, 186; jury duty for, 94; in legal profession, 94, 105; legal treatment of, 40, 93, 95, 100, 136–138, 162, 181–187; police and, 60, 188; as "second-class citizen," 94
"neighborhood law office," 100
"neutral principles of constitutional law," 186
New Deal, 50, 103
New Economic Policy (NEP), Soviet Union, 116–117
"New Property, The" (Reich), 97
New York City, law and lawyers in, 98, 104, 151, 174–175
"nonaction" as a form of action, 48
norm(s), "basic" (Kelsen), 27–28; distinguishing between law and, 73–79; legal, 28, 81, 131, 160–161, 174, 179, 202; of "living law," 38; in moshav, 71; "patterned evasion" of, 133; in private systems, 125–126; procedural, 53–56, 125, 198–201; racial segregation, 93; reinstitutionalization of, 77; social, 58, 73, 75, 131; stated and actual, 180; within legal profession, 172–177
"normative" ideals, 5, 140
"normative systems," 54
Northrop, F. S. C., 38
Nuremberg Laws, 90
"Nuremberg principle," 65
Nuremberg trials, 63–67

obedience, concept of, 58–67, 76, 85
O'Gorman, Hubert J., 175–176
On the Division of Labor in Society (Durkheim), 110
order, law and, 68–106, 139–140

organic solidarity, 110
organization, large-scale, 121–122, 124–125

Page, Charles H., 7
"parental law," 120
Parsons, Talcott, 80, 172–173
"Path of the Law, The" (Holmes), 44
"patterned evasion" of norms, 133
Peltason, Jack, 153
penology, sociological research in, 34, 153
People's Courts in Soviet Union, 116–117
personal-injury suits, 146, 175–176, 199–200
Piliavin, Irving, 158
pleasure-pain psychology, 131
police, 111–112; corruption in, 134; international, 129; juveniles and, 158, 161–162; pressures on, 176; secret, 116; violence by, 159
policy-making, judicial, 123, 177
"political justice," 66, 86
political parties, 151
political rights, 87
political scientists, 146–150
political systems, Parsons on, 81, 83
political trials, 66
poor, legal needs of the, 141
Poor Pay More, The (Caplovitz), 98
positive law, 23, 28, 37–38, 52
positivistic jurisprudence, 24, 26, 29
Pound, Roscoe, 25, 36, 39–43, 121, 127
power, 85–106; bargaining, 121–122; characteristics of, 85; law, class, and, 92–101; of legal functionaries, 85, 101; legal system and, 85–88
prejudice: jury, 145; racial, 161; reduction of, 135–137
pressure groups, 152
"primary rules" (Hart), 76–77
primitive law, 73, 86, 107
Pritchett, C. Herman, 147
private legal systems, 125–126, 188

private morality, 132
"procedural natural law," 53
procedural norms, 53–56, 125, 198–201; see also norm(s)
procedure: administrative, 123–126; adversary, 13, 46–48, 56, 124, 188, 198–201; grievance, 125; juvenile court, 189–190; legality and, 55–56, 198–201; mental commitment, 194–198; organizational due process and, 125–126; substance and, 12–13, 202–203
Prohibition, 133
property law, 78, 115
prostitution, 132–134, 159
psychiatric commitment, 194–198
Psychiatric Justice (Szasz), 196
psychiatrists, law and, 195–198
psychoanalysis, Freudian, 50
public opinion, law and, 177–182
public assistance, 97
public defender, 160
punishment: Bentham on, 34; capital, 7, 119, 131; social functions of, 113
"pure theory of law," 27

"quasi-legal" phenomena, 125

race relations, legal reform in, 105
racial prejudice, 90–95, 135, 161, 182
racial segregation, 93, 185
Radcliffe-Brown, H., 74
rape, 184
rationality, substantive and formal, 13–14, 84, 108–110
reciprocity principle, 73–74, 86
regulatory crimes, 199
"rehabilitative ideal," 190, 194
Reich, Charles, 97
repressive law, 110–113
restitutive law, 110–113
"revolt against formalism," 50
Rheinstein, Max, 75
Riesman, David, 6, 165
rights: civil, see civil rights; indi-

vidual, 136; minority, 136–137; Negro's, *see* Negro, the; political, 87; "right to resist," 61

roles: analysis of, in legal system, 4; judges', nature of and constraints in, 47–50, 55–57, 81, 85, 146–152; lawyers', in stratification order, 101–106; lawyers', variety of, 163–177; of police, 158–160; of psychiatrists, 194–198; of public defenders, 160

Roman Catholicism, natural law and, 52–54

Rose, Arnold, 83

Ross, Edward A., 40

"rule of law," 53, 67, 89

"rule of men," 67

rules: adjudication, 77; of change, 76; primary, 76–77, 123; of recognition, 76; secondary, 76–77; substantive, 201

"rule skepticism," 46

"rules of war," 128

Russian law, 117, 120

sanctions, legal and social, 7, 59, 73, 75, 130–131, 154–157; *see also* norm(s)

Savigny, Friedrich Karl von, 25, 30–32

Scandinavia, central planning in, 92

Scheff, Thomas, 197–198

Schermerhorn, Richard A., 85

Schwartz, Richard, 71–72, 111–112, 157

"scientific" justice: legality and, 183–204; social science and, 184–188; specialized tribunals and, 188–201

secondary rules, 76–77

segregation, 185–187; institutionalized, 192

Selznick, Philip, 7, 51, 54–59, 76, 121–122, 125, 200

sensate values, 115

sexual offenses, 134

Simmel, Georg, 86

Simon, Rita James, 145

Skolnick, Jerome, 125, 157, 159, 161, 198

Small, Albion, 40–41

Smigel, Erwin, 102, 166

social change, law and, 107–141

social control: formal and informal, 7, 35, 70–72, 77, 127; law as mechanism of, 7, 39–41, 80; by law, limits of, 35, 42, 127–139; within legal profession, 172–177; *see also* norm(s), sanctions

Social Darwinism, 127

social psychologists on race, 187

social sciences, evidence from, 179–181, 184–188

"social utilitarianism," 36

socialization system ("pattern maintenance"), 82

societal reactions, deviance and, 154–157

society: American, 7, 69, 92, 104, 121; heterogeneous, 37–38; homogeneous, 32; industrial, 109, 113, 202; mass, 121, 198; primitive, 70, 86; socialist, 116–119; Western, 108, 115, 122

sociological jurists and jurisprudence, 25, 37–38, 42–43, 142

sociologists: as expert witnesses, 184–188; assessment of public opinion by, 177–182; cultural relativism of, 56–58, 63; lawyers and, communication between, 6, 163–164, 204; neglect of jurisprudence by, 17; neglect of law by, 5–8; normative realm and, 5, 17–18, 54–57; orientations to legal system of, 4–5, 8–14, 68–70, 108–115, 127, 140, 202–204; recruitment to sociology of law of, 8–9; studies of law in action by, 141–182

Sorokin, Pitirim, 115–116

South Africa, Republic of, 90

Soviet Union, 63, 90–91, 116–121

Spencer, Herbert, 127

"status-degradation ceremony," 155

status-to-contract trend (Maine), 13, 32, 113
Stinchcombe, Arthur L., 159
Stone, Julius, 26
stratification, 85–106, 161, 164; in legal profession, 104, 114, 174; in Soviet Union, 91; see also class and law in United States, minority groups, power
Stringfellow, William, 182
substance, procedure and, 12–13
substantive law, 12–14, 42, 83, 92, 115, 120, 122–123, 176, 203
Sumner, William Graham, 35, 127
"Suppression of Communism Act," 90
suppressive regime, 90
Sutherland, Edwin, 131, 153
Szasz, Thomas S., 195–196, 201

Tappan, Paul, 192
tax avoidance or evasion, 173
"therapeutic state," 201
Thoreau, Henry David, 60
Third Reich, see Germany
Tocqueville, Alexis de, 101
tort law, 122, 199
totalitarian regime, 92
trade unions, 126
"traditional" authority, 109
transactions, commercial, 122, 130
trial courts, 49, 142, 146, 200–201
trial judges, 47
trials: criminal, 188, 190, 196; jury, 201; political, 66; war-crimes, 62–67
tribunals, 123–124; international, 64, 128; specialized, 188–194

Trobriand Islanders, 73–74
trusts, 78

unemployment compensation, 97
United Nations, strengthening of, 129
United States Supreme Court, 49, 100, 121, 135, 147, 184–185
"unity of State and law," Kelsen on, 28
utilitarianism, 25, 33–43

Veblen, Thorstein, 102
vice, law and, 132–136, 159
Volksgeist, 30–31
voting blocs, judges and, 147–148

Wall Street Lawyer, The (Smigel), 102, 166
war-crimes trials, 62–67
Ward, Lester, 40–41, 127
Weber, Max, 13, 33, 48, 75 76, 108 109, 113, 126
Wechsler, Herbert, 186
welfare law, 96–97, 200
Western law, 113, 120
Westley, William, 159
White, Morton, 50
white-collar offenses, 199
"white man's justice," 182
wills, 78, 96
Wolfenden Report, 132–133
workmen's compensation laws, 124, 175, 188, 199
world law, 64